*Sound Advice*

# Sound Advice

## Becoming a Better
## Children's Choir Conductor

JEAN ASHWORTH BARTLE

OXFORD
UNIVERSITY PRESS

2003

# OXFORD
UNIVERSITY PRESS

Oxford   New York

Auckland   Bangkok   Buenos Aires   Cape Town   Chennai
Dar es Salaam   Delhi   Hong Kong   Istanbul   Karachi   Kolkata
Kuala Lumpur   Madrid   Melbourne   Mexico City   Mumbai
Nairobi   São Paulo   Shanghai   Taipei   Tokyo   Toronto

Published by Oxford University Press, Inc.
198 Madison Avenue, New York, New York, 10016

www.oup.com

Oxford is a registered trademark of Oxford University Press

Library of Congress Cataloging-in-Publication Data
Bartle, Jean Ashworth.
Sound advice: becoming a better children's choir conductor / Jean Ashworth Bartle.
    p.   cm.
Includes bibliographical references and index.
ISBN 0-19-514178-4
1. Choral conducting.   2. Children's choirs.
3. Choral singing—Instruction and study—Juvenile.   I. Title.
MT88 .B35 2002
782.7'145—dc21      2002002112

18  17  16  15  14  13  12  11

Printed in the United States of America
on acid-free paper

ACKNOWLEDGMENTS

During the past thirty years, children's choirs have become instruments of artistic excellence treated with the same respect that has usually been reserved for adult choirs, orchestras, and opera companies. Many colleagues have worked faithfully to achieve this and have graciously endorsed this book or are listed in the bibliography. What a privilege it is to work with them!

I wish to express my gratitude to several individuals who have offered their own "sound advice" during the writing of this book: Matthew Baird, producer, Canadian Broadcasting Corporation, for his invaluable insights on the making of recordings; John McGuigan for his computer skills; musicians Rebecca Davies, Russell Hartenberger, Karen Henderson, and David Miller for their input to the chapter titled "Conducting an Orchestra"; and composers Derek Holman and Ruth Watson Henderson for their assistance with the section on the commissioning of new works and repertoire evaluation.

I also offer my heartfelt thanks to photographers Linda Locke and Maura Mc-Groarty; to my computer guru, Heather Dunford, a teacher with infinite patience and tact; to Toronto Children's Chorus administrative staff members Beth Anderson, Rebecca Davies, Jennifer Kirner, and Heather Wood; and to my personal assistant, Carol Stairs, whose composure, devotion, enthusiasm, and formidable editing skills have made this book possible.

Mentoring plays a vital role in the life of every teacher. This book is dedicated with much love and gratitude to four great mentors in my life: Lloyd Bradshaw (1929–1994), music director of St. George's United Church, Toronto, 1960–1970; Dr. Elmer Iseler (1927–1998), music director of the Toronto Mendelssohn Choir, 1964–1997, the Festival Singers of Canada, 1954–1977, and the Elmer Iseler Singers, 1979–1998; Sir Andrew Davis, music director of the Toronto Symphony

Orchestra, 1975–1988; and Sir David Willcocks, artistic director of the London Bach Choir, 1950–1998, music director of Kings' College Cambridge, 1957–1973, and director of the Royal College of Music, London, England, 1974–1984.

To the thousands of children I have had the privilege of teaching, I say a humble, "Thank you. You have been the best teachers of all."

And finally, to my husband, Don, soul mate and love of my life, thank you for your unwavering support of my work, for the countless ways in which you show it, and for sharing with me the joy of children and music.

Jean Ashworth Bartle is a superb musician, master conductor and teacher. She writes this book from her years of experience building the Toronto Children's Chorus, one of the finest choral instruments in the world today. *Sound Advice* is a 'must have.' You will use it your whole career.

> Lydia Adams
> Artistic Director, Elmer Iseler Singers
> Music Director, Amadeus Choir
> Toronto, Ontario

In the end, with Jean Ashworth Bartle it is all about the music. She has nurtured and encouraged the love, the beauty, and the skills of music in young singers and, as a consequence, has put the children's choir right at the front in musical life.

> Bob Chilcott
> Composer & Former Member of The Kings Singers
> Oxford, England

Jean Ashworth Bartle has opened the eyes and ears of the world to the artistry of the child's voice. Her dedication and devotion to the choral art have created standards of performance that will benefit generations of children for years to come. Jean continues to share her wealth of experience with choral directors around the world. Who better to turn to for "sound advice"?

> Barbara Clark, C.M.
> Artistic Director, Central Children's Choir of Ottawa-Carleton
> Ottawa, Ontario

Jean Ashworth Bartle is Canada's consummate conductor of children's choirs. Her articulate and insightful commentary not only on the fundamentals of choral conducting and rehearsing, but also on the preparation of major works, new repertoire, and the subtleties of successful chorus management is truly "sound advice" for all conductors of the unchanged voice. This is an invaluable resource—a rich and multifaceted compendium of choral excellence.

> Robert Cooper
> Conductor & Executive Producer of Choral Concert, CBC
> Radio Two
> Toronto, Ontario

Jean Ashworth Bartle is a great inspiration to me. It is a joy and an educational experience to observe Jean in action with her choirs, each section of her rehearsal ideally planned and creatively executed. The respect she shows the children as musicians and as human beings is reflected by their behavior in rehearsal, onstage and interacting with one another. The quality of vocal production of her singers is rounded, clear and simply a beautiful tone complimenting the young voice. TCC performances are always of the highest quality. With great admiration I congratulate Jean on her fine work and thank her for her contributions to the world of choral singing.

> Debra Damron
> Founder and Director of the Internationaler Oberurseler
> Kinderchor, Germany.

Jean Ashworth Bartle's *Sound Advice* manages to pack a lifetime of experience and reflection into one book. The range of topics—from vocal technique through recording, repertoire and "other things you need to know that you likely were not taught in music school"—will make this book a valuable resource and a fascinating read for conductors of any choir, not only children's choirs.

> Morna Edmundson
> Executive Director, World of Children's Choirs–2001
> Co-Director, Elektra Women's Choir
> Vancouver, British Columbia
> Associate Artistic Director, Coastal Sounds Music Academy

Jean Ashworth Bartle is one of the world's leading authorities on children's choirs. Her exemplary work as conductor, teacher, and champion of contemporary composers has consistently set high standards for children's choirs. *Sound Advice*, with its artistic and practical information, is a gift to the choral community from a master teacher. Jean has amazing knowledge of the young voice and what is required to lead a choir to sing beautifully. This is a "must have" for anyone involved with children's choirs.

> Dr. Janet Galván
> Professor of Music
> Ithaca College, Ithaca, New York

Jean Ashworth Bartle has a complete and awe-inspiring knowledge of the conductor's art; she is also a great humanist. We who know her are grateful for her profound love of music and people. Her heart is as big as the world. When she conducts my compositions, she has the uncanny ability to reach in and touch the heart and soul of my feelings.

> Srul Irving Glick, C.M.
> Composer and Conductor
> Toronto, Ontario

Jean Ashworth Bartle is dedicated to the children with whom she works and to the artistic expression of the music she conducts. While striving for the highest musical goals, she still manages to make rehearsals enjoyable and rewarding for her choirs. The choristers are always treated as artists, not as mechanical robots, and their singing conveys a musical sensitivity far beyond what one would expect from young singers. Drawn from her wealth of knowledge and experience, Jean's new book will be of great interest to all conductors of children's choirs.

> Ruth Watson Henderson
> Composer and Pianist
> Accompanist, Toronto Children's Chorus
> Toronto, Ontario

Jean Ashworth Bartle is an integral part of the Toronto artistic pyramid. Her musicianship is world-renowned. She is inspired and inspirational. Her secrets are out! A "must read"!

> Jessie Iseler
> Manager, Elmer Iseler Singers
> Toronto, Ontario

When Jean Ashworth Bartle's Toronto Children's Chorus first appeared at the National ACDA Convention in San Antonio, Texas, in 1987, we in the audience were dazzled by their stunning tone, their ambitious repertoire, and their glorious musicianship. Jean is a master teacher, a wonderful musician, and an inspiration. Her new book is a "must have."

> Dr. Ann Howard Jones
> Professor and Director of Choral Activities
> Boston University School for the Arts
> Boston, Massachusetts

Another gift to treasure! In *Sound Advice*, Jean Ashworth Bartle generously shares her experience and expertise, her philosophy and passion. She challenges each of us to become better at the magical work we have chosen to do—direct children's choirs. I know Jean's newest literary creation will be a most valuable resource.

> Helen Kemp
> Professor Emeritus of Voice and Church Music
> Westminster Choir College of Rider University
> Princeton, New Jersey

The trinity of Jean Ashworth Bartle's special gift to the musical world has been expectation, encouragement, and possibility. Through her belief in the abilities of young choristers, she has been successful in raising the bar of choral artistry to hitherto unattainable levels. Jean has also generously shared the new knowledge and understanding she has gained on her journey by affirming and inspiring colleagues worldwide.

> Susan Knight
> Founder/Director, Newfoundland Symphony Youth Choir
> Founder/Artistic Co-Director, Festival 500
> St. John's, Newfoundland

When I began conducting children's choirs over fifteen years ago *Lifeline for Children's Choir Directors* became one of the most important sources for my growth as a conductor of children's ensembles. Jean Ashworth Bartle has always been an inspiration and teacher to me. After having worn out several editions of her previous book and having used it as a textbook with hundreds of college students, I am delighted she will be taking us to another level. This exciting new book will undoubtedly become an essential component to the training of any children's choir director.

> Henry H. Leck
> Founder and Artistic Director, Indianapolis Children's Choir
> Director of Choral Activities, Butler University
> Indianapolis, Indiana

Any conductor who has read Jean Ashworth Bartle's *Lifeline for Children's Choir Directors* will be cheering that there is a sequel. Jean has a wonderful ability to combine significant ideas with a treasury of experience to create thoughtful, practical, intelligent, and illuminating information applicable to all levels of teaching. She is a master teacher from whom we've all been privileged to learn. What a joy to welcome her second volume of skills and sage advice to my resource desk!

> Diane Loomer, C.M.
> Artistic Director, Elektra Women's Choir and Chor Leoni Men's Choir
> Vancouver, British Columbia

Oxford University Press has shown sound judgement and superb wisdom in publishing Jean Ashworth Bartle's *Sound Advice*. Every child on this tired planet deserves the opportunity to sing and celebrate, and a battered, cynical world needs to listen, understand, and be made more loving and human. As the preeminent authority on teaching children to sing with intelligence, musical sensitivity, and a glorious sound, Jean has traveled the world, as a consultant and adjudicator and most often with her magnificent Toronto Children's Chorus. It is her lifetime gift to all of us and we are blessed indeed.

> Dr. Walter Pitman
> Educator and Author
> Toronto, Ontario

Jean Ashworth Bartle is one of the great personalities in the children's and youth choir movement worldwide. The sharing of her noble expertise and experience through *Sound Advice* should be an absolute Must for every colleague in our field.

> Erkki Pohjola
> Founder /Artistic Director, Tapiola Choir (1963–1995)
> Espoo, Finland

I remember when Jean Ashworth Bartle agreed to conduct the American Choral Director Association's first honor choir—the 1983 ACDA National Honor Children's Chorus! From that magical moment in Nashville, Tennessee, I knew that our vision for the future of children's choirs in the United States and Canada was a reality! Now from Jean's vision and lifetime experience leading Canada's incomparable Toronto Children's Chorus, she brings her renowned teaching expertise, unbounded musical devotion, and disciplined craft to the world of conductors and teachers. Through the power of Jean's experience and the magic of her musical spirit *Sound Advice: Becoming a Better Children's Choir Conductor* will surely enrich the professional development of committed professionals worldwide.

> Dr. Doreen Rao
> Elmer Iseler Chair in Conducting
> Director of Choral Programs, University of Toronto
> Toronto, Ontario
> Founder/Chair ACDA National Committee on Children's
> Choirs 1979–1999

Not only has Jean Ashworth Bartle founded one of the finest children's choirs in the world, but also her work and service to the choral professional for over 20 years is consummate. This book is a practical guide for all conductors working with children because it is written by one of the leading authorities on organizing, running, and training children's choirs whom I have ever had the privilege to know.

> Marie Stultz
> Founder & Artistic Director, The Treble Chorus of New England
> Boston, Massachusetts

Jean Ashworth Bartle is one of the world's leading experts on children's choirs. Her dedication to artistic excellence and teaching has enriched the choral profession. This book is a "must read."

> Dr. Barbara Tagg
> Artistic Director/Founder, Syracuse Children's Chorus
> Affiliate Artist, Syracuse University, New York

Jean Ashworth Bartle continues to set the standard of excellence for children's choirs and conductors. Her comprehensive knowledge of the choral art for children and her deep sense of beauty, are an inspiration. She is a master.

> Anne Tomlinson
> Artistic Director, Los Angeles Children's Chorus

*Sound Advice: Becoming a Better Children's Choir Conductor* is an indispensable resource for the beginning children's choir conductor as well as the seasoned professional. Children's choruses, their artistic and management staffs, and all who care about children who sing in choruses, will value the comprehensive and thoughtful information shared in Jean Ashworth Bartle's newest book.

> Judith Willoughby
> Founder and Music Director, Temple University Children's Choir
> Philadelphia, Pennsylvania
> Associate Professor of Conducting and Music Education
> Northwestern University, Evanston, Illinois

# CONTENTS

# FOREWORD

I have admired Jean Ashworth Bartle's outstanding work with children's choirs for more than a quarter of a century. I have also witnessed the steady development of the Toronto Children's Chorus under her inspired direction since its founding in 1978. The chorus has gone on to achieve worldwide acclaim for its excellence, and several generations of children are grateful, not only for the wonderful training in singing they have received but also for the lifelong love of music that Jean has instilled. Those who have been privileged to see Jean at work with children will already know some of her secrets!

Jean is successful not just with children who have been auditioned and selected for their musical gifts; I have seen her work with children who do not possess great talent but who respond to her imaginative training in a remarkable way. A glance at the contents of this book will reveal the comprehensive nature of Jean's "sound advice"—advice based on wide experience and keen observation. This book will be of great interest and benefit not only to conductors of children's choirs but also to parents and all those who are interested in education in a broad context.

Sir David Willcocks
*Cambridge, England*
*August 2001*

*Sound Advice*

# Introduction

This book is based on the premise that all children can and should learn to sing. This wide-ranging resource book has been compiled for conductors of children's community choirs and elementary school choirs. It is my hope that the information will be valuable to many diverse groups:

- those who are considering a career in training children's choirs
- those who conduct choirs in primary school but are seeking more ideas for training the child's voice and finding suggestions for effective repertoire
- those who have recently become artistic directors of children's community choirs
- those who are experienced directors of children's community choirs
- composers, parents, volunteers, administrators, and board members
- those members of the community who are interested in all aspects of children's choir training

Several chapters are devoted to the pedagogy that helps children sing with skill and enjoyment. In addition, because of the prodigious growth in the children's choir movement over the last two decades, the book includes many concepts that will also assist the artistic director: preparing a children's chorus to sing a major work with orchestra; organizational skills and effective long-range planning; working with management, volunteers, and a board of directors; conducting an orchestra; and commissioning, recording, and touring. (Because of the inevitable overlapping of certain ideas and concepts in such a wide-ranging study, there is a small amount of repetition for the reader's benefit.)

Chapter 12 is devoted solely to the children. In a series of letters, the children express their thoughts and deepest feelings about singing in a children's choir and the influence it has had on their lives.

The book's detailed appendices also contain much useful information. These include a comprehensive list of works for orchestra and children's choir; warm-ups and skill-building sheets for children of all ages; a sight-singing curriculum guide; and repertoire lists for children of all ages and stages of development. There is also a list of compact discs made by the Toronto Children's Chorus, accompanied by repertoire lists with voicing and publishers.

Next to effective parenting, teaching children is perhaps the most important job in the world. Teaching children to sing, and to sing well in a fine choir, is work that embraces far more than the actual singing. We mold lives. We teach values. We develop tastes. We inspire and nurture talent and creativity. Each of us must continually strive to improve our skills, our craft, and our knowledge of great music making. In addition, we must ever be mindful of the way in which we interact and work with people—such an important, yet neglected, task— in order to meet this formidable responsibility.

It is my sincere hope that this "sound advice" will prove helpful as you pursue your vitally important work with renewed enthusiasm, dedication, and skill.

# CHAPTER ONE

# The Formative Years

*It is in the first years of Primary School that the first laying of foundations, the collecting of the first, decisive musical experience begins. What the child learns here, he will never forget: it becomes his flesh and blood. It will affect the public taste of the whole country. This very idea warns us that the first songs are to be chosen with special care. And I would advise my young colleagues, the composers of symphonies, to drop in at the kindergartens, too. It is there that it is decided whether there will be anybody to understand their works in twenty years' time.*
—Zoltán Kodály, *The Selected Writings*

Although this chapter deals with teaching singing to six- and seven-year-olds and is based on a first-grade curriculum, I recommend it to music teachers of all levels. Many of the ideas, strategies, and routines outlined here could, and perhaps should, be applied in all stages of music education.

First grade is the most important year in a child's school life. During this school year, the growth of a child physically, mentally, socially, and emotionally is greater than in any other school year. Children in the first grade have no inhibitions about singing alone. They are not self-conscious about trying to match pitch. Boys have not yet developed any resistance to singing. All are eager to learn. If the children experience great joy and satisfaction in their singing in first grade, they are often hooked for life. Having taught music to first graders for more than three decades, I have much I would like to share with you.

## Quality of the Teacher's Singing Voice

Ideally, six- and seven-year-olds should be singing every day, at various times of the day, with their regular classroom teacher. Quite often, however, these teachers have not been trained in singing; many sing in a chest voice that is far too low. Children need to hear a voice that is bright, pure, light, free of excessive vibrato, and capable of singing in the keys of E flat, E, and F major. I strongly recommend that male teachers sing in their falsetto range initially, until the children are used to hearing a "head-tone" quality and learn to imitate it. Youngsters initially learn to sing through imitation. It is critical, particularly during the months of September and October, that the children hear from the teacher the quality of sound that they need to reproduce. Although this may be vocally exhausting for the teacher, it is nonetheless a vital step in the process of teaching first graders to sing. Should the teacher find this impossible, there are two other ways of giving the children a role model: the first is to invite a soprano with the voice described here to come in regularly to do tone matching; the second is to invite the four or five children in the class who were "born" with this sound to be role models. With any group of twenty-five six-year-olds, there most likely is a small group of them who not only can match pitch but also can sing with a beautiful head-tone quality.

## The Prepared Environment

Masterful teaching requires detailed preparation and organization. In this preparation, potential problems must be anticipated and prevented. Having children knowledgeable and comfortable about routines prevents many problems from happening. A room that is bright, clean, child-centered, well ventilated, and spacious is ideal. Fresh flowers or foliage plants give the room a lift. Sadly, I have visited music rooms where discipline was a problem because the children didn't have enough space or fresh air. Brains don't function well without a healthy supply of oxygen. I must confess, however, that one of the best lessons I have ever seen taught to about forty ten-year-olds occurred in Hungary in a room with bare green walls that hadn't seen a coat of paint in decades. The children sat in rows of desks that were nailed to the floor and used booklets with tissue-paper-thin pages. Fortunately, the windows were open and the room was well ventilated; the children were happy and focused. The instructor, a delightful woman who had been teaching for over twenty years, sparkled with enthusiasm, and the joy she created was infectious. The work was challenging, but the ten-year-olds were succeeding. These young children individually sang the modes by memory and then were asked to identify the modes the teacher sang.

It is beneficial to have the classroom teacher bring the class to the music room and help them line up single file outside the music room. The music teacher should then guide them into the room. Ideally, first graders need an area in the room that is carpeted, with room enough for all children to sit comfortably at least six inches away from one another. They need to be able to stand and do actions easily. If they are sitting too closely to one another, they are bound to become uncomfortable and restless. I always had the children sit on chairs for about eight minutes out of the thirty so they could get used to sitting in a seating plan. Using the entire room for part of the lesson is a concept I introduced the third week of school.

A list of the children's names printed neatly on experience-chart paper, with a small passportlike photo mounted to each name, gives the children a sense of belonging in that room. The photos, requested early in the year from the children's parents, are also an excellent way to learn new names quickly. Rhythm instruments, visible yet out of reach, should be introduced one at a time early in the school year. The instruments are there to enhance the singing, not obliterate it. Large, colorful flashcards with neatly printed blank rhythms, that is, one-measure rhythms without pitch, should be visible on walls or cupboards. Having a soft and slow recording of a piece such as the slow movement of a Mozart piano concerto playing in the background helps the children prepare psychologically for the lesson. Use the same recording during every lesson for two weeks.

I am aware that there are many schools where every room contains a grade class and there isn't a spare room available for the music teacher. I, too, have trekked from class to class with my equipment on a trolley. Needless to say, this is less than ideal. Traveling from room to room is exhausting for the music teacher, and remaining in their regular classroom is limiting for the children, since desks and chairs prevent easy movement. Music teachers need to try to convince principals and parents that a music room is a high priority. The room need not come equipped with the latest expensive technology; it is perhaps better if it does not. A piano is helpful, though not essential.

## Effective Use of the Speaking Voice

A teacher's speaking voice, used wisely, is a powerful teaching tool. It can be used to set the desired atmosphere in a room; it can be used for classroom management; it can give the children a sense of comfort and well-being. In first grade, a teacher's speaking voice needs to be as soft as it can be with the children still able to hear. It should have the air of both authority and kindness. Vocabulary that does not talk down to the children should be used. There should be enthusiasm along with a sense of expectation in the voice. (A loud and nasal voice tends to elicit a loud response from the children. The louder the teacher speaks, the louder the children respond. Eventually the teacher's speaking voice is so loud that the children stop listening altogether.) Teachers should be encouraged to tape their lessons and listen objectively to the sound of their own speaking voices.

## Teaching First Graders to Find Their Singing Voices and Match Pitch

In my experience, in September in a new class of thirty first graders, five would be able to match pitch and twenty-five would not. By June, however, twenty-five would be able to match pitch and five would not. Let us examine the reasons so many children at this age cannot match pitch. Most come under the categories of inexperience and lack of exposure:

1. They have not yet identified with nor heard anyone sing with a head tone. Children learn by imitation. If they have not heard it, they cannot imitate it.
2. They have not yet sung in an environment where they have been encouraged to sing alone with tone matching. They have always sung with the entire class, in too low a range, and accompanied by a piano.

3. They have poor concentration and an inability to focus. Children with underdeveloped auditory memory are often deprived of the joy of silence. They are constantly barraged from morning until night with some form of distraction.
4. They are from homes where their parents do not have time to sing to them or with them or where the music they hear on tapes and videos is not conducive to developing the beauty in a child's voice.
5. They are shy and lack self-confidence or may be experiencing difficulties learning in school.
6. They are simply not interested, since the music teacher perhaps does not provide a stimulating and positive environment where the energy is high and the activities interesting. The teaching style may not be as warm and supportive as it should be.
7. They lack the coordination needed to be able to experience the sensation of engaging the breath and reproducing the sounds.
8. They are accustomed to using a raspy voice as they speak. The speaking voice and singing voice are closely related. Many children have allergies that may cause raspy or husky speech, or they may use their speaking voices inappropriately or in a stressful way that causes vocal nodules or polyps to appear.

All children can be taught to sing if they begin their personal vocal discovery at a very early age and if they are taught by someone who not only believes all children can sing but also has the pedagogical skills to teach them to sing. Children must never, ever, be told that they cannot sing or be told to just mouth the words.

## Ways to Develop the Child's Singing Voice

### Exploring Sounds

The singing voice comes from the speaking voice. Start with the speaking voice and ways it can be used with high and low sounds. The siren, the wind, Santa Claus, and the train can be explored frequently at the beginning of first grade. Make this an individual activity within the class, since children will be more successful if they sing alone than with a group. "Who can make the sound of a fire siren like me? Raise your hand if you would like to try." "Good, John. Who can make a siren that goes higher than John's?" Eventually the teacher can go directly from the speaking voice to the singing voice with, "I can go there very, very soon," and on the word "soon" speak it with a sung pitch that slides from a fourth-line D down a fifth. Simple words and phrases such as "Wow!" and "Oh no!" can easily be taken from the speaking voice to the singing voice.

The circle game is an excellent way for six- and seven-year-old children to sing individually while working in a group. All children stand in a circle. One child, Tom, is in the center and has a large ball. Tom sings in descending minor thirds as he bounces the ball: "This is my ball. Now I'll pass to Stephen." Tom keeps bouncing the ball until Stephen comes into the center. Tom then sits in his place in the circle. Stephen continues to bounce the ball and sings, "This is my ball. Now I'll pass to Ursula." Stephen continues to bounce the ball until Ursula comes into the center and starts to bounce the ball. Stephen then sits in his place in the circle. The game continues until all children are sitting in the circle. The great thing about this game is that all children have a chance to sing individually and all are absorbed in the bouncing ball and are not concerned about voices that are not yet matching pitch.

### Choosing Appropriate Song Material

The selection of song material, the key of the song, and the voice the children hear singing it are probably the most important factors in developing the child's singing voice. The keys of D, E flat, and E, both major and minor, are best. The American folk song "Little Liza Jane" in E-flat major is ideal. It is pentatonic and repetitive and goes up to high "doh" twice. First graders enjoy raising their arms up high and turning around when on high "doh" and keeping a steady and light beat on their knees for the rest of the song. Songs written in C major should be avoided, as should songs that have difficult leaps. "Raindrops Keep Falling on My Head" may be a song you love, but it is not appropriate for teaching children to develop head voices; the range is too great and the leaps are too awkward. It is best not to use piano accompaniment on a daily basis, since it clutters the texture and confuses the child, and the piano is not an ideal instrument to imitate.

### Individual Questioning

The use of sung questions and answers on the descending minor third interval on B flat and G is highly effective. "What day is it today?" The children sing, "Monday." "What month is this?" "September." "What's your gym teacher's name?" "Mr. Macdonald." On lesson 4 or 5, when you have gained the children's trust and know some who can match pitch correctly, sing individually to each of them, "My name's Mrs. Bartle. What's your name?" The others will hear their answers and imitate. It is a process that needs to be done in every lesson. They *will* eventually develop their voices and learn to match pitch accurately.

When you sing individually and get two low A's from one child as a response, do not react. This takes much tact, skill, love, and patience. Early in the year, there likely will not be any giggles. Whatever you do, make sure the child who has sung the two low A's feels no discomfort or embarrassment. If you must, perhaps say, "Some of us have low voices and some of us have high voices; some of us have big hands, and some of us have smaller hands. Isn't it wonderful that all of us are different? How dull it would be if we were all the same." You need to create an environment of trust so no child is ever afraid to make a mistake. In great teaching, there are no wrong answers, just poorly set up questions.

### Making Tapes

Make a tape of four or five songs in appropriate keys that children can listen to at home. They need to hear the model head voice regularly.

One of the most effective things I did while teaching first grade was help each child make a tape as a Christmas or Hanukkah gift for his or her parents. Since each tape was only about nine or ten minutes long, I was able to make three in a half hour. It was well worth the investment of my time. By early December I had taught at least twelve songs by rote. I had the words of each song printed on twelve separate pages, and the children would actually point to the words as they sang the song. Often they would point to the wrong words, but that did not matter; they would draw a picture of the song on the page. In fact, the classroom teacher would often assist with this project, since it helped the children's reading skills. The tape and word sheets would then be carefully wrapped and I told the children how important it was to keep this as a surprise. The response from grateful parents was overwhelming. The tape was a priceless treasure and a permanent memory in song of their child's voice. The children were always proud of the tape made for mom and dad, mom and stepdad, stepmom and dad, and so on. They often asked that their tapes be duplicated for their extended families. By January, the children were proud of their accomplishments and were well on their way to matching pitch, and the parents were even more supportive of the music program than earlier.

## Teaching Strategies

Ideally, first graders need a minimum of three half-hour lessons each week. Often they have only two, but the learning value of that extra thirty minutes cannot be overstated. Let us assume, for the purposes of this book, that the children have three half-hour lessons each week. During the first four months, the children can learn about twelve songs. The skills and games must be incorporated into these songs in a program that is song-based. The ultimate goal should be to nurture a love of singing and music, develop skill in using the singing voice, and build self-confidence and self-esteem.

### The First Lesson

The first lesson is such an important one. How you start on day one and on the next few days will influence your year's work, and the lesson will help to prepare a path for the rest of the year that will bring you and the children success and a feeling of accomplishment. If possible visit the kindergarten the previous spring, not to teach but just to observe and have the children get to know you. The children will feel more content walking into a strange room if there is a familiar face.

1. Ask the classroom teachers to provide large name tags for the children. It is essential to learn the children's names quickly and to always call a child by name. Meet the children outside the door before they come in and set a tone of expectation and organization. If they are noisy, have them line up in single file beside the wall. Praise the children who are doing well. "I like the way that John and Mark are ready for music." Wait quietly and patiently until they all are ready. It may take two or three minutes or even longer. Your face, eyes, smile, stance, and self-assuredness are critical.

2. When the children are ready, have them sit on a carpet in front of your chair. Stress the importance of leaving a gap as wide as they are between them. (Space relationships are often difficult for children, so illustrate by showing them an example.) Discipline problems are bound to occur if they are sitting too close to one another.

3. Begin by speaking very briefly about the singing voice. Explain that our singing voices are different from our speaking voices and that the singing voice they hear from you may seem strange at first, just as many new situations do. Then, to give the children an activity immediately, as you are beating a hand drum lightly (about a quarter at 80 m.m.) say with them, "Put the beat on your knees," several times, then, "Put the beat on your shoulders." Some will do it loudly, while others will be too shy to do anything. Say (with the beat), "I don't want to hear it; I just want to see it." As they are keeping the beat, sing your first song, "Mrs. Jenny Wren," in the key of E flat, by memory and without the piano. Guided listening questions are very important, since they make the listening purposeful. Ask the children to listen and tell you how many times you sing "Jenny Wren." The timbre of your voice, the intonation, and the musicality with which you sing the song through are critical. The second time you sing the song, have the words printed neatly on large chart paper. Children in first grade are very excited about learning to read. The second guided question should be one where the answer is close to the end of the song, because you want them to listen to as much of the song as possible. Set up the question so you are certain to get the correct answer. The art of questioning is one that teachers must pursue throughout their careers. Only respond to those children who have their hands raised. Getting this idea across takes time, patience, and insistence. However, it is essential for good classroom management and for giving children an opportunity to answer alone and develop the self-esteem they need to sing well. The children need to hear the entire song a minimum of three times before you begin to teach it line by line. The line by line, phrase by phrase, echo approach must be presented rhythmically, so there is a natural uninterrupted response from the children. If they are not able to sing each line or phrase back to you, you must retrace your steps and sing the song again for them using a different approach. You could have them stand up and follow your actions as you describe the lines of the song through gesture. You could have them keep four beats on their heads, shoulders, knees, and toes as you sing it through. You could have one child, with a stick pointer, come and point to the words as you sing it through while three or four other children accompany softly on drums. They will then be ready to sing line by line/phrase by phrase. Your reaction to their singing must always be positive and encouraging. I would not correct any pitches on the first day.

4. Effective teaching means that you are accomplishing several skills at once. (You drive down six lanes of the highway simultaneously!) Having started to learn "Mrs. Jenny Wren," the children need to learn a poem that you can use as a stretch break, to teach beat patterns, and to develop spatial awareness. Have the children stand and again use their arms to distance themselves from the other children.

I'm All Made of Hinges (Anonymous)

| | |
|---|---|
| I'm all made of hinges | *large circles with the arms* |
| 'Cause everything bends | *crouch down and touch toes* |
| From the top of my head | *both hands on head as you stand up* |
| Way down to my ends | *crouch all the way down again* |
| I'm hinges in front | *hands on shoulders* |
| I'm hinges in back | *hands behind back touching spine* |
| But I have to have hinges | *wide circles with arms* |
| Or else I will crack! | *clap hands once* |

5. Do some tone matching during the first lesson. Use a metallophone, since the overtones make it an effective tone-matching instrument. Start with D2 to D1. Play it and then sing the words high and low on those pitches. If you see a confident singer who is matching, ask him/her to sing it alone. Have two children come up and, with one crouching and one standing tall with arms in the air, they can illustrate high low or low high with their bodies.

6. Have the children read some simple musical notation the first day with something as easy as

This is my first day of school.

Do your best here. That's the rule.

Have the rhythm, not the words, on the blackboard and point to the quarter notes as you say the text rhythmically.

7. At the end of the lesson, ask the children if they have a favorite song they can all sing together. This can be dangerous, because you might hear something like "I've Been Working on the Railroad" with a loud, raucous chest sound. If that is how they sing it, stop them, put your hands over your ears, and say, "Is that your singing voice or your schoolyard yelling voice?" Illustrate the kind of sound you want by singing the song properly for them The chances are very good that they will then sing it somewhat better, even on their first day!

8. At the end of the lesson, a Singer of the Day Award can be given to one child who is trying his/her best, listening well, and exhibiting the kind of behavior you are hoping to get from every child. The award can be a simple pinned ribbon or even a small badge with the child's name printed by a computer. An "S" is also placed beside the child's name on a class list printed on chart paper and hung on the wall. This kind of positive reinforcement is very important but requires much care and tact. Eventually, all children must receive the awards, and the last dozen may be given to children in small groups rather than individually so that no child's feelings are hurt. The award reinforces and nourishes the classroom environment you wish to foster and prevents discipline problems. Improvement of children's self-esteem through positive reinforcement and the provision of satisfying musical experiences that give them a feeling of accomplishment are essential ingredients of every music lesson and choir rehearsal.

9. Each child needs to leave the class with a letter that goes home to his/her parents. (The letter should have the child's name at the top; otherwise the letter is sure to get mislaid.) The letter outlines what you are planning to accomplish this year in the first-grade music program. It should also request that a passport-size photograph of the child be given to the classroom teacher in an envelope and that the child's name be printed on the back of the photograph. The photograph will then be stapled next to the name of the child on the class list on the wall. You should be able to memorize all of the children's names by the end of September. The letter to parents accomplishes several things: it stresses that music is important, tells them that you want their children to have maximum benefit from the program, and establishes a vital link to the child's family.

It is important to begin dismissal routines on the first day. After years of trying to find a safe, efficient, and effective way to do this, I have come to the conclusion that the best way is by alphabetical order of last names. (It sounds like something that might have been done in schools two hundred years ago, but it works!) The first few times, you need to call out the children's last names a few at a time. By the third or fourth lesson, one of the children could read the list. (There will likely be a child who can read alone or with a prompter. Eventually they will all want to be chosen to read the list.) This type of organized dismissal prevents rushing and butting in; it also ensures that the eager ones are not always at the front while the stragglers lag behind. Halfway through the year, you might start with Z and go back to A or call first names instead of last names. Again, encourage one of the children to read the list.

## *Excellent Repertoire to Use in the First-Grade Classroom or for Six- and Seven-Year-Olds in a Community Choir*

| | | | |
|---|---|---|---|
| Cradle Song | W. H. Anderson | GVT/Warner/Chappell | VG-144 |
| Children Singing | Violet Archer | GVT/Warner/Chappell | VG-259 |
| Mrs. Jenny Wren | Arthur Baynon | Boosey & Hawkes | No. 88 |
| Rabbits | W. H. Belyea | Leslie Music (Brodt in USA) | 1151 |
| The Zoo | W. H. Belyea | Leslie Music (ten songs in this collection) | |
| Just Like Me and The Telephone Wires | Marilyn Broughton | GVT/Warner/Chappell | VG-1003 |
| My Caterpillar | Marilyn Broughton | GVT/Warner/Chappell | G-185 |
| Nursery Rhyme Nonsense | Marilyn Broughton | GVT/Warner/Chappell | VG-184 |
| The Scarecrow | John Clements | Elkin | 16 0131 08 |
| My Dog Spot | Clifford Curwin | Curwen/G. Schirmer | 72621 |
| Orion | Donald Ford | GVT/Warner/Chappell | G-140 |
| Song for a Little House | Donald Ford | GVT/Warner/Chappell | G-147 |
| The Laughing Brook | Cyril Hampshire | Jarman | |
| Man in the Moon | Cyril Hampshire | Jarman | |
| Bessie the Black Cat | Peter Jenkyns | Elkin | 16 0110 |

| | | | |
|---|---|---|---|
| New Shoes and Purr, Purr | Burton Keith | Western/Vancouver | 1071 |
| Haida | Leck/Gerber | Plymouth | HL-516 |
| Adventure | Havelock Nelson | GVT/Warner/Chappell | VG-1016 |
| Cheerily | David Ouchterlony | GVT/Warner/Chappell | G-161 |
| Three Songs for Very Young People | David Ouchterlony | Leslie Music | 1124 |
| 1. Walk, Run, Jump; | | | |
| 2. Some Day; | | | |
| 3. Almost Asleep | | | |
| Pigeons | George Rathbone | Curwen | 71934 |
| Wee Willie Winkie | Arr. Hugh Roberton | Roberton | 75022 |
| The Grandfather Clock | Alec Rowley | Western (Vancouver) | 1023 |
| The Kangaroo | Alec Rowley | Novello | SMR395 |
| The Windmill | Evelyn Sharpe | Cramer (Leslie Music) | 1654 |
| A Room of My Own | Eric Thiman | Curwen/Boosey & Hawkes | 72355 |
| The Man in the Moon | Eric Thiman | Curwen/Boosey & Hawkes | 72413 |
| The Path to the Moon | Eric Thiman | Boosey & Hawkes | OCUB6114 |
| The Grasshopper | Stuart Young | Curwen/Boosey & Hawkes | 72022 |

For ways in which a conductor should choose suitable repertoire, please see appendix 4A.

Teaching six- and seven-year-olds to discover and use their singing voices, to develop a love of singing, and to use their ears to listen discriminatingly is critically important. These accomplishments begin to build a solid foundation for the skills that are to be developed in subsequent years.

# CHAPTER TWO

# Training Eight- to Fourteen-Year-Old Children to Sing

To build an outstanding children's choir, the conductor must understand the basic tenets of singing. Exquisite tone, effective breath support, clear diction, musical phrasing, and perfect intonation are among the concepts that need to be nurtured during every rehearsal. When these concepts have been mastered, children should be introduced to a variety of musical styles and the communication needed to interpret and perform them. The selection of suitable repertoire is of paramount importance if the children are going to succeed in all of these areas.

## Exquisite Tone

The tone of a children's choir is more a reflection of its conductor than the collective sound of individual voices. While membership varies from one year to the next, the tone of the choir under the same conductor remains remarkably consistent. Each conductor has his or her own concept of exquisite tone. This is a good thing, since it would be rather dull if all choirs tried to sound the same. As the choir matures and the children gain more skill, the timbre of the choir should be varied, depending on the style of music that is being sung. Initially, however, it is crucial that young children develop good habits that will enable them to sing with exquisite tone.

The qualities of exquisite tone that one should try to develop in young voices are the following:

1. Ringing: A ringing or resonant tone has a buoyancy and projection that is thrilling to the listener. The overtones enable even a small voice to be heard in a large hall.

2. Purity: A pure tone, unencumbered by excessive vibrato or a distinctive color, has clarity and sweetness.
3. Brightness: A bright tone is easy to tune and blend. It glimmers and shines. There is a hint of the "oo" vowel sound in every vowel sung.
4. Freedom: A free tone is completely unrestricted. It is without any form of tension. It is not driven or forced. It brings a sense of composure to the listener.

The ability of the conductor to develop these qualities in the choir's tone depends on five things:

- the consistent teaching of pure, uniform vowel sounds
- the warm-up exercises used to develop the voices
- the teaching of good breath support
- the repertoire that the teacher has selected for the children to study
- the positive teaching atmosphere created by the conductor in the rehearsal

It helps a great deal if the teacher is able to demonstrate the qualities of exquisite tone with his or her own voice. It is also necessary to correct poorly produced tone as soon as it is detected.

The consistent weekly warm-up of descending E-flat major scales using tonic-solfa syllables is the initial way in which a young singer can begin to develop and appreciate the importance of correct vowel formation and unification. All vowel sounds except "oo" are learned in the tonic-solfa scale. These scales also help to engage the breath support if four notes are sung in one breath. (A list of warm-ups suitable for this age group is found in appendix 1.) The children need to tape these scales on their small tape recorders during the rehearsal and practice them daily. Singing the scales helps develop the musculature needed for good singing. If children arrive early for rehearsal, it is a good idea to have them line up at the piano and sing one of their pieces for you. In two or three minutes you are able to assess such problems as raised tongues or tight jaws and give individual help. It is essential that children learn to appreciate the physical sensation in their faces when singing with a beautiful tone in order for them to do it naturally and consistently. Children need to sense an open throat with much space at the back of the throat. The sensation one has just before yawning is ideal. If any problems occur during the brief singing "lesson" before rehearsal begins, the warm-up exercises should be modified to address them.

A common problem that impedes exquisite tone often involves a raised, tight tongue. The exercise "flee, flay, flah, flow, floo" on a descending five-note scale pattern will help. It will loosen and lower the tongue, create more space in the mouth, and reduce tension. Another common problem is the desire of young children to sing with a chest sound before they have developed the upper range and before they have developed the strong breathing apparatus necessary for successful singing in the chest register. The best exercise for this is an ascending broken triad that starts on second-space A flat, uses the syllable "pa," and ascends in half steps to a C. Children can not sing in the chest in this register. Once they get used to that "ringing" feeling, the children need to bring that quality of tone into their middle register and then down to an E flat above middle C, through the descending tonic-solfa scale. During the rehearsal, it is essential for the conductor to correct throaty-chesty singing as soon as it occurs. If the conductor can use his or her own voice to demonstrate both the "head-tone" and the "chesty-throaty" tone, the children will sense what is acceptable and what is not.

## Effective Breath Support

The most important aspect of developing exquisite tone, and of good singing in general, is breath support. During children's early training in singing they must be made aware that we need more breath for singing than we need for speaking. They should be told that taking in sufficient breath for singing is similar to putting sufficient gas into the tank of the car. Without adequate breath that is coordinated with the voice, the children will not be able to develop fully the beauty of their singing voices. Several of these ideas could help make the children aware of the mechanics of good breath support:

1. During early rehearsals hold a belt around your own rib cage and ask the children to count the number of notches it moves when you take a breath for singing. At the same time, have a child put his or her hands on your shoulders to see if your shoulders rise. When the children see that the rib cage expands for singing while the shoulders remain relaxed, low, and still, they get a much clearer picture of what you are trying to teach them. Afterward, reverse this procedure as you gently place one hand on a child's rib cage and the other on the shoulder. It is crucial that the children do not raise their shoulders when breathing. See figure 2.1.

2. Have the children raise their arms over their heads. The rib cage is now high. Then let their arms hang loosely at their sides with shoulders low and relaxed. The children can now pretend to sip through a straw with quick stops and starts until plenty of air has been taken in. The air can now be released in a slow hiss, trying to keep the rib cage expanded. Repeat five times at the beginning of every rehearsal.

3. Beginning with the same exercise as in 2., the children can put one hand on the waist and one hand on the ribs and pant like a dog. They should be able to feel the expansion and movement around the waist that occurs during a prepared breath.

4. Ask the children to line up one behind the other in choir rows, with only an arm's distance between them. (When they put one arm on the person in front of them, they should not have to lean forward. See figure 2.2.) One hand rests on the shoulder of the person in front and the other hand goes on his/her rib cage. As each child sips through the imaginary straw, the child behind checks to make sure that the shoulders are not moving and that the rib cage is expanding. A brief peer evaluation session should take place after the exercise.

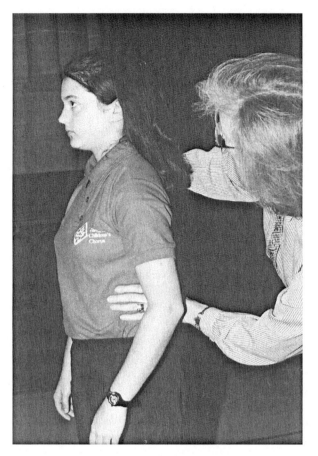

Figure 2.1

5. Ask the children to bring their own long belts or scarves to rehearsal. While they lie on the floor, have them loosely wrap the belts and scarves around their rib cages. On your signal, they will all sip through their imaginary straws and feel the belts or scarves tighten.

6. To activate and feel the diaphragm muscle, have the children repeat "puh, tuh, kuh, fuh, shhhh" rhythmically while placing their hands on their rib cages.

These pre-warm-up activities are intended to give the children a sense of breath support for good singing and should be introduced at the beginning of the season. Much patience is then needed, since the breathing mechanism takes time to develop. The conductor must learn to detect during successive warm-ups whether the children are engaging their breath correctly.

Effective conducting gesture and lack of tension in the room can aid dramatically in this process. One of the most common problems is that young children try to take in too much breath and hold the breath. Their shoulders will be raised

Figure 2.2

and tense. Conductors can help their singers with conducting gestures that are wide instead of high or horizontal instead of vertical. Conductors should be able to look at a choir and tell if their singers' breathing needs work after seeing them sing one phrase. Children need lots of room to breathe easily, and conductors should make sure that the children are not standing too closely on risers or sitting too closely together on chairs. (The general rule of thumb is one chair space between each chair and the width of one person between each two people standing.)

Once the children understand the need for good breathing habits, the conductor must begin to teach breathing during warm-ups and repertoire. (Spending 25 percent of a choir rehearsal on breathing techniques is not a wise use of time.) Lecturing on the minute details of diaphragmatic breathing is almost useless to a child. How many of us understand the complexities involved in the coordination of muscles and joints it takes for a child to run a race? Would the gym teacher spend time lecturing on that? The wise conductor will teach breathing and vocal technique while the children are making music.

Correct posture is critical for correct singing. Children must get used to standing on the balls of their feet with their knees flexed, not locked. Their arms must be loose at their sides, not held in front or behind. Shoulders need to be low and without tension. Chins need to be low and jaws relaxed. If the children are sitting on chairs, several problems need to be resolved. Often the chairs are too high for the children. Rather than having the children sit on the edge of their seat, which causes a swayback and impedes good breath support, have them sit tall on the chair with their bottom at the back of the chair. Move your singers to at least three places during a rehearsal— sitting on the chair, standing in front of the chair, and standing around the room. Allow them to stretch several times at twenty-minute intervals during a rehearsal, always coming back to the "singer's posture." If children are standing and holding choir folders, the folders must be lower than their mouths and must be held with the elbows relaxed and slightly away from the waist.

Conductors would be wise to use the term "breath support" during every rehearsal and teach breath coordination with each musical phrase. The breath needs to feel connected to the resonance chambers, and hence the initial exercise of "h'ng" and "h'ng-ee-oh" sung on D2 works extraordinarily well. The breath needs to be used efficiently without the singers trying to conserve it. Often the phrase "convert your breath into beautiful tone" helps the young singer.

## Clear Diction

When children are asked to explain the difference between singers and instrumentalists, the response is invariably something like "singers have their voices inside them and instrumentalists hold their instruments" or "singers have to get the notes from their heads and instrumentalists put their fingers down on something to get the right note." Rarely, if ever, do the children come up with the notion that singers have words and instrumentalists do not. Words are the meat and potatoes of singers. Words are the reason that singers and choirs sing. Words give a whole new dimension to music making that goes beyond the scope of an instrumentalist. Composers of choral music start with the text as their inspiration. How many of us, however, have listened to a choir that makes a beautiful sound, but any attempt to understand what they are singing about is futile? Children's choirs need to be taught to enunciate and articulate text clearly, without impeding the line of a phrase, and with such intensity and feeling that the audience cannot help but be moved by their performance. Children must always understand the meaning of the text they are singing and use the appropriate facial expression to convey the meaning.

Madeleine Marshall devotes twenty-two chapters to consonants in her book, *The Singer's Manual of English Diction*. This book should be in every choral conductor's library. In addition, Ron Jeffers's *Sacred Latin Texts*, volume 1 of *Translations and Annotations of Choral Repertoire*, contains an excellent pronunciation guide and translations of all of the common Latin texts. I devoted chapter 4 in my first book, *Lifeline for Children's Choir Directors*, to diction. The chapter outlines nine activities a children's choir director can use to promote good diction. What bears repeating here and cannot be emphasized strongly enough is the need for children's choir directors to speak like singers and encourage their singers to do the same. One of the huge benefits of singing in a choir is that choristers will generally speak more clearly than someone who has not been trained in a choir.

The obvious reason for a choir to sing text clearly is so that the audience can hear the words and follow their meaning. Consonants give choral sound vitality as well as clarity, energy as well as beauty, and definition as well as intensity. Vowel sounds give choral music its color and vibrancy, and pure vowel sounds give the choir its distinctive sound. To illustrate the importance of consonants, have the children sing pieces with vowels only. This will be quite difficult at first, but what a great lesson! The choral conductor must insist that the children use their lips, tongue, and teeth as they enunciate words clearly and that this looks natural and not contrived. A good exercise for the children is to watch a video of them singing but with the sound turned off. If their faces on the video appear lifeless and they are unable to detect any of the words, then the children will realize that they need to work on their diction.

Good conducting gestures help the choir with diction, although children should mark in their music where final consonants come. A conductor's preparation beat needs to be effective enough to give the children time to breathe and sing the initial consonant strongly together. The softer the vowels get, the louder and more intense the consonants must be; otherwise soft singing loses its vitality. While the conducting gesture for soft singing is small, this is one place where the conductor could mouth the words to help the children maintain intensity. One or two children need to be chosen to come up to the front of a rehearsal and listen for clear text and watch those children who are doing well. Peer evaluation in a positive, constructive way can help reinforce many important concepts.

Live acoustics can play havoc with diction. It is always wise to have the text printed in the program, but in a hall or church with live acoustics it is essential. Make sure that whoever is responsible for preparing the printed program is aware of page turns at natural breaks in the text *and* in the music. Nothing is more annoying during a performance than hearing all members of the audience turn a page at the same time during a soft passage of music.

## Common Diction Errors

- The letters "gr" at the beginning of a phrase will not be heard unless they are exaggerated.
- The word "Lord" is often mistreated because of the "aw" vowel and too much "r." The "r" should hardly be heard, and the vowel sound should be close to a long "o."
- The initial consonants "f" and "v" will not be heard unless exaggerated as in words such as "life," "live," and "fire."
- The letter "r" is a major problem in the middle of a word or at the end of a word. Generally there is too much of it. The words "further" and "ever" must be sung with the "r" softened. The word "bird" must almost be sung

"buhd," again without it sounding contrived. The word "world" must almost sound "wuhld" when sung.

- Two-syllable words such as "angels," "singing," "many," "voices," "glory," and countless others must have a lighter second syllable.
- Words such as "tune" and "new" should be sung as "tyoon" and "nyoo" instead of "toon" and "noo."
- "Our" should be sung as "aoor" instead of "are."
- The third syllable of the word "instruments" is often sung too loudly. A case in point is the phrase "All the instruments of joy" in Henry Purcell's "Sound the Trumpet."
- The initial consonant "c," especially at the beginning of a phrase, is usually not strong enough.
- Diphthongs such as the one in the word "sound" are often mistreated. It must be sung as "sahoond," without any hint of a nasal quality, and similarly with the words "down," "around," "out," and "mountain."
- The final "p" at the end of a word must be exaggerated or it will not be heard. For example, in the case of the words "pipe" and "harp" the children need to be taught to sing "pipuh" and "harpuh."
- The word "spirit" is a great test of any choir. It is not "speerit." Both "i" vowels are short "i"s. The "r" needs to be light. The second syllable needs to be lighter than the first.
- The "ay" vowel in the words "day" and "brave" must be a modified "eh" rather than the spread diphthong so often sung.
- Final "t"s are easy. (In many cases they are too loud and the conductor needs to remind the choir that the final consonant must be in proportion with the volume of the phrase itself. The conducting gesture helps here.) Final "d"s such as in the word "God," however, need to be exaggerated.
- The word "beauty" must have an "oo" vowel sound in it, and the sooner the choir sings it, the better.
- The words "which," "why," "when," "where," and "what" need an exaggerated "wh." This is done by a quick diaphragmatic breath and the vowel sound "oo" at the beginning of the word.
- The final "t" in the word "that" acts as a springboard to the following word and needs to be exaggerated. The children will then sing "that day" rather than the more familiar "tha day."
- The letters "pr" at the beginning of a word need to be exaggerated and the "r" even rolled slightly for greater definition, especially when coloring words such as "praise."
- "Doubt" and "about" are words that cause problems similar to those caused by "around" and "sound," since the diphthong is the same. Care should be taken to have the children sing an "ah/oo" combination for these vowels.
- Having children sing in foreign languages is very good for their diction, since they don't bring any preconceived ideas of vowel sounds with them. The four most common errors children make when they sing in Latin are

the following: "Kyrie Eleison" often is pronounced "Kee-ree-ay ay-lay-ee-zon" instead of the correct "Kee-ree-eh eh-leh-ee-sawn." In the "Gloria in excelsis" the children sing "Glaw-ree-ah in" (not the correct "een"!) "ekkshehl-sees." The children sing "ahgnoos" rather than "Ahg-nyus," with the soft "g." The "J" is often pronounced as a "j" as in "Jean" rather than a "y" as in "you." "Jubilate" must be sung "yoo-bee-lah-te" and "Jesu" is "Yeh-su." (When children sing "Jesu, Joy of Man's Desiring" in English, they must sing "Geez-yoo," since this is the English pronunciation.)

When the children are singing in foreign languages, invite an expert in that language to coach them. Make sure the parameters of the lesson are clearly understood beforehand, and explain any time constraints to the expert.

Good diction involves more than having the audience hear words clearly. How words are strung together, note by note, takes us to the next major tenet of great singing, and that is phrasing. Children can learn to sing phrases musically if the conductor is sensitive to text and vocal line and can provide a model for the children, either with his or her voice or on the piano or violin.


## Musical Phrasing

A great Canadian choral conductor once said he did not know of any hymns in four-four time; they are all in two. A great American choral conductor once said that all choral conductors need to spend time studying and singing Gregorian chant—only then would they know how to teach their choirs to sing with a legato line. If we combine these two ideas, we can form the basis of what makes a musical phrase. Heavy stress on unimportant syllables is the death knell of a musical phrase. Countless words that we sing have two syllables, and the second one must be sung lighter than the first. Choral music does not move note by note, syllable by syllable, but by phrases. Choral conductors need to spend time deciding on a phrase length. The most common would be four or eight measures. The following important questions need to be asked: Where is the phrase going? What is the most important word in the phrase? What is there harmonically that determines the length of the phrase? All music is either going somewhere or coming back from somewhere. All music has energy and forward motion. It is not lifeless. Choral conductors need to study the poetry first, since an excellent choral composer will write in musical phrases that complement the phrase lengths of the poem. Consider the Twenty-third Psalm, which has inspired countless choral composers, including the great Franz Schubert. There is a beautiful natural rhythm to the words when they are spoken. Why would choirs sing the second syllables of "shepherd," "pastures," "valley," "mercy," "goodness," and "shadows" with the same weight as the first syllables? Why would choirs sing the word "and" with the same importance as the words "rod" and "staff"? It makes no phrase sense at all, yet many choirs sing it that way.

One of the problems in teaching children's choirs is that often the notes are learned in isolation before the text is added. I think this is a huge mistake, since the children tend to phrase the notes in the way the piano has played them and if the pianist is not sensitive to the text, the phrasing will be unmusical. When you are teaching younger children, it is much safer to teach the words and their phrase length along with the notes. A conductor of children's choirs can develop his or her own sensitivity to text, line, and phrase shape by listening to excellent singers, by singing in an excellent choir, or by listening to outstanding children's choirs on compact discs.

The conductor's effective gesture is vitally important in getting the choir to sing musically. The gesture must reflect the kind of phrasing one expects from the children. If the conductor is merely beating time and starting and stopping the choir, the result will be unmusical phrasing. Gestures can be precise and still convey musical line and shape.

Let us consider "My Country 'Tis of Thee," or, as it is known in the United Kingdom and Canada, "God Save the Queen," in terms of the phrase possibilities. Most conductors, I suspect, would think of this piece as seven two-measure phrases. There is nothing wrong with that, particularly if the tempo is slow. However, the larger picture could be that there are three phrases in the entire piece. The first is six measures long. A breath could be taken after the fourth measure, but it is not the end of the phrase. The second phrase is also six measures long and builds in intensity up to "over us" or "mountainside." The final triumphant phrase is two measures long and is the place where the first two phrases have wanted to take us. We must resist the temptation to have each measure strong, weak, weak, since that is how we were once taught that three-four time is played. This leads to pedantic, unmusical singing. Bar lines are perhaps the worst thing that were ever invented for choral conductors—while they help organize the notes in some fashion, they must not overly influence phrasing. Every note after every bar line is not necessarily a strong beat.

Phrasing is a difficult concept because it is not either "correct" or "incorrect." It is not like tuning. A note or chord either is in tune or is not. As Robert Shaw once said during a rehearsal, chords and notes cannot be partly in tune, just as a woman cannot be partly pregnant! Sensitive phrasing, however, is another matter. It has everything to do with a choral conductor's taste, experience, and musical maturity. Children can be taught to sing with great sensitivity and can develop discriminating listening skills. These skills are bound to develop if the children sing in a choir where emphasis is placed on musical singing at each rehearsal.

## Perfect Intonation

There is only one reason that a choir sings out of tune, and that is because someone lets them. Singing in tune should become a habit. Singers do not sing out of tune deliberately. The challenging task for the conductor is to hear the faulty into-nation, analyze why it is out of tune, and then correct it. This is all done in a mat-ter of seconds. Less-experienced conductors would be wise to tape their rehearsals and listen to them several times at home. Often these conductors are concentrat-ing on so many tasks during the rehearsal that they cannot hear faulty intonation. It is essential that the conductor's ear improve with experience.

Singing in tune becomes a habit for the children if faulty intonation is cor-rected immediately. Their ears must be trained to discriminate between notes that are in tune and notes that are out of tune. At the first rehearsal, if the conductor sings a descending E-flat major scale and asks the children to stand when they hear a note out of tune, it is astonishing how many of them stand up in the right spot. Their ears are already learning to discriminate. If the pianist plays a pitch and the conductor sings the exact pitch and then a slightly lower one, the children will be able to identify which is correct.

Warm-up exercises and scales must be sung in tune. Chromatic scales and whole-tone scales help the children discriminate between whole steps and half steps. This is essential if the choir is going to sing with correct intonation. Con-ductors need to study their scores to decide where faulty intonation is likely to take place and be prepared to correct it in the rehearsal. These spots often involve the following:

- ascending whole steps and descending half steps
- major thirds that are not high enough
- key changes and sensing the new tonality
- repeating the same note several times
- leading notes that are not high enough

Many choirs tend to sing flat. Some sing sharp. Following are lists of reasons for both.

## Reasons for Singing Flat

1. Breath support is inadequate and posture poor.
2. There is a lack of uniformity and brightness in the vowels. (See figures 2.3a and 2.3b, which illustrate how the conductor can encourage correct vowel formation.)
3. Lethargy and general lack of concentration prevail.
4. The piece is in a key that is not conducive to good intonation. The worst keys for this tend to be C and F major. Transpose the pieces up a half step if your choir has difficulty singing them in tune.
5. The intervals are too close in ascending passages and too far apart in de-scending passages.
6. Leading tones and thirds are neither bright enough nor high enough.

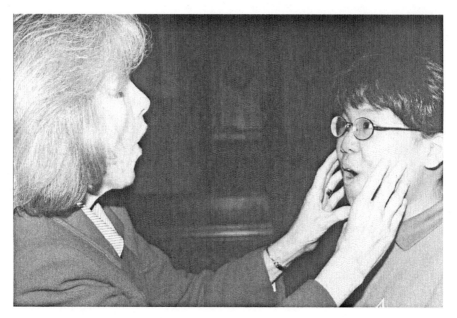

Figure 2.3a

7. The rehearsal has gone on too long. Too much time has been spent on one piece.
8. Boredom and fatigue on the part of the children occur as the result of an uninspiring director with an uninspiring rehearsal technique.
9. Too much slow music is rehearsed, and there is not enough variety in the rehearsal.
10. The conductor fails to correct faulty intonation straightaway and the children have not learned independent listening.
11. The children have come to depend far too much on the piano and have not spent enough time on a cappella music.
12. Children are sitting according to the same seating plan week after week. Children need to sit or stand in a variety of seating plans and be placed next to those who are singing harmony parts.
13. The conductor does not know the children's individual voices well enough to put children with strong voices next to those with lighter ones or those with an excellent ear next to those with a more modest ear.
14. The choir is singing the same piece for too long in the same key. Often transposing up a half step solves the faulty intonation problem.
15. Children are sitting in the same place during the rehearsal without stretching or moving around the room. The chairs are too close together in straight instead of curved lines and the children cannot hear anyone except the person on either side of them.

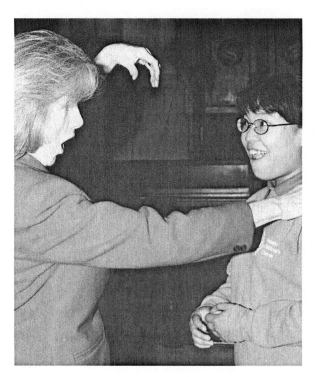

Figure 2.3b

16. The children do not understand the harmony. The conductor needs to have the piece sung in slow motion and stop on the chords to tune them vertically. The children need to learn, hear, and understand the feeling of singing a major triad or a dominant seventh chord in tune.

## Reasons for Singing Sharp

1. Vocal production is faulty.
2. Too much tension exists in the jaw, lips, teeth, and tongue. (Encourage the children to relax the jaw. See figure 2.4.)
3. Vowels are pinched.
4. The conductor shows too much tension and nervousness in his or her stance, gestures, and face.
5. The children have been singing far too long and are overcompensating.
6. The conductor sings sharp and the children imitate.
7. The conductor fails to hear the problem and correct it immediately.
8. The children are singing too loud to produce a beautiful sound.
9. The children are keyed up because of a major performance.

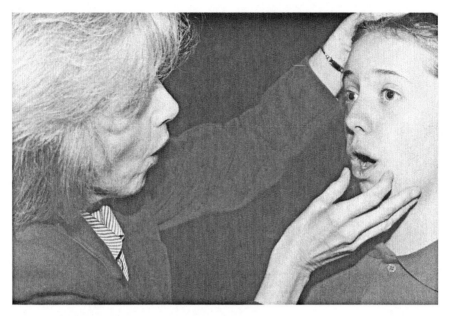

Figure 2.4

10. There is too much stress in the warm-up room beforehand, and too many changes are made at the last minute.

Singing in tune can and should become a habit in all children's choirs.

## Style

Children need to be taught folk song arrangements and art songs at an early age. Simpler pieces by Bach, Handel, and Schubert are essential songs for the nine-, ten-, and eleven-year-old singer. Choral conductors need to be very fussy with tempo as they are preparing their rehearsals. What is reasonable for the piece and what is in the best interests of the developing child's voice should be questions the choral conductor tries to answer. The range and tessitura are also very important considerations. A range from middle C to F above third-space C is enough at this early stage. The twelve-year-olds and older can certainly handle two octaves from A to A, depending on the vowels on the highest and lowest notes.

During the last twenty years, many composers have written music for treble choirs that covers a great variety of styles. Children are now singing jazz, gospel, bebop, pop, and many forms of multicultural music. This is certainly a good thing, and it has opened up a new world for children's choirs, their directors, and composers. Conductors must now understand and learn about styles of music with which they may be unfamiliar and even uncomfortable.

Before children venture out and experiment with different ways of using their singing voices and different ways of singing words, they must have a healthy vocal technique and an understanding of good singing and good diction in the traditional sense. Having a nine-year-old belt out songs from the musical *Annie* in a chest voice that is out of control is disastrous pedagogy and is worse than if the child did not sing at all. Children should not be using the chest voice until they are twelve years old and have been singing in a children's choir for a minimum of three years. The chest voice should not be used without some head voice in it and the same forward placement they have when singing an "ee" vowel sound in head voice. Conductors must be vigilant to make sure their choristers are always singing with a healthy technique, with a resonant singing voice, and with effective breath support. Children should not complain of sore throats. If they do, the voice is not supported on the breath or they have been singing too long in a rehearsal with repertoire that is too high or too low, with too much tension in the jaw and neck.

## Communication

The essence of great choral singing is the communication that takes place between the choral conductor and the choir and between the choir and the audience. The children's faces must radiate what they are singing about. How often have we seen joyous songs sung by children who have been rehearsing up to the last minute, so that every last ounce of joy has gone out of them? Our emotions can influence the essence of the performance and the very tone of the choir. If the children are being yelled at to keep quiet in a small room before a performance, how on earth can they go out onstage and radiate anything but frustration? There must be a quiet, reflective, and inspirational time before they go out onstage.

## Repertoire

Choral conductors can teach the art of singing through repertoire carefully chosen to develop resonant and buoyant tone, musical phrasing, good vocal habits, and musical taste in young children. Always examine the vocal range of a piece. Avoid pieces in C major that begin on middle C. Choose instead pieces that develop the mid- and upper ranges. The conductor needs to develop a sense of the tessitura that is conducive to developing good singing habits. Here is a list of pieces that I have found particularly effective in developing beautiful tone and musical phrasing with young children. (Other repertoire can be found in appendices 4B and 9.)

## Unison Songs for Seven-, Eight-, and Nine-Year-Olds

| | | | |
|---|---|---|---|
| How Brightly Shines the Morning Star | Bach, arr. Rao | Boosey & Hawkes | 6418 |
| The Zoo | W. H. Belyea | Leslie | 1980 |
| A New Year Carol | Benjamin Britten | Boosey & Hawkes | 5615 |
| My Caterpillar | Marilyn Broughton | GVT/Warner/Chappell | G-185 |
| The Little Birch Tree | Mary Goetze | Boosey & Hawkes | 6130 |
| Bessie the Black Cat | Peter Jenkyns | Elkin | 16 0110 |
| Adventure | Havelock Nelson | GVT/Warner/Chappell | VG-1016 |
| If I Were . . . and The Moon (especially The Moon: Transpose up a half step to F sharp major.) | Elizabeth Pollmer | GVT/Warner/Chappell | G-151 |
| The Kangaroo | Alec Rowley | Novello | 395 |
| Sleep, My Baby | Arr. Alec Rowley | Boosey & Hawkes | 5449 |
| We Will Sing for Joy | Domenico Scarlatti, arr. Helenclair Lowe | Choristers Guild | CGA-202 |
| To the Moon | Schubert, arr. Barron | McGroarty | MMP-16 |
| The Hand of Spring | Eric Thiman | Cramer | 134 |
| The Path to the Moon | Eric Thiman | Boosey & Hawkes | 18160Unison |

## Unison Songs for Children Ten and Older

| | | | |
|---|---|---|---|
| Bist du bei mir | Bach, arr. Calvert | GVT/Warner/Chappell | GVTVG-183 |
| Lullaby | Johannes Brahms | Hinshaw | HMC1536 |
| The Birds | Benjamin Britten | Boosey & Hawkes | OCTB6524 |
| The Child | Bob Chilcott | Oxford | U170 |
| And God Shall Wipe Away All Tears | Eleanor Daley | Hinshaw | HMC1284 |
| The Birds | Eleanor Daley | GVT/Warner/Chappell | GVTVG-1011 |
| Sweet Was the Song the Virgin Sang | Eleanor Daley | Hinshaw | HMC1461 |
| As I Hear the Sweet Lark Sing | Richard DeLong | Plymouth | HL-518 |
| Pie Jesu | Robert Evans | GVT/Warner/Chappell | VG-1010 |
| The Lord's Prayer | David Fanshawe | Hal Leonard | 085955499 |
| Pie Jesu | Gabriel Fauré | Boosey & Hawkes | OCTB6631 |
| Art Thou Troubled? | Handel, ed. Bartle | Hinshaw | HMC1431 |
| She's like the Swallow | Arr. Godfrey Ridout | GVT/Warner/Chappell | VG-1024SA |
| Litanei and Nacht und Traume | Schubert | GVT/Warner/Chappell | G-191 |

| The Man in the Moon | Eric Thiman | Curwen/Boosey & Hawkes | 72413 |
| Orpheus with His Lute | Ralph Vaughan Williams | OUP | OCS 52 |

## Two-Part Songs for Children Ten and Older

| Nigra Sum | Pablo Casals | Tetra Music Corp. | Tc 120 |
| Mid-Winter | Bob Chilcott | OUP | OUP T121 |
| My Heart Soars | Ruth Watson Henderson | Hinshaw | HMC1238 |
| Psalm 23 | Srul Irving Glick | earthsongs | |
| Bashana Haba-a | Hirsh, ed. Leck | Posthorn Press | C1019 |
| Nodle Kangbyon | Wallace Hornady | earthsongs | |
| Evening Prayer | Humperdinck | Leslie Music | 2003 |
| Good Night | Kabalevsky, arr. Rao | Boosey & Hawkes | OCUB6441 |
| Al Shlosha D'Varim | Allan Naplan | Boosey & Hawkes | M051-46783-9 |
| Stabat Mater | Pergolesi | Hinshaw | HMB209 |
| For the Beauty of the Earth | John Rutter | Hinshaw | HMC469 |
| I Will Sing with the Spirit | John Rutter | Hinshaw | HMC1387 |
| The Lord Bless You and Keep You | John Rutter | Hinshaw | HMC1169 |
| Can You Count the Stars? | Jonathan Willcocks | OUP | E156 |

## Three-Part Songs for Children Ten and Older

| Donna, Donna | Arr. C. B. Agnestig | Walton | WTC-1008 |
| Blessing | Katie Moran Bart | Curtis/Kjos | C8425 |
| The May Day Carol | Arr. Betty Bertaux | Boosey & Hawkes | 6358 |
| Jubilate Deo | David Brunner | Boosey & Hawkes | M051-47169-0 |
| Non Nobis, Domine | Byrd, arr. Bartle | Hinshaw | HMC1161 |
| D'où viens-tu, bergère? | Arr. Howard Cable | Hinshaw | HMC1188 |
| Fare Thee Well, Love | Arr. Stuart Calvert | GVT/Warner/Chappell | VG-350 |
| Kookaburra | Arr. Carolee Curtright | Boosey & Hawkes | OCTB6255 |
| Each Child | Eleanor Daley | McGroarty | MMP-07 |
| Seven Songs Home | Peter Maxwell Davies | Chester | 55436 |
| Cantique de Jean Racine | Gabriel Fauré | Hinshaw | HMC1730 |
| Voices of Light | Paul Halley | Pelagos | |
| La Lluvia | Stephen Hatfield | Boosey & Hawkes | M051-46941-3 |
| Vus Vet Zayn | Stephen Hatfield | Plymouth | HL-231 |
| Go Down, Moses | Arr. Mark Hayes | Hinshaw | HMC1302 |
| The Ships of Arcady | Michael Head | Boosey & Hawkes | H.15322 |
| The Sow Took the Measles | Arr. Stuart Hunt | Hinshaw | HMC1432 |
| Stars | Larysa Kuzmenko | Boosey & Hawkes | OCTB6767 |
| Cape Breton Lullaby | Leslie, arr. Calvert | GVT/Warner/Chappell | VG-327 |

| A Clare Benediction | John Rutter | Hinshaw | HMC1634 |
| Glory to Thee, My God, This Night (Tallis Canon) | Tallis, arr. Brown | OUP | OUP 40.922 |
| The Magic Store | Alexander Tilley | Frederick Harris | 8547 |

## Conclusion

Training eight- to fourteen-year-old children to sing is a highly satisfying task. Collectively, these children can become an artistic instrument of great versatility, flexibility, and musicality. It is essential that the children are in the care of skilled and knowledgeable pedagogues who are also fine musicians.

# CHAPTER THREE

# Checklist for Ideal Rehearsals and Preparation for Complete Artistic Performances

What makes a children's choir performance inspirational rather than perfunctory? Why does one performance move us to tears while another may leave us only satisfied? How should a conductor sow the seeds for a complete artistic performance? It is in well-organized, thoroughly prepared, and dynamic rehearsals that the children become an artistic instrument and a vital rapport is established between choir and conductor. Only then can the music begin to touch the soul.

An excellent rehearsal is perhaps an art form in itself. Conducting a rehearsal requires total concentration and the complete integration of body, mind, and spirit; as a result, it is mentally and physically exhausting. The pacing of a rehearsal is critical. The conductor must emit much positive energy, while the singers should feel a sense of accomplishment and well-being. Most children come to a rehearsal because they love music, they want to improve their singing, they want to feel fulfilled, and they want to enjoy one another's company. At the end of the rehearsal, the children must be "on a high."

## Before the Rehearsal Begins

The Physical Arrangement

- The conductor arrives in plenty of time to make sure the setup is conducive to an effective and efficient rehearsal.
- Loose chairs are much better than fixed seating. Chairs that support good singing posture are ideal. The chairs should be arranged so that the conductor can see everyone and should be spaced out and not crowded.

- There must be adequate light, a comfortable temperature, and as much fresh air as possible. Nothing can ruin a rehearsal more quickly than a stuffy, poorly lit room.
- The accompanist should have adequate light and the piano should be positioned so the accompanist can see the conductor easily without blocking the children. The lid should be open on the short stick.
- The conductor's music stand or stands should be no higher than the hips of the conductor and should have proper lighting.
- A side table placed near the conductor's music stand should have room for scores, a water bottle, and personal items. A box of tissues and a jar of pencils should be in reach of the children.
- Also on this side table should be taped large labeled envelopes for collecting any paper that the children or rehearsal assistants have to hand in to the conductor. These could include notes from parents, the attendance forms, the attendance sheet, applications for apprentice-trainers, and written sight-singing exercises. Having separate labeled envelopes helps organize the steady stream of paperwork received each week.
- Adequate microphones need to be in place if the conductor is working with a large choir in a big room where a normal speaking voice cannot be heard.
- A blackboard or chart that lists the pieces in the order that they will be rehearsed should be in place.
- The rehearsal area must look neat and tidy. A messy room does not encourage the children to be fastidious or organized. There should be a trash can in the room. Music should never be on the floor but rather be kept in individual music bags.

## Musical Preparation

- The conductor must have thoroughly marked his or her own score with the breath marks, phrasing, and articulation. If the children are preparing a newly commissioned work that is to be photocopied, the conductor can save valuable rehearsal time by marking in phrasing, breath marks, and voice parts before it is run off. Difficulties should be anticipated and noted. Places in the score that help singers find pitches and relate to pitches should also be marked.
- The conductor, from the initial rehearsal, needs to have a concept in mind of what he or she wishes the ultimate performance of each piece to be, while at the same time being realistic about the possible limitations of the choir.
- The accompanist's score needs to be marked, and the conductor and accompanist, particularly if they are not used to working with each other, should go over the music together before the first rehearsal.
- When the first rehearsal begins, ideally the conductor should have the score in his or her head and not in the score.

## Arrival of the Children

- The children sign in at the registration desk, manned by parent volunteers, and pick up their memos and any new music.
- A seating plan has been organized so they know where to sit. If the children are in the first or second grade, names are put on their chairs.
- Hats come off; coats go on the backs of the chair; mittens and scarves go down the sleeves. Music bags are placed beside the right chair legs. All other bags, such as school bags, go under the chair. With older children, Walkmans, sunglasses, and hats come off. Tape recorders are ready to record.
- The children must put their music in order before they socialize. If they arrive early, children can come and sing individually at the piano or do the weekly sight-singing exercise printed at the top of each memo.

## The Start of the Rehearsal

- Never, ever yell to get children's attention. A good method of getting their attention when you wish to begin is to have them repeat the conductor's A on a beautifully formed "oo" vowel sound and sustain it. The conductor can then start conducting the pitch A and give gestures to *crescendo* and *decrescendo.* When the choir is seated, focused, and singing *pianissimo,* the conductor may then speak quietly.
- For a list of warm-ups, please see appendix 1. Warm-ups must be used to warm up the mind as well as the voice and get the children focused. Warm-ups should never be routine or they become monotonous. They should always aim to teach breath support and good singing habits. They should also be tailor-made from difficult passages in the music the children are about to learn, which will make the music about to be rehearsed easier to read and more meaningful.

Sometimes the children need to be stimulated or calmed, depending on the time of day and what they have been doing beforehand. Use your speaking voice effectively, in a kind, quiet, relaxed, yet authoritative manner. Never talk over the noise. Do not nag. Use echo clapping as a way of focusing young children, and then speak to them always, always, always with respect.

## The Rehearsal

- All rehearsals have an energy and momentum that emanates from the conductor and the music. In addition to being thoroughly prepared musically, the conductor must be positive, in command, self-assured, and up! The conductor must connect with the singers via face, eyes, and gesture. Use a conductor's stool if you need to, but stand when the singers are asked to stand.

- All rehearsals differ, but generally speaking, the choir should be singing for 90 percent of the time, with the conductor talking only 10 percent of the time.
- The pieces need to vary in tempo, style, and tessitura. Let the children sing through a piece for the first five minutes. Work on the most challenging pieces about one-third through the rehearsal. Don't have the children singing high for endless periods of time. Do not expect everything to be learned instantly. Have them sing the most difficult passages with the less-experienced section of the choir in unison. In the Toronto Children's Chorus the less-experienced section is the first sopranos. Rehearsals must never be drudgery or dull routine. The pacing of the rehearsal is critical. Keep singers alert, fresh, and responsive by adding an element of surprise. Humor is most effective if spontaneous and derived from the rehearsal itself. Capitalize on these moments. They can add much vitality to a rehearsal and energize the singers.
- When you stop to correct something, never just ask the children to repeat a passage. Always make sure you give them a specific reason for repeating it. Use brief to-the-point statements such as, "that's much better," "very good," "that's the idea," "well-done," "improving," and "not quite as good that time—try it once more," and then go on. Do not use overblown praise unless they indeed do something that is extraordinary. If the conductor keeps saying "brilliant," then either the material is too easy or the conductor's standard is not high enough.
- Work on short sections, then put them together and have the children sing the piece through even if they make mistakes. Sometime mistakes correct themselves; psychologically it is good for the singers and the pacing of the rehearsal to ignore insignificant errors for the moment.
- Be flexible with your rehearsal plan. Be prepared to go in a different direction occasionally.
- Always reserve time in the rehearsal for unaccompanied singing. Singers must learn to listen to one another and not constantly rely on the piano.
- Have children stand and sit regularly. With older groups who have learned the music well, have them stand around the room in quartets.
- As the children become familiar with the notes, encourage them to look up and follow the conducting gestures. Praise those singers who are watching and following. The gestures must be effective, clear, and consistent. If they are, children follow and respond. Speed up and slow down occasionally to see who is watching. Exaggerate the changes of tempi and dynamics. The humor derived from this will help children remember essential concepts you are trying to teach and will add momentum to the rehearsal.
- Rely on the intelligence of the singers. Do not spoon-feed them, particularly the ones who have had one or two years' experience in the choir. Work to the top third of the choir. The other two-thirds will come along.

- Encourage involvement of the children by having them come up to the front to evaluate the progress of a piece. "Is the piece in tune?" "Are the parts balanced?" "Is the diction clear?" "Who is working particularly hard today?" "Who is trying to improve?" "Is the blend satisfactory or are voices standing out?"
- Rehearsing many small pieces is challenging for the conductor because momentum can be lost. After a song has been rehearsed, encourage the singers to put the piece back in the proper order in their music bags and then stand if they were able to put it away without talking. Praise those children who are able to change pieces without talking.
- There should not be any need for the children to chat to one another during rehearsal, but socializing during the breaks is a vital part of choir life. The break is a good time. Food and juice at break, organized by parent volunteers, are essential, as is a place to move. After the break, let the children sing though pieces—it is a poor time in the rehearsal to work on refined detail.
- The length of the rehearsal is not as important as how well rehearsal time is used and what is accomplished. Effective, thoroughly prepared conductors can accomplish in one hour what others can do in two.

The following could be a checklist for the ideal rehearsal. The rehearsal:

- began and ended on time
- was well planned, with a list of pieces to be worked on and activities to be done listed on a board that all could see
- began with greeting the children with warm smiles and calling a singer by name each time an interaction took place between the conductor and the singer
- continued with an appropriate warm-up, geared not only to the voices but also to skill building related to pieces being rehearsed
- started with pieces that were familiar and needed polishing and went on to new material that needed much concentration
- finished with something the choir sang well, leaving the singers on a high
- taught skills in sight-reading and improved musical knowledge
- was mostly singing, with minimal talking from the conductor
- contained a few elements of humor to break any tension that may have gathered
- included space changes when there was a lull or the children were restless
- created opportunities for peer evaluation and assessment
- rewarded excellence with a gesture, a word, or a tangible thing like a star or badge
- enabled children to predict what was coming next but also had a few elements of surprise
- gave the children a feeling of satisfaction, enjoyment, accomplishment, and importance

- created opportunities for challenges without frustrations
- left the children eager to come back to the next rehearsal

This list is ideal and could be used to evaluate a rehearsal or help a conductor come to terms with a rehearsal that he or she deemed unsuccessful. Vibrancy, energy, imagination, and humor are the hallmarks of an effective and successful rehearsal. One hopes that the conductor can hear what he or she sees in the score and react quickly. If not, the conductor should record the rehearsal and listen to the tape at home. The conductor should then try to write out the vocal parts by memory. This is really the only way to improve one's inner hearing. Hearing what one sees in the score is an essential prerequisite for every choral conductor.

The following could be a checklist of poor rehearsal techniques. The conductor:

- wastes precious rehearsal time with personal anecdotes
- wastes precious rehearsal time on lengthy analyses of the score to make sure the choir is aware of how talented and knowledgeable he or she is
- spends an unnecessary amount of time getting, for example, a final "t" on a consonant, while the rest of the score is not learned
- yells over the talking of the singers, so no one listens and explanations have to be repeated
- belittles the singers, has a condescending manner, and uses sarcasm
- tells the singers everything is wonderful
- uses words such as "fantastic," "brilliant," "great," and "marvelous"
- asks open-ended questions so everyone gets to help make decisions on the interpretation of the music and respond to the open-ended questions simultaneously
- constantly sings with the choir and as a result never really hears the choir
- overrehearses easy things and leaves challenging pieces hanging in the balance
- thinks choral discipline is unnecessary because he or she wants everyone to have a good time

## The Dress Rehearsal

The dress rehearsal can present a host of new problems, which the conductor must try to solve. This rehearsal must be very carefully timed, because there are many details to be addressed. In a performance hall or church, adjustments may have to be made because of acoustic changes. Ideally, a choir rehearses in a somewhat dead hall where mistakes are easily heard and the singers do not get a false concept of the choir's sound. The performance in a live hall can enhance the quality of the choir's sound and even mask problem voices and poor blends. Singing fast pieces in a live hall can be disastrous when singers cannot hear one another. Adjustments in tempo will have to be made to remedy this, or drop the piece from the program. To create even more problems, the presence of a huge audience, especially wearing heavy winter coats, will change the acoustics again.

The final rehearsal must not be one where musical details are drilled. These should have been covered in the regular rehearsals. The singers should not be physically or vocally fatigued. The best singing must be saved for the concert, and children must be reminded about saving their voices. Details such as entrances and exits must be worked out, preferably by someone else, but the conductor still needs to be aware of what is happening. It is much better if the children are given these details in writing as well as verbally. The verbal directions need to be given by someone who understands children and how they learn. An effective, well-organized dress rehearsal should have a positive impact on the quality of the performance.

The fifteen minutes before the concert are critical. Children need to focus with the conductor and have a time of quiet reflection. If the children are out of control with excitement, hours of preparation can be harmed and a poor performance can result. The conductor needs to be with the children for this special time. Older children can also be encouraged to mentor here and show leadership with the conductor present. The children must learn to conserve their energy so that it can be released at the time of performance. It is vitally important that the children are not left in the hands of someone who may not understand the delicacy of the situation and tries to gain control by yelling. The last thing the children need at this juncture is to have their confidence and self-esteem suppressed. They are indeed justifiably excited and can be loud. This energy just needs to be harnessed by the conductor, who must also be a highly skilled pedagogue.

## Further Thoughts on Rehearsals

- Always provide the children with translations of foreign-language text, since it is crucial for them to understand the words they are singing. Good editions of octavos should contain translations and explanations of text. If you are having an outsider come in to assist with pronunciation, try to get someone who knows something about teaching children. Give the person a time limit. Work beside him or her on the podium and kindly assist in the teaching. It would be wise if the person had sat in for a good portion of the rehearsal beforehand to give him or her some idea of how you work and the pacing of the rehearsal.
- Remember birthdays and acknowledge them at break.
- Have a nonverbal rehearsal occasionally and see how well the children respond to your face and gesture.
- Answer questions at appropriate times so the impetus of the rehearsal will not be continuously disrupted.
- Do not copy someone else's rehearsal style. The manner, speech, and charisma that one conductor has will not necessarily work for you. Instead, analyze why the choir sings well under his/her direction and think about

the musical ideas that the conductor uses to bring the score to life. Then develop a style that suits your unique personality and nature.

Conductors need to tape their rehearsals and analyze them. Rehearsal techniques need to be honed by even the most experienced conductors. Rehearsals need to have variety and be stimulating. They need to engage the singers to evaluate themselves. They need to be purposeful. They need to be creative and thought-provoking. There should be merely a second or two when the conductor stops the choir and makes a comment. Longer than this will lose the choir. The conductor must, at the speed of lightning, recognize what the problem is and articulate a plan to correct it. Children are seldom able to correct more than two or three things at a time. Young ones need to correct one thing at a time, depending on the nature of the problem.

## Pitches and Rhythms

Incorrect pitches and rhythms must be corrected first. This can be done in a variety of ways, depending upon why the children are singing the incorrect notes and rhythms in the first place. In order for them to fix anything purposefully, the children must be aware of what it is that is incorrect. The conductor should sing or play a passage two ways and ask which they think is correct, then ask one singer to sing the passage correctly. Having the children repeat a passage several times in several keys is also effective. Teaching the children that ascending whole steps and half steps are wide while descending whole steps and half steps are narrow is the most important thing a conductor can do to make his or her choir sing in tune. The conductor must also insist that leading tones are high and thirds are high. If children have been taught to sing sequentials, whole-tone scales, and chromatic scales in tune, they will have little difficulty singing pieces in tune.

In order to reinforce this learning there has to be repetition or drill. Repetition always the same way will not improve the accuracy of rhythm and pitches, but repetition in imaginative and different ways will. "Everyone wearing blue jeans, sing it." "Everyone who has a birthday in October, sing it." "Everyone who has three brothers, sing it." "Everyone who lives in a house or an apartment with a number four in the address, sing it." "Everyone who has a dog, sing it." "Everyone who wishes they had a dog, sing it." Obviously, the number of times this is repeated should not exceed the number of times required to learn the concept, but great pedagogues say the average person must hear something five times in order to remember it. A conductor must use his or her imagination to develop creative ways of correcting rhythms and pitches in the rehearsal. These ideas are the essence of effective teaching.

## Intonation

Intonation is the next thing that must be corrected. There is only one reason that a choir sings out of tune, and that is because someone lets them. Intonation is a habit. The conductor needs to correct it so the children can themselves tell whether something is out of tune or not. The rehearsal atmosphere affects intonation in many ways. Children can sing out of tune

- if the conductor creates a tense working environment
- if they cannot hear one another
- if they cannot see the conductor
- if the conductor cannot see all of the children
- if they cannot hear the piano
- if the room is stuffy and the children aren't getting enough oxygen to the brain
- if they have spent too much time on the same piece and are bored with it
- if the lighting is dull
- if the ceiling is too low
- if the acoustics are too live or too dry
- if the rehearsal space is too small
- if they have not been placed strategically for vocal and social reasons
- if the chairs are placed too close together

## Vowel Sounds

Uniform vowel sounds give a choir its unique tone and color. The vowels must be beautifully shaped and properly supported. Again, role modeling by the conductor is the most expedient way to achieve the desired results.

## Diction

Impeccable diction is the next thing to go after. The children can be taught through the conducting gestures to put final consonants on correctly. Young children enjoy learning how to give a cut-off gesture themselves, and it helps reinforce this concept. For a more in-depth study of both intonation and diction, please refer to chapter 2.

Children working in pairs can learn a great deal by watching and evaluating each other. Jaws must be dropped and all tension in the face should be eliminated if children are to sing with a free, unrestricted tone. Peer evaluation is most helpful here.

## Blend

Blend is usually not a great problem with children's choirs unless a child develops a unique sound. This unique "solo" quality sound often occurs when a girl is fourteen or fifteen and with boys' voices a year before the change begins. The best solution to this problem is placement. The conductor needs to work with a variety of seating plans to find the best blend.

## Balance

Balance is a major concern for children's choirs, since the instrument as a whole changes and develops over a season. What worked in September does not necessarily work in May. The younger children are often reluctant to sing out early in the year, but after learning the material and gaining confidence these children, often first sopranos, sing out and the choir balance becomes top-heavy. One remedy is to have the children learn more than one part and gradually increase the number of altos as the year goes by.

## Phrasing, Style, and Interpretation

Appropriate phrasing, style, and interpretation are usually the last things a conductor tries to achieve in a rehearsal. Children can be and should be taught to mark the breathing in the score. Phrasing, style, and interpretation can often be taught through imagery. A conductor needs a host of life experiences and an understanding of children's minds to use imagery effectively. Imagery used effectively is one of a conductor's greatest assets, since the singers will remember vividly what has been taught.

## The Complete Artistic Performance

Having worked out the preceding fundamental concepts of choral music, the conductor needs to turn his or her attention to the most challenging aspect of all music making. The work needed to train the choir to give an exceptional performance will now be discussed.

## Preparation

Sometimes a performance is note-perfect and in tune. The directions in the score are followed closely and implemented. The tempo is exactly as the composer wished. The venue is more than satisfactory, with good acoustics and good lighting. The conductor's gestures are clear. The diction is clean and words clearly understood. The parts are well balanced, and the blend is perfection. Yet despite the many hours of preparation that had been given to the performance, the performance is perfunctory and uninspiring. The emotions of the audience are not stirred. Why this happens is somewhat of a mystery. Moving performances are rare but are thrilling to hear. Thrilling artistic performances are what all of us try to achieve but rarely give.

It has been mentioned previously that thorough score preparation is essential before a complete artistic performance can be realized. It cannot be stated often enough that before the first rehearsal begins the conductor must do a thorough analysis of the piece and have a complete understanding of it. The conductor needs to begin, as it were, with the end in mind and needs to hear the ideal performance of the work in his or her own inner ear. All further preparation and rehearsals will be organized with this ideal performance in mind.

While some conductors prefer pencil markings, others prepare their score using colored markers, since the coloring helps them memorize the piece. Specific colors are for specific ideas, and each conductor has his or her own system. For example, red may be used for dynamics beyond a *mezzo forte*. Blue may be used for dynamics less than a *mezzo piano*. Orange may be used to highlight thematic material, while green may be used to highlight tempo changes. Whatever the system, it must be consistent.

When approaching a new piece of music, the conductor should sing or play through all the parts. This enables one to discover passages that will be most difficult for the children and build the rehearsal strategies around them. It is important to find out as much as possible about the composer and style. Is this a Bach duet that will require Baroque articulation, or is it a folk song that requires simplicity and directness? Is the texture complex, with four-part contemporary harmony, as in a work by the great Finnish composer Rautavaara, or is the texture simplicity itself, as in a unison line by Brahms? If the composer is living, is it possible to contact him or her to discuss the work? Is the piece written in a style, such as jazz or gospel, that is perhaps not comfortable for the conductor, and would it be helpful to contact an expert? What is the text? How is the text married to the music? What is known about the poet or librettist? Does the accompaniment double the vocal line or is it completely independent? Questions such as these, and others, can be answered only by thorough preparation beforehand.

As the work is studied and analyzed, it is important to consider the kind of conducting gesture that will be used to express the meaning of the music. The conductor of a children's choir can elicit style and articulation from the singers through effective conducting technique; it is often not necessary to express the emotion in words. Conducting is far more than setting the correct tempo and keeping the piece together. If a work that demands a legato line is conducted with a non-*espressivo* pattern or if a Baroque piece that needs a *marcato* beat is conducted with a relaxed *espressivo* pattern, a truly artistic performance will never be realized. The gesture must always reflect the musical style. Children's choir conductors who have not formally studied stick technique should consider doing so. The benefits are extensive: the rehearsals will be much more efficient, working with orchestral players will be much more rewarding; children will watch much more carefully when their conductor is highly skilled, and the choir will find it easier to work with many different conductors.

## Tempo

Setting the correct tempo is fundamental to good conducting. Conductors must be able to find metronome markings easily in their heads, since playing a piece too quickly or too slowly can ruin it. Tempo considerations must be done during score preparation, but there should be room for some flexibility in rehearsal. Metronome markings in a score are not infallible; they are a guide. Conductors need to take into account the choir's vocal abilities, the style of the work, the acoustics of the performing venue, and whether or not the text can be clearly enunciated and heard at a particular speed.

## Text

The text must be clearly heard. It is the consonants that give the performance its much-needed vitality and definition. Beautifully placed, uniform vowel sounds are not enough; they must be clothed in consonants. Children need to be taught where in the measure to place the final consonants and then be shown with a clear gesture. During rehearsal enjoyable games can be introduced in which the children themselves conduct and put final consonants on words. Two or three children could be invited to come to the front to see if the text can be heard and if the consonants are exactly together. These children can then choose two or three others whose faces they think reflect the spirit of the music. Watching and listening to the choir gives choristers a totally different perspective from standing in the middle of it and singing.

Foreign-language texts must be sung with great clarity and expression so the audience will be captivated by the piece. The audience's enjoyment and understanding will be further enhanced by an excellent translation available in their programs.

Tasteful word coloring can take a performance of a work to new heights. The children must think of the meaning of words such as "beauty," "slumber," "fear," and "angel" when they are singing them and give these words a thoughtful inflection. Children must be taught not to stress syllables equally. Most two-syllable words need to be sung by singing the second syllable softer. (The obvious exceptions to this rule are words such as: "rejoice," "today," "intent," "mistake," "distress," and "outside.") Three-syllable words must be sung by making the weight of two of the syllables lighter: for example, the second and third syllables of the word "beautiful" and the first and third syllables of the word "redeemer."

The major difference between orchestral and choral music is text. The main reason for choral music is to give singers an opportunity to express text. The conductor's countenance and the countenances of the children must express the text. The children—and their faces—must be totally involved in the performance. How often have we heard children singing about joy when there is little on their faces?

## The Tyranny of the Bar Lines

Conductors are often slaves to the bar line. They feel that all measures need a strong beat and that the strongest beat must come after the bar line. As a result, what is often heard is a series of wooden, foursquare, mechanical phrases. To avoid this common trap, the conductor must think of musical phrases horizontally, not vertically. All vocal lines are either moving forward toward the peak of a musical phrase or retreating from it. It is the text, melody, and harmony that help dictate the shape of a phrase, not the bar lines. Sometimes the subtle use of rubato, with careful attention being given to harmonic shifts and text, can vastly improve the standard of a performance.

Composers must organize the notes in some fashion, and the way it has been done for the past five hundred years has worked. It is up to the tasteful imagination of the conductor, however, to give the music a soul of its own. To achieve an inspired musical performance, the conductor must get the notes off the page and breathe life into them. The technique of the conductor or the singers must never get in the way of the music. Indeed, the technique needs to be so secure that the audience is not even aware of it. The notes and words on the page are a means to an end; they are not "the" end. A composer cannot write down all that is needed. I would go so far as to say that what makes music inspiring is very difficult to express in words. The soul of the music is not in black and white. Making the music live and have a soul of its own requires imagination, inspiration, and a thorough understanding of the text and how the music relates to the text. The musicality and sensitivity of the conductor—the conductor's heart, mind, and spirit—are revealed in this process. The ability of the conductor to effectively communicate these aspects of art to the ensemble is of paramount importance. This communication is achieved through elegant gestures, through words, and through the conductor's face and eyes. It is also achieved through charm, poise, personality, and charisma. When working on the podium, the conductor has nowhere to hide. His or her persona is transparent. The more willing the conductor is to be vulnerable, the greater the depth of music making. The lines of communication between the conductor and the ensemble must always transmit energy, confidence, faith, and trust.

The inspiration comes from the music itself and the conductor's burning desire to bring the music alive through the singers. The imagination comes from the very essence of the conductor's being and from the ability to motivate the singers to release their own imaginations in rehearsal and performance. Art is not prepackaged and then delivered. Great conductors do not tie up a tidy parcel in rehearsal and then present it in performance. Artistry is a live process and great artists often "seize the moment" in live performance and go with it. As a result, no two great performances are ever the same. This is one of the true joys of music making.

Inspiring performances conclude a conductor's long and challenging journey. They are the result of many musical experiences and a lifetime of study and reflection. A conductor must not get discouraged along the way. Giving children the opportunity to create great art is surely one of life's noblest tasks.

# CHAPTER FOUR

# *Developing Literacy*

One of the long-term goals of all children's choir directors must be to develop reading skills that foster independence. Teaching children music exclusively by rote in the choral rehearsal is equivalent to reading stories to a second- or third-grade class without ever letting the children read stories by themselves. It is a great disservice to the children if they are not taught to read music well. In the same way that very young children can master new language, the earlier they are taught to read music, the better. When they can read well, they receive enormous personal satisfaction and can be much more effective in the rehearsal. Learning to read music is perhaps the greatest of all challenges for a children's choir, but it must be done.

Many choral directors want to teach literacy skills but feel they are too pressed for time; instead, they choose to spend valuable time polishing repertoire for the upcoming concert. The irony is that if the children learn to read music well, much time will be saved in the rehearsal and advanced work on the repertoire can be done. The ideas explored in this chapter will help children become independent readers.

## Opportunities to Read Independently

In every rehearsal there must be opportunities for the children to read independently. This encompasses all levels of ability—from the youngest training choir member to the most advanced singer.

Sight-reading has much to do with tonal memory. On day one, the children should be listening to pitch discriminately. They need to hear the conductor sing a descending E-flat major scale, in tonic-solfa syllables, perfectly in tune. With the teacher pointing to the names of the notes (i.e. "doh," "te," "lah," in descending order) the children can be asked which note comes next. The answer is obvious, but what the children are doing is hearing the major scale sung perfectly. The conductor then can repeat the scale but sing one of the pitches noticeably flat and ask the children to stand when they hear the pitch that is out of tune. Seven- and eight-year-olds enjoy this experience because they think they are playing a game. The children are then encouraged to sing the descending E-flat major scale perfectly in tune. Afterward, the conductor may sense that one child can sing it alone but should request this only if quite certain that it will be done correctly. (If it is not done correctly, the conductor must not let the child lose face but should move on to something new.)

The conductor must try to make the reading skills relevant to the repertoire that the children are singing. It is extremely important for the children to have authentic music in front of them. A sheet with only words is like a story with only pictures. Children must develop a love of the printed score and a yearning to hear in their inner ear what they see on the printed page. The best way, of course, is to isolate four measures of blank rhythm and write them on the board. This could be something as simple as clapping in four-four time with eighths and quarters and stopping on one of the notes. A child then has to tell you what note you stopped on by coming up to the board and pointing to it. After several examples, the children are ready to clap the rhythms themselves and are able to find the four measures in their score.

It is wise, with a community chorus, to teach the children to count rather than give them "taa" symbols. When they learn to count, they can learn subdivisions, whereas "taa" is arbitrary and often has no relevance to other notes in the measure. (See appendix 12 for examples of counting.) Putting the last four measures of the song in musical notation on the chalkboard and singing it to them in tonic-solfa syllables while pointing to the notes is an important teaching device in the early years. Guided questioning, such as asking one of the children to point to the highest/lowest/longest/shortest note, will guide the children to an awareness of reading the score.

## Tonic Triad

Children must sing the tonic triad in solfa syllables for every piece they sing. Tonic-solfa syllables using movable "doh" are the best way to help many children learn to read and hear well. Key signatures in both major and minor, with up to five sharps and flats, should be on the wall. If you are teaching the "Tallis Canon" in G major, for example (see appendix 7), have the children sing "doh," "me," and "soh," in G major. The conductor should sing it through for them using the tonic-solfa syllables. Then have one child come up and show you which note you stopped on, which was the highest, and which was the lowest for a total of about five times sung completely through. The next time, the children could sing all the "doh" pitches when you get to them and you could sing all the rest of the pitches. The next time through, the children could sing all the "me" pitches and then the high "soh" pitch. Eventually, the children should be able to sing the complete "Tallis Canon" to tonic-solfa names.

Christmas carols are excellent pieces for tonic-solfa singing with very young children. The single line of notes, without accompaniment, can be given out, with the syllables hand-printed beneath. Since many of the tunes are familiar, the children are able to concentrate on the syllables and key signatures. The solfa syllables of "Oh, Come, All Ye Faithful" and "Away in a Manger" should be memorized and sung from memory each successive year.

Sequentials can also be mastered early in a child's progress through a community choir or through the third, fourth, and fifth grades of school. (See appendix 3 for a list of sequentials.) These sequentials can be used each week as warm-ups, to teach the children to sing beautiful, uniform vowels, to remember the many different vocal patterns they will use in their songs, to sing in harmony when the piece is sung as a round, and to sing in tune. The sequentials are an important tool on the way to independent sight-singing. After the fourth sequential has been mastered, the syllable names can be changed to "major second," "major third," and "perfect fourth," as the progression is sung. Games can then be incorporated so that the children only sing aloud when your hand is open and must sing silently when your hand is closed.

## Dummy Keyboard

The road to independent reading is not straight, nor is it exactly the same for all people. Having a cardboard dummy keyboard helps some children learn to read music, particularly if they have had a background in piano and particularly if they are visual learners. Showing the relationship between "soh" and "lah," and "te" and "doh," will help them understand whole tones and semitones. With a C major scale, seeing the distance from "doh" to "soh," or C to G, can help them remember a perfect fifth.

## Private Instrumental Study

There is no question that a child who studies an instrument such as the piano or violin independently can learn to read music more easily than can the child with no instrumental background. If it is not possible for your students to study instruments, consider bringing in some inexpensive recorders. Even a thirty-minute weekly lesson with a group of no more than fifteen students will help the children become better readers.

Invite some of your instrumentalists to play at Training Choir concerts. This has many benefits. It gives the child an opportunity to play in public. It gives other children a chance to appreciate the work of their peers. It gives parents continued validation for their investment in instrumental music lessons. It adds variety to the challenging programming for Training Choir concerts. It embraces the work of both choral and instrumental music with a focus on complete music making. A child who can sing a phrase with shape, line, and direction will play it more musically than a child who has had no vocal training. It is perhaps easier for children to achieve a more sophisticated level of music making in choral music than in instrumental music because they do not have to be concerned with the great challenges of such things as fingering, hand position, and bowing technique.

## Weekly Sight-Reading

Along with the many perfunctory details that need to go into community choir's weekly memo should be an exercise for each child to sight-read. At the beginning of the memo, write out a four-measure passage in C major with corresponding tonic-solfa syllables. The children may arrive early if they come from great distances— take this opportunity to hear their sight-reading individually. If they are successful (or even if they are not; use your discretion), give them a paper badge that says "Super Sight-Reader" or something similar. The badge should be simple and easy to duplicate, with a place for the child's name and the date. When the rehearsal begins, use the sight-reading passage as a warm-up for the whole choir. With very young children, you can accomplish several things in just a minute and a half. Ask who can name the highest note, the longest note, the shortest note, and the kinds of rests. Ask who can clap the rhythm, who can sing the notes, and who can clap and sing it. Ask what key it would be in if it were a tone higher. How many sharps would that key have? (Remember that an attractive chart with the key signatures is on the wall.) Ask those who came early and sang the sight-singing passage successfully to stand up and sing it together.

In a school situation, when there are no memos to hand out, the sight-singing should be written on the board. The first person to figure it out receives a badge.

If the children are not motivated to do this, it is likely because the work is either too difficult or too easy. Motivation is one of the most significant keys to learning. The work has to be easy enough for them to eventually sing correctly yet challenging enough to teach them something new. In order to make their work relevant, there should be some kind of tangible reward. Discovering what makes a classroom or choir "tick" is one of the great challenges of teaching. If a few of the children get the sight-singing passages correct each week, perhaps offer them a ten-minute independent study session at the beginning of each lesson. A leader should be appointed, and at the end of the ten minutes the group returns to sing for the class. Often incidental teaching brings greater rewards than a formal lesson. Using every minute wisely is one of the hallmarks of great teaching.

## The Five-Minute Silent Study and Drill

When introducing a brand-new piece, do not always begin with rote learning. Give the choir five minutes for silent study to discover as much as they can about the piece. Initially, the results they give you may be elementary in the extreme, but at least they are examining the score. After they have told you how many sharps or flats the key signature has, write the key on the chalkboard with "doh," "me," and "soh" written in whole notes. Do a short drill from "doh" to "soh," "soh" to "me," "doh" to "me," and so on. When the children have mastered this, put the entire scale on the board and drill the intervals, beginning with very easy ones such as "doh" to "ray." All the work done on sequentials will now begin to bear fruit.

Example: Ask the children if they can find any patterns in the music. Do any sections repeat, or is every measure different? Does the key stay the same throughout, or does it change? Does the music go very high or very low? Is the rhythm tricky or easy? Is there any section of the piece they can sight-read? Does it start on "doh" or another degree of the scale? Are there any "doh"–"soh" intervals or "doh"–"me" intervals? After the quiz let the children sing the music. Initially it does not matter if they make lots of mistakes. Their ability to sight-read will improve with time. Sing the music correctly for them and ask where their mistakes were made. Then ask them to follow along and tell you on what note you stop. Ask them to stand up and sit down each time you sing a "doh" or a "me." The number of questions is endless and will reflect the conductor's creativity and vivid imagination. The point is to keep the children involved in the teaching process by following the score. As they sight-read a new piece, the children should be allowed to make mistakes and not be overly concerned about them.

## New Skills

New skills must be taught in every new piece. Cumulative learning is critical when one is learning a language or learning to read music. Skills must be carried over from one piece to the next. When children in a Level 2 Training Choir study a piece such as "The Path to the Moon," by Eric Thiman (Boosey & Hawkes), they must learn about compound time. Children will have great difficulty thinking an eighth note gets one beat if no one has ever explained six-eight time to them. Having them read and sing-count "The Farmer in the Dell" would be a wonderful preparatory lesson before they begin "The Path," since likely all of them will know the tune. It would be helpful if it were in the same key as "The Path" to prevent further complications. The children should have "The Farmer" written out on a page with the counting written underneath the pitches. Several measures should be isolated for drill afterward. When you are teaching "The Path" it would be very wise to have the children sing-count the first four measures by rote at first. After the children have done this, the blank rhythms with solfa syllables underneath for the first verse should be sung from the chalkboard. In a community choir, the children should tape it and memorize it for the next rehearsal. In a school choir, the children should sing it during three or four subsequent lessons. Different blank rhythms in six-eight time should then be drilled at every lesson.

In a piece such as "Non Nobis, Domine," for example (Byrd/Bartle: Hinshaw), several skills can be found that can be carried over to other pieces. The concept of the dotted quarter note followed by an eighth note is always difficult for children to grasp. The conductor should isolate it on the blackboard and then sing-count the entire piece, asking the children to stand each time a dotted quarter followed by an eighth is sung. This concept does not have to be mastered in one lesson, but as the children become more familiar with the piece, they will come to an understanding of it. This piece is also effective for teaching beautiful, uniform vowels with relatively easy Latin and in teaching a three-measure arched phrase within an easy tessitura. After the unison line has been mastered, the piece can be sung as a round—an easy way to introduce the children to three-part harmony.

When choosing repertoire, conductors should always consider pieces from which the children can learn new skills in sight- reading.


## Theory

Sight-reading skills will be developed and understood more effectively if the children are given the opportunity to learn basic theory. Ten to 15 percent of each rehearsal could be devoted to theory lessons, if theory cannot be taught in isolation in small groups. Marking an entire choir's theory homework can be a logistical problem: In the Toronto Children's Chorus, four parent volunteers mark the children's theory workbooks each week. In addition, I give three tests each season that I mark myself so that I can tell how well the children are progressing and if I have to do some remedial work.

It is vitally important that theory not become a burden. Make it fun. The children should never be discouraged or frustrated because of onerous theory homework. For a list of concepts to be learned by the end of Training Choir I, Training Choir II, and Training Choir III, please see appendix 5.


## Sight-Singing and Ear-Training at a Summer Music Camp

Having the main choir attend a music camp for seven to ten days during the summer months has many advantages. An enormous amount of new music can be covered when the children are away from their regular routines of school, sports, music lessons, and other activities. It is also possible to offer the children an hour a day of sight-singing and ear-training.

During the re-audition process in May and June, choristers should be asked to sight-sing several examples of four-measure phrases to tonic solfa (see appendix 12). The examples should range from something quite easy to a passage that is very challenging. The children also should be given melodic and rhythmic dictation and be asked to write out a familiar song, such as "Happy Birthday" in B-flat major, "Jingle Bells" in G major, "Oh, Come, All Ye Faithful" in A-flat major, or "The Farmer in the Dell" in F major. The results of these activities will tell you everything you need to know about the children's musical literacy. For camp sight-singing and ear-training you will now be able to group the children into varying ability levels. The smaller the group the better—I would suggest no fewer than eight and no more than twelve children in each group. The re-audition results can also assist you in developing a relevant curriculum, not only for camp but also for the following season.

The Toronto Children's Chorus is grouped into six levels (see appendix 6), with three or four groups in Levels 1, 2, and 3. Beyond Level 6 is the Independent Level, made up of eighteen to twenty-four highly skilled singers. In this group, I try to balance the Sopranos I and II and Altos I and II evenly, but this is not always possible. The best sight reader who also possesses strong leadership skills is appointed the leader, and four section leaders are also appointed. At the beginning of camp, two or three pieces that the Independent group is given are prepared by the children for the final concert.

Two main goals of training children in the art of choral music must be musical literacy and musical independence. Only when the children are able to hear and reproduce what they see on the page have we done our jobs thoroughly.


## From Unison to Harmony

### Rounds

*Lesson 1*

In order for children to move comfortably from singing in unison texture to singing pieces in two and three parts, they must advance through various stages. In about the third grade, when the children are eight or nine years old, they are introduced to harmony through rounds, which can be printed out along with the tonic-solfa syllables and words. (See appendix 7.) Begin with simpler rounds like "Fire's Burning," the "Tallis Canon," and "White Coral Bells" and gradually teach more complex ones such as "Dona Nobis Pacem" and "Non Nobis, Domine." Use the rounds as warm-ups before rehearsal begins.

The young children must be looking at the round either on the printed page or on the chalkboard. The latter allows all the children to focus as the teacher points to certain things.

"Fire's Burning" should be in A-flat major, enabling these young children to sing in their best range, from E flat to E flat. The conductor should sing the entire piece first. The conductor should use a light head voice and sing with perfect intonation. Even a simple round can be sung with exquisite phrasing, without equal syllabic stress, and at a suitable tempo. Correct modeling for the children cannot be overemphasized. Guided questions need to be used each time a round is sung to maintain the children's interest and to give them a purpose for listening. "What note did I stop on?" "Where is the lowest note of the song?" "Where is the highest?" "How many high notes are there?" "Where are they?" "Name the note that follows the one on which I stop." "Name the notes in measure three, in measure four." "Stand up if I sing an incorrect note." "Can you identify the note I sang incorrectly?" "Name the pickup note." "Can you think of another song that has a pickup note?" The conductor claps the rhythm as the children keep a silent beat with two fingers on their arm. "Which word or note did I stop on?" A child comes to the board and identifies it. The children may be ready to sing the round all the way through. If they are not, teach it in two-measure phrases by imitation. At this point in the lesson, if you know the children's abilities well you may be wise to ask a child to sing it alone and ask another child to tell you which note the child stopped on. Ask another who can sing it through with words, with tonic-solfa syllables, with sing-counting. Leave the round now until the next lesson.

*Lesson 2*

Hum the round at some point during the rehearsal and ask if anyone can identify it. When part of the round is hummed a second time, ask a child if he/she can hum the next note. If more review is needed, ask a child to be ready to substitute the last word for another word and sing it. (Instead of "merry," a child might sing "happy," "sad," "funny," "scared," or any emotion; it need not have two syllables.) This is an opportunity for solo singing, which is necessary in every lesson. Eventually, the class or choir will be able to sing "Fire's Burning" all the way through. Only when they can sing it with ease should the attempt be made to sing it in two parts.

*Lesson 3*

Divide the class into two even groups and ask each group to sing the round alone. If one group is noticeably weaker, try to balance the voices by moving a few of the children. Success will only occur if the groups are evenly matched. Now have one group sing the song alone as you sing the second part. The children will be able to hear the harmony before they sing it. Then have the two groups sing the song as a round.

*Lesson 4*

If the children are able to sing the two-part round with ease, divide them into three groups of equal ability and try it as a three-part round. If this doesn't work, go back to singing it in two parts for several weeks.

*Subsequent Lessons*

Teach the children to sing the round in three parts. When this has been mastered, divide the class or choir according to birthdays. For example, those born from January to April will sing part 1, those born from May to August will sing part 2, and those born from September to December will sing part 3. The odds are that the children sitting next to each other will be singing different parts—the acid test comes when three children can sing the round as a trio. The children who find this relatively easy will be your altos or those who will be singing the harmony part.

## Two-Part Songs

### Sequentials

Sequentials provide excellent preparation for the study of two-part songs. Sequentials 2, 3, 4, and 5 can be sung in two or three parts after they have been mastered in unison. Begin as you did when teaching "Fire's Burning." After making sure that the two groups are of equal ability, have them sing first in two parts as groups, then three parts. Divide them up arbitrarily into three groups, by birthdays or by some other method, and try to make sure you do not have a cluster of children who are singing the same part. Try to find three children who can sing a sequential as a trio. These children would make good altos.

### Choosing the Altos

The fourth and fifth grade is an appropriate time to begin singing in two parts. At this age, altos are chosen for their excellent ear, not for their voice color, and the ratio of sopranos to altos should be about two-thirds sopranos to one-third altos. From the work the children have done in rounds and sequentials the conductor should already have a fair idea of those children who possess the stronger ears. Several exercises to validate your ideas should be carried out during a rehearsal:

1. Divide the children into two equal groups. One group sings repeatedly the following passage in G major: "doh," "me," "soh," "me," "me," "ray," "doh," in quarter notes. The other group sings a half-note "doh," half-note low "soh," quarter-note low "lah," quarter-note low "te," and quarter-note "doh." You should walk around group two while singing the tune of group one. The child who can hold his or her part while you sing the other part has a good musical ear. Tap that child lightly on the shoulder.
2. With the children still in the same groups, sing two melodies again, the lower one being more challenging. Walk around and tap those children who can sing the lower part successfully while you sing the other.
3. Repeat the entire procedure with the two groups singing the opposite melody.
4. Ask those children who were tapped twice on the shoulder to come to the front of the room. Ideally, one-third will come forward. If not, the children are not yet ready to sing in harmony. If more than one-third were selected, sing a third set of more challenging melodies and repeat the entire process.
5. When selecting altos who have great ears, you must be careful not to completely deplete the soprano section of those children with beautiful high

notes. (Remember at this stage, it is likely that some of your best altos are also outstanding sopranos.) The final step would be to have the "sopranos" sing an octave scale G to G. If the sopranos are breathy and feeble and the "altos" have a strong sound, many with a good high G, some of those altos will have to go to the soprano section.

6. A seating plan, drawn up by an assistant or even by one of the children, should be prepared for the next rehearsal. Be sure to distribute the strength in the soprano section so weaker singers sit next to a strong singer—if you have enough strong singers, have two of them sit together, with a weaker one on either side.

Two-part repertoire appropriate for a fourth- or fifth-grade class or for a second-year Training Choir in a community choir can be found in appendix 9.

### Sectional Rehearsals

It is better pedagogically to teach small sections of a work in harmony than to teach an entire work in sectionals. Children have a richer musical experience if they learn their parts simultaneously. The parts are often related, and children should be taught those relationships during the rehearsal. If they are going to achieve success, the sopranos and altos should be able to sing their parts a cappella.

After small sections have been taught separately in the combined rehearsal, the accompanist can be asked to double the alto line while the conductor sings the soprano line, or vice versa. This helps reinforce the parts if necessary. Conductors should avoid singing "over" the choir, as it prevents the singers from listening intently.

Although small sections are ideal pedagogically, there is no doubt that sometimes sectionals are necessary and save time, particularly if the children are weak readers and have not had the benefit of a background rich in rounds and sequentials.

Having mastered two-part harmony, eventually children will be able to sing in three- and four-part. Then they should have advanced reading skills and not need the crutch of sectionals. Three-part repertoire should generally be started in the sixth grade and four-part in the seventh. There are always exceptions, but these grades are a wise guideline. In some choirs, repertoire with a four-part texture may have to be avoided altogether if the second alto line lies consistently between middle C and low G and the singers are not comfortable singing in this range.

As far as seating is concerned, I prefer the sopranos to sit on my left and the altos on my right. The voice parts then correspond with the seating plan of an orchestra, where the first violins are on the left and cellos are on the right. When the children know their parts well, it is effective to jumble the seating to encourage the singers to be more independent. The children enjoy having this opportunity to sit next to someone new. Sitting or standing in trios or quartets is also a very effective way of encouraging independent parts and the necessary listening skills. Often a choir's ideal blend is achieved in trios or quartets.

Following are some sample teaching strategies for easy two-part songs.

*"Hand Me Down My Silver Trumpet" (arr. Bartle: Hinshaw, HMC1535)*

This is an effective piece for introducing two-part harmony to less-experienced singers because of the natural call and response of the refrain. Conductors are often concerned when teaching one part that the children learning the other part will be distracted. This piece minimizes that concern. It is important, however, to give each part a "listening question." After the verse has been taught, the following should occur:

1. The conductor sings the soprano line while the accompanist (or conductor) plays the alto line. Children listen for the number of times the word "down" is sung.
2. The conductor sings the soprano line and stops partway through. The children say which word comes next. (Repeat three times.)
3. The conductor sings the soprano line and stops on a note. A child is asked to identify the type of note (i.e., a half, a dotted half, a quarter, or an eighth), and one of the altos writes it on the chalkboard.
4. The conductor sings four measures of the soprano line and the sopranos then imitate it. The conductor or accompanist is still playing the alto part.
5. The sopranos should now be able to sing the line in its entirety without assistance.
6. Write measures 13 and 14 of the alto line on the chalkboard, since the children often need help locating their place in the score. Children identify the eighth and quarter rests.
7. All children are asked to follow the alto line in their scores as the conductor sings it. The conductor stops and the children identify where they are in the score.
8. The conductor or accompanist plays the soprano part as the conductor sings the alto part. The altos follow the alto line and sopranos follow the soprano line.
9. The conductor sings the alto line and stops to ask for the next word. Repeat four times.
10. The conductor sings tonic-solfa syllables from measures 16 to 20 and asks how many "lah"/"te" repetitions there are before "lah"/"te" "doh" occurs.
11. The altos sing their part through a cappella.
12. Sopranos and altos should now be able to sing their parts through independently. If they are unable to manage it, group the altos around the piano and have the pianist double their part. The conductor can then sing the soprano part with the sopranos. If this still does not work, teach each part separately and have each section sing their part a cappella.
13. When it is time to sing the third ending, the altos will need to be drilled on

the problematic minor sixth leap. The altos can sing measure 18 and stop on measure 20 to listen to the sopranos sing the C. Do this several times and then have the altos join the sopranos on the C.

14. In the third ending, children always have trouble with the repeated C's. Both parts should be asked how many C's they have in a row. (The sopranos have six and the altos have five.) Have each part sing separately and slowly, and then put both parts together slowly. Have them stop on the "ver" of "silver" to listen to the major second. If they are able to do this, the third ending up to speed will be easy for them. If they are not, repeat it slowly and separately until they can sing it.

### "To Music" (Arr. Betty Bertaux: Boosey & Hawkes, OCTB6573)

Children should be encouraged to sing this SA piece by heart. The noble text is reassuring for all of us who work in this great art, and we are grateful to Betty Bertaux for setting it.

1. All singers can be taught the descant line. The conductor begins by writing measures 53 and 54 on the chalkboard and teaching these measures by rote in four eighth-note groupings to "lah" (legato) and "hah" (staccato.) The conductor should sing each of the four-note groupings and stop on a note that one of the children should identify. The children should also sing the four eighth-note patterns and, when they have mastered it, sing all twelve, stopping on the quarter note F sharp.
2. The conductor asks the children to identify any octave leaps, eighth-note patterns, or accidentals each time he or she sings it.
3. The conductor asks the children to listen as he or she sings it and tell how the descant differs from the tune and how it is the same.
4. The conductor teaches by rote in phrase fragments.
5. In a fourth- or fifth-grade choir, the altos (the singers with the strongest ears) should sing the descant while the sopranos sing the tune.

### "Sing Me a Song" (Leonard Enns: Warner/GVT, VG-1026)

This is a very popular song with children. It is a good opening piece for a concert and also makes an effective encore. The optional harmony part is sometimes an alto line and sometimes a soprano line.

1. Before beginning to sing this piece, the conductor isolates the following three passages in the soprano line and writes them on the chalkboard:
   a. measures 9 and 10
   b. measures 17 and 18
   c. measures 45 and 46

Since these passages are somewhat similar, they cause great difficulties for students who are nonreaders. These measures, however, provide excellent opportunities to develop reading skills.

2. The conductor sings the three examples for the children.
3. The conductor asks the children how the passages are similar and how they are different.
4. The conductor removes the ties and sings the passage. The conductor then adds the ties and sings the passage and asks how the two versions are different. The children then sing the passage with and without the ties.
5. The conductor should then teach the soprano part over a three-lesson time frame, beginning each time by reviewing those three measures that were previously isolated. Part 1 is complete at the first beat of measure 18, part 2 is complete on the third beat of measure 38, and part 3 ends the piece.
6. Only when all the children have mastered the soprano part should the harmony parts be taught. The conductor should teach them by rote in the same three-lesson time frame as the sopranos were taught and with a teaching strategy similar to that used in "Hand Me Down My Silver Trumpet." The pianist doubles in octaves the alto line as the conductor sings with the sopranos.

One of the most effective ways to reinforce what has been taught, particularly in a community choir, is to have the children bring hand-held tape recorders to all rehearsals. Listening to the tape during the car pool drive or at home during independent study helps all choristers a great deal. (Further details on the use of recorders during the rehearsal will be given in chapter 6.)

# CHAPTER FIVE

# *Discipline*

It would be ideal if all children came into rehearsal bursting with enthusiasm and energy, sat quietly in their seats, prepared their music, and looked directly at you for the downbeat. This is perhaps impossible, but many of the ideas expressed in this chapter may help you get closer to the ideal and make music making more enjoyable for you and your students. One of the major concerns of teacher/conductors is discipline; hence this chapter has been devoted to exploring ways of preventing discipline problems from happening. A great part of the success of any rehearsal has to do with the preparation made before it. It goes without saying that you must know the music thoroughly. Despite knowing the music thoroughly, however, if the mechanical preparation has not taken place, the rehearsal is doomed to failure.

## Establishing and Implementing Routines

### Seating Plans

Children respond well to predictability but become frustrated in chaotic environments. It is important to have a seating plan that is easy to follow and takes into account factors such as the children's varying heights, voice types, and behavior patterns. Some time has to have been spent with each child or a group of children before the first rehearsal takes place in either a formal audition or an informal "getting to know your voice" session. "Getting to know your voice" sessions can be as simple as having a group of six children singing "Happy Birthday." It is important to know the voices you are working with. Early in the season it likely will be nec-

Figure 5.1

essary to experiment with various seating plans until you find the one that works. If the group is multiaged and possesses various skill levels, I find it beneficial to have a mentoring system where the older singers assist the younger ones. Such an apprentice/apprentice-trainer system provides excellent opportunities for leadership. Apprentice-trainers can help the apprentices by helping them put their music in rehearsal order, pointing out the line they are on in the music, encouraging good singing posture, helping mark scores correctly, and so on. (See figure 5.1 which illustrates this.)

*Hints:*
- I never place a boy between two girls, but I would never have the boys all clumped together.
- I prefer to place two singers with good ears next to each other, each sitting beside a child with a more modest ear.

- I have different seating plans for the rehearsal and the performance. When notes are learned and the children are secure, I place them according to height in a performance seating plan. Apprentices do not stand next to their apprentice-trainers in the performance seating plan.

## Chairs

Chairs must be arranged with the greatest of care if the rehearsal is going to be effective, without discipline incidents.

- They need to be placed with one chair width between them.
- They need to be placed with two chair lengths between the rows.
- They need to be staggered like bricks of a house so that every child can see and be seen. The conductor needs to be able to have eye contact with every child in the choir—every single child in that room is important to the success of the rehearsal.
- The chairs need to be placed in a curve so that those children sitting at the ends do not feel left out.
- The piano, if one is used, should be placed directly in front of the conductor or at the side so that the accompanist and all the children can see the conductor.

## Music Materials

The materials need to be well organized. For very young children, the music should go into a three-ring binder with each piece color-coded in the top right-hand corner for easy recognition. It is also helpful to photocopy skill-building loose sheets onto different colors of paper. Each child needs to have his or her own materials.

Older children need to have a repertoire list if they are working with more than four or five pieces. Music should have the child's name or the chorister's number on it. Pieces can then be divided up into colored file folders so the children can find them easily. Some conductors prefer to punch three holes in the octavos in order to keep them in binders. Use the system that is best for you—as long as the music does not fall on the floor or get lost, which encourages the children to squabble.

## The Room Itself

The ideal rehearsal space is well lit and well ventilated. There should be a clock on the wall and a list on a chalkboard of all the work that is to be accomplished that day. This list needs to contain review work, new work, and the children's own choice. The list needs to be set up so that the children will feel a sense of accomplishment, not frustration. One child can act as secretary and cross off the items on the list as they are covered. If it is a large rehearsal space, the conductor needs to use a microphone. The rehearsal must begin and end on time.

## Know the Children

The teacher/conductor needs to learn the names of everyone in the room and be able to address each child by name. Making a photograph chart of the seating plan is particularly helpful when dealing with large groups of children. Memorize their names from the chart. It is vital that you be sincerely interested in the well-being and development of the children. Find out what their interests are, and if you see them in the hall or when they come early to rehearsal speak to them by name. Ask them about the nonmusical aspects of their lives.

## The Speaking Voice

A teacher's speaking voice is a most important asset as well as a powerful tool. The finest musicians in the world can stand before a children's choir, but if they mumble, they will lose the children's attention and little will be accomplished. Depending on the size of the room and the size of your voice, it may be imperative to use a microphone.

An effective speaking voice should:

1. Be well modulated: The speaking voice must have a variety of sounds that are pleasing to the ear. Generally, good singers speak well, with the inflections used in singing also used in speech. A nasal, high-pitched, or loud, bellowing voice is grating to the ear and is not an effective teaching tool.
2. Be confident and calm: An effective speaking voice must have an air of confidence and charm that encourages the listener to listen. Nervous, irritating, or nagging voices encourage the children to lose their concentration, and if they get caught up in the hyperactivity they may even sing sharp. A calm speaking voice encourages the children to relax, thereby projecting a free sound that is in tune.
3. Be well paced and child-centered: An effective speaking voice is well paced—neither too fast nor too slow. I do not advocate talking down to children, since this insults their intelligence; instead the conductor's vocabulary and pacing should be child-centered and age-appropriate. Instructions need to be clear and precise, not long-winded and flowery. If the choristers do not understand the instructions, it is the instructor's fault, not theirs.
4. Use grammatical language: While effective teachers and conductors need not feel that they are broadcasting on the radio, it is essential that they speak correctly. Such colloquialisms as "you guys," "ya know," "ugh," "like," and "sort of" should be avoided. Instructions such as "OK, kids, get over here

right now" are degrading to the children. In very subtle ways, poor speech leads to an environment where discipline can become an issue.

## During the Rehearsal

### Establish an Effective Method of Getting Control at the Beginning

I have yet to see a children's choir where silence occurs and the rehearsal begins when the director walks onto the podium and raises the baton. I have seen echo clapping used effectively. I have also seen managers, teachers, and conductors yell to establish control. There are more humane ways to begin the artistic process. I prefer to sing on the pitch A, "Sing loo"; the children then sing "loo" on the pitch A and go immediately to their places to begin. They cannot talk when they are singing and they must sustain the pitch until they are seated with their music in front of them. (Choristers must look at the rehearsal list on the chalkboard before the rehearsal begins and get their music in order before they socialize.) Sometimes asking the chorister who is in place first to come up and give the cutoff motivates them to get ready on time.

If you use a podium, stand on it only to conduct. Do not use it to make announcements or for any other nonconducting activity. In this way, the children subconsciously begin to develop a respect for the podium and the person who stands on it. If your chorus sings with a variety of professional conductors, this is a very important routine to establish.

Involve the senior members of the group. They can sing the "loo" and get the rehearsal started. Some senior members will even be skilful enough to do the warm-ups.

Discipline in a chorus means mutual respect—between the choristers and the director and among the choristers themselves. A conductor's presence, manner, and deportment can enhance this respect or detract from it. To create the correct ambience for an effective, productive, and polished rehearsal, a conductor needs to have a presence that is not only an extension of his or her personality but also polished enough to command respect.

### Use Peer Evaluation

All the children need to be recognized in positive ways. Good behavior should be rewarded. If, for example, you have just asked for appropriate facial expression in a song that has been learned well and is approaching performance standard, choose two or three children to come up to the podium. Ask them to see if they can find a chorister who not only has a dropped, relaxed jaw but also knows the words perfectly and shows a facial expression that reflects the meaning of the text. This technique encourages those who may not be giving 100 percent to try a bit harder and be recognized for their efforts.

Figure 5.2

## Use Praise Effectively

Build a choral rehearsal dynamic through reinforcing positive self-esteem. During a rehearsal, it is important to make comments such as, "Hilary, thank you for sitting with excellent posture. I know you must be making a beautiful sound." Or, "Tristan, I can tell you have been practicing this week. You have all of the French text memorized. Good for you!" (See figure 5.2. This apprentice has just sung a French phrase correctly.) Of course, praise can be overdone and utmost care must be taken to ensure it is done tastefully and honestly. Children can tell instantly if they are being patronized, which makes them feel most uncomfortable.

## Vary the Activities

If children, at any age, are asked to sit in a chair and concentrate for forty-five minutes, discipline problems will inevitably occur. Use the skills and songs you are teaching in creative ways. A teacher's imagination and the ability to think of things on the spot are necessary assets. If the children can read words, ask them to stand when you sing an incorrect word. Ask them to stand each time you sing a whole note. If the children can read pitches, ask them to stand each time you sing an F sharp. If they have a song learned, have them stand and use their arms to demonstrate phrase lengths. Ask them to stand and conduct. Have older ones stand in groups around the room facing one another in a circle with two first sopranos, two second sopranos, and two altos in each group. Use songs that incorporate movement—there are many fine octavo works for treble choirs available. ("Haida" in Henry Leck's Plymouth Music Series is ideal, and I use it with the young ones every year. They love it!) Make up your own movement, especially in spirited folk songs, rhythmic spirituals, and African music.

Rehearsals must never be dull and uninspiring. Time should pass quickly. Even learning the most challenging music must never be drudgery. If the children cannot cope, it is not their fault. On the one hand, if the music is too difficult, the children may not have the background necessary to learn it. This is rarely the case, however. On the other hand, if the music is too easy, the children may get bored. Perhaps the conductor keeps rehearsing a passage over and over again without telling the choristers how to improve it; perhaps too much time is spent on one piece; perhaps the teaching is too predictable. When drilling an idea or skill, use humor. For example, if you are after a louder "k" in the word "make" on beat 3, have the children sing on one pitch "one, two, kuh," then ask them how to do it row by row; finally, have the row with the most accurate "kuh" add several words with "kuh"—you may end up with them singing on one pitch, "Bake and take the cake I make for goodness' sake; it's not a fake!" The children will remember the "kuh" in "make" the next time it is sung!

## Have Realistic Expectations

It is admirable to have high expectations, but having expectations that are unrealistic is bound to lead to discipline problems. The following questions, answered honestly, may help you evaluate and prevent discipline problems that arise.

1. Where were the children before they got to rehearsal? Were they in a gym class and now need to settle down? Were they in a math class and now need to move? When was the last time they ate? Were they stuck in traffic in a cramped car pool for an hour?
2. How long and how frequent are the rehearsals?
3. What repertoire did they sing last season? What values and artistic aspirations did their previous director have?
4. Should they really be singing in four languages? Do the children have meaningful translations? Should you put the Purcell away for now and work on something equally valuable that they can better relate to and learn from?
5. Are the children motivated by you or by themselves?
6. How much time do you spend at every rehearsal listening? How much time do you spend talking? How much time do you spend nagging? How much time do you spend whining?
7. How tired were you at the beginning of the rehearsal? Why were you losing your temper?

It is not possible to create glorious singing in a nagging, tension-filled environment. We must stretch ourselves continuously to find creative ways of teaching and engage the children in a positive, caring, and respectful manner.

CHAPTER SIX

# *The Importance of Organization*

## Personal Time Management and the Effect It Has on Your Work

Spending time organizing your projects, your priorities, and your thoughts is one of the most valuable things a children's choir director will ever do. All of us have the same amount of time—that is, twenty-four hours a day, seven days a week, and fifty-two weeks a year. If we use our time judiciously, we will not only accomplish more, but we will also accomplish what is important. Stephen R. Covey, in his powerful books *The Seven Habits of Highly Effective People* and *Principle-Centered Leadership,* establishes quadrants in which to organize time, list projects, and prioritize them. The first quadrant is labeled "Important and Urgent"; the second, "Important and Not Urgent"; the third, "Not Important but Urgent"; and the fourth, "Not Important and Not Urgent." Covey's quadrants can be most helpful to children's choir directors. In the "Important and Urgent" quadrant would come the daily and weekly commitments such as rehearsals, some meetings, upcoming concerts, some correspondence, and deadlines. The second quadrant, which many of us never seem to get to, is the most important one: "Important and Not Urgent." Serious score study, long-range planning, vacation time with family and friends, meditation, learning new skills, thinking, meaningful dialogue with colleagues, and significant reading belong in this quadrant. In the "Not Important but Urgent" quadrant are the many details that can overtake us and wear us down. These include many meetings, paperwork, phone calls, E-mails, and other people's minor issues. These are things we need to find someone else to do. Some items in this quadrant relate to putting out fires that might never have started if serious long-range planning that began with an effective mission statement had been in place. Much time is wasted in the "Not Important and Not Urgent" quadrant, and we will never get that time back. Watching television and meaningless reading come into this quadrant. Some telephone calls, many E-mails, and cruising the Internet can be great time wasters. Each time you agree to do something in this quadrant, it means you are sacrificing something from the "Important and Not Urgent" quadrant. Artistic directors are leaders, and leaders must be gracious with people and ruthless with their time. I heartily recommend Stephen Covey's books. They offer much more than time-management theories—they are life-changing and life-enhancing documents.

The following is a list of time savers that I have developed over the years:

- Always work from a prioritized list.
- Invest time in training people to do things for you that you do not need to do. Ask yourself frequently when you are working at a task, "Can someone else do this, so I can spend my time on the music?"
- Find a student to work for you on Saturdays and have him/her file music away. Keep music you need to study in a box and take time every week to give it away, throw it away, or file it. Keep a box for music to give away— repertoire that is worthwhile but that you won't use.
- Skim periodicals once a week. Tear out or photocopy articles that you know you will use and need. Make sure to record the name and the date of the journal on each. File them in a "Professional Articles" file folder for easy access. Throw out all periodicals that are over three years old.
- When attending a conference obtain a copy of the program as soon as it is available. Read ahead and plan to attend the sessions that will be the most beneficial to you. Take file folders with you that are already labeled to each session and insert material and notes from that session. Keep business cards that you collect at the conference in alphabetical order. Put them into your business card Rolodex as soon as you return to your office.
- If you do not know where your time is going and you do not feel as though you are accomplishing anything, keep a time log for a week—or, better yet, a month. Write down everything you do. Ask yourself at the end of each week what you are doing that really does not need to be done at all, what could be done by someone else, and what you do that wastes other people's time.
- Share projects with colleagues. Divide and conquer. Two heads are better than one and the whole is indeed greater than the sum of its parts.
- If you teach two training choirs as I do, rehearse them on the same evening with a thirty- or forty-five-minute change-around time. Try to have a least a day each week when you have no rehearsals or meetings scheduled and the office staff has been asked not to contact you.
- Try to get up early each day. Meditate; pray; look at your day and promise yourself that you will spend some time that day on projects in the "Important but Not Urgent" quadrant.
- Ensure that there is time every week for family, exercise, and leisure activi-

ties. You skimp on this at your peril. If there isn't enough time for these things, you are doing too much and need to address the problem. Someone else needs to share the load. Always ask yourself, "What is the worst thing that could happen if I don't get this all done?" If the answer is, "I could lose this job," perhaps you had better look for another one. No one can do it all, nor should he/she be expected to.

- Have breakfast meetings between 7:30 and 9:00 in the morning. Much can be accomplished at that time of day, and most people will need to leave by 8:45.
- Know how you spend your time. Know when your peak performance times during the day are. Plan for tomorrow tonight. Delegate wisely. Ask yourself often throughout the day why you are doing what you are doing. An artistic director must organize the amount of time spent with staff, board, committees, parents, and choristers to ensure that adequate time remains for the most important aspects of your job, score preparation and conducting.

Remember this Chinese proverb: "Besides the noble art of getting things done, there is the noble art of leaving things undone. The wisdom of life lies in eliminating the nonessentials."

## Effective Routines That Save Time and Maximize Results

### A June Parent Meeting

Auditions for the Toronto Children's Chorus are held on five Saturdays during February, March, April, and May for the following season. A meeting of all current and new parents is held in June and the new season's calendar is given out. It outlines all rehearsals, concerts, tours, recording sessions, and any other projects and activities for the year. The Chorister Handbook, which contains rules, regulations, routines, and expectations, is also given out, along with a separate Agreement for Membership in the Chorus, to be signed by each chorister and parent. The June meeting gives parents an opportunity to meet and bond with one another, to volunteer, to express concerns, and to ask questions. This procedure gives all concerned an opportunity to organize their time, family vacations, and activities around the chorus schedule. It also gives parents and choristers an opportunity to reconsider membership if they feel they cannot make the necessary commitment.

### Rehearsal Times

The Toronto Children's Chorus Training Choirs rehearse once a week for an hour. Membership in the Training Choir is based on skill, not age. (For a list of skills necessary to move up, see appendix 5A.) Generally, Training Choir I is second to fifth grade; Training Choir II is third to sixth grade; Training Choir III is fourth to eighth grade. The Main Choir, which is made up of two choirs, Cantare and Chamber from fifth through twelfth grade, rehearses twice a week, for two and a quarter hours on Tuesday and one and a half hours on Friday.

Rehearsals must be planned with great care so they can begin and end exactly on time. Respect other people's time and they will respect yours.

## Weekly Memos

All children in the Toronto Children's Chorus receive a detailed memo each week with information they need and with theory homework and memory work listed. The children get used to receiving the weekly memos and reading them. As the year progresses, an appropriate sight-singing passage can be written at the top of the memo. When the children have figured it out, prior to the start of the rehearsal they come up to me and sing it softly in my ear. If it is correct, they put a star beside their name on the large photo-seating plan. There are always children who arrive early, and this gives them something worthwhile to do. Parents, who are invited to sit in at every rehearsal, must sign the memo that is checked the following week at the sign-in desk by the volunteer rehearsal assistants. The artistic director makes the follow-up phone calls each week, to those families that did not sign the memo. Time spent on the telephone with new parents early in the year is well worth it. (See appendix 5B for the first four memos as an example. Memos are now available to our parents electronically.)

Weekly memos are color-coded for easy identification; Training Choir I, yellow; TC II, blue; TCIII, green; Main Choir, pink; Office, orange. The chorister must place memos each week into a soft-covered inexpensive three-hole booklet or a three-ring binder. The artistic director or rehearsal assistants check the binders in the music bags to make sure they are there in order.

The librarian gives out all of the music that will be used for the first term in their music bags at the first rehearsal. Music must be numbered and children must learn to respect and look after their music. The preparation by the music director, who works closely with the librarian, in making sure the children have everything in the bags they need to be organized and ready is of paramount importance. No time should be wasted in rehearsals looking for music.

Memos play a vital role in a very busy and active organization. The time spent in establishing routines early in the year with the Training Choirs is very important. It sets the year and their life in the chorus on a smooth course. Members of the Main Choir also receive extensive memos with weekly assignments. Without the memos, routines, and expectations, it is inevitable that uncertainties, misunderstandings, confusion, and even fear and chaos will develop.

## Seating Plans

Seating plans, given out to the children at the sign-in desk, are time savers as they help children find their places quickly. In the Toronto Children's Chorus, attendance is taken by having the children cross their names off the master seating plan at the sign-in desk. Early in the season, the artistic director should follow up any unexpected absences with a phone call. Later in the season, a volunteer should make these calls.

For each Training Choir, a large seating plan that displays the children's names and passport-size photos should be made by the artistic director or assistant during the summer. This enables one to learn the children's names before the first rehearsal. It can also be used for stars and other rewards throughout the year. All children should have received some stars by the end of the first few months.

Voice parts are also indicated on the seating plan. This is not difficult with Training Choirs I and II, since they generally sing only in two parts, but for the Main Choir it is an important document that can save hours of rehearsal time if used effectively. In this choir, unlike the Training Choirs, parts are assigned according to voice color, not just ear. A rehearsal seating plan is made up with the results of the re-audition in hand and is often modified after the first few rehearsals. Those singers who switch from Soprano II to Alto I in four-part divisi need to have good ears and a rich sound. Balance is a major issue with treble choirs that have a large age span. Generally in a choir of 100 singers it is wise to have the younger, less-experienced ones singing Soprano I with a dozen outstanding experienced sopranos. Soprano IIs and Alto Is need to be versatile and able to follow an SSAA score. Alto IIs need a resonant low G. A rehearsal seating plan is used at all preliminary rehearsals to give the apprentice-trainers ample opportunity to sit next to and work with their apprentices. When the notes are secure, a performance plan can be used, with the children placed according to height as well as voice. (At the August Music Camp, a week-long music camp for the Main Choir, heights are written down, from the tallest to shortest, for Sopranos I and II and Altos I and II.) For a sample rehearsal seating plan, please see appendix 11.

### Absence Forms/Rehearsal Assistants

If a child must miss a rehearsal because of school commitments, such as concerts, trips, or high-school exams, a rehearsal absence form, obtained from a volunteer at the sign-in desk, must be completed and given to the conductor at least three weeks before the event. If a child is ill the day of a rehearsal or concert, the parent must call the conductor and the office. The rehearsal assistant, a parent volunteer, lists the names of the absentees, makes notes of the absences in the attendance book kept at the sign-in desk, and calls the parents of any children who are absent without notification. This safety check is extremely important, particularly in a city where children may travel to choir by city transit rather than by car pool.

### Use of the Blackboard

Before every rehearsal there should be a list on a blackboard of the pieces, exercises, theory and sight-singing to be covered in the rehearsal. A younger child often enjoys small jobs such as the rehearsal secretary, so they can come up and cross off each piece as it is completed. The blackboard list saves precious rehearsal time, but it also has a psychological function. All people feel more satisfied when they know they have accomplished something and can see it checked off on a list. In addition, while an hour of rehearsal for an artistic director may feel like a short period of time because there is so much to do, for an eight- or nine-year-old an hour seems like an eternity. Seeing, for example, number eight checked off a list of ten items helps the children realize the end is in sight!

## Use of Tape Recorders

In the Toronto Children's Chorus, the Training Choirs and weaker readers in the Main Choir tape their rehearsals each week with their own tapes and tape recorders. This is a great time saver. Small Sony tape recorders seem to do the job and are easy for the younger children to learn how to use and transport. It is essential for all choristers to listen to the tape as often as it takes them to learn the notes. This is usually about three half hours each week. Parents also find the tapes a useful tool for helping their young choristers, particularly if they do not read music or play the piano. In the Main Choir, once the choristers have sung through the notes of a piece, they are expected to know them. This enables the choir to learn an enormous amount of repertoire, with much rehearsal time spent on interpretation, musicality, and style.

## Three Sharp Pencils

All choristers in the Toronto Children's Chorus are asked to keep three sharpened HB pencils in their music bags. (HB pencil markings are easy to erase. Any light pencil will do.) They must learn the important skill of marking music effectively and carefully. Sample markings are outlined at the back of the Chorister Handbooks.

## Sight-Singing and Ear-Training

When I am teaching formal sight-singing, ear-training, and theory to the Training Choirs, the choristers gather on the floor in front of the blackboard for the last twelve minutes of each rehearsal. While I teach a new concept, parent volunteers place the marked theory homework books on the children's chairs. The books used by the Toronto Children's Chorus are: *Keyboard Theory: Preparatory Books A, B, and C,* by Grace Vandendool (Frederick Harris), and *The Folk Song Sight Singing Series,* books 1–6, edited by Edgar Crowe, Annie Lawton, and W. Gillies Whittaker (Oxford University Press).

Sight-singing, ear-training, and theory must also be taught incidentally and imaginatively throughout the rehearsal, as the pieces are being taught. It is in this context that they are highly valuable and memorable. I have not yet found the perfect theory book or sight-singing book for choristers to complement the songs they are studying.

## The Season Calendar

The season calendar that the Toronto Children's Chorus parents receive at the June meeting has been in the planning stages for six months. The artistic director works closely with the choir manager and staff to ensure that all details are in place, including consideration of various religious holidays. In addition to listing the dates, times, and locations of all rehearsals and concerts, the calendar must include substantial breaks—a minimum of two weeks at least two or three times a year. Choristers need these breaks to maintain optimum health and creativity. These breaks also provide the conductor great opportunities for score study, for serious reading, and for professional development. The administrative staff needs blocks of time to work when there are no rehearsals or performances. Interestingly enough, in Italy every young person starting out in his first job is legally entitled to six weeks of paid vacation every year. Would that North Americans could adopt this wise policy!

## Your Personal Calendar

Once the season has begun, personal weekly plans need to be developed. Always plan at least a week ahead, since day-to-day planning results in crisis management. There are several excellent personal planners on the market, but you need to find one that works for you. Do not use a planner in which you have to keep transferring information. Never work with more than one calendar. I prefer a planner that offers two pages a day, with blank sections at the beginning for personal project descriptions. Set aside time each week to fill out the four Covey quadrants; blocks of time must be found each week for those projects that come under the "Important but Not Urgent" quadrant; otherwise your entire week will be taken up with items in the "Important and Urgent" quadrant.

## Planning a Concert Season and Long-Range Strategic Planning with Management, Volunteers, and a Board of Directors

Choirs, like individuals, families, and all organizations, need mission statements. Mission statements clarify who you are, where you want to go, and how you are going to get there. A mission statement is as important for a school, church, or synagogue choir as it is for a community choir. Without a mission statement to which everyone is committed, long- and short-term goals cannot be developed or realized. As I write, the mission statement of the Toronto Children's Chorus, which is written and revised every two years by the board of directors, the artistic director, and the general manager, is as follows:

The mission of the Toronto Children's Chorus is to maintain its position as one of the finest treble choirs in the world. It provides unique musical and educational opportunities for children by performing the finest repertoire available, especially Canadian works and new commissions by Canadian composers; and it records this material and performs it in Canada and all over the world.

A community children's chorus also needs to develop a five-year plan in which ideas are prioritized and broken down into yearly segments. A two-year plan then can be adopted, and programs and projects for a season can begin to take shape.

Ideally, detailed planning for a season begins in the fall of the previous season and is in place by January—eight months before the new season begins. (For sample programs, see appendix 3.) Although one cannot be certain how many children will return or audition, it is still vital to plan ahead and map out the season. One of the committees of the board of directors needs to be a program committee that meets for half a day twice a year, preferably away from the regular office. Saturday morning is an ideal time. Seven or eight people should sit on the program committee along with the artistic director, the choir manager, and the marketing director. Each and every idea should be brought to the table and welcomed. This creative process is energizing and fruitful. The program committee needs creative people from the community who are familiar with the aspirations and standards of the choir—composers, artists from other disciplines, artistic directors and managers of other musical arts organizations, music teachers, educators, and effective leaders in the community. A week or so before the program committee meeting takes place, the artistic director should give the members of the program committee an agenda and a two-page handout. The handout should begin with the mission statement in bold type and contain ideas and thoughts that the artistic director wishes to bring to the table. This handout is only a guideline to help focus the meeting. It is not a blueprint for the season.

The artistic director needs to keep an open mind during these meetings. Quite often, ideas from members of the committee may seem quite "off the wall" but, when discussed and shaped, can prove quite innovative and worthwhile. Careful minutes need to be taken and distributed to committee members. The artistic director and choir manager follow up with a proposed program in terms of number and types of concerts, performance venues, guest engagements, tours, and recordings that the choir can accommodate. This plan then needs to be taken to the board chair and treasurer for further discussion and preparation of a preliminary budget. The season outline and preliminary budget are finally taken to the board, which analyzes the financial implications of the season, not the program content.

The number of concerts the choir gives each year depends on many factors, including the ability of children in the choir to learn new material, the cost of scores and hall rental, the number of choirs in the organization, and the number of choral concerts given annually in the community. Many choirs give two concerts, one in December and one in May. Choirs that wish to offer subscription series, however, need to offer a minimum of three concerts. The Toronto Children's Chorus performs four concerts each year in its own subscription series, with some concerts being repeated; in addition, the three Training Choirs sing two of their own programs each season.

Performing opportunities are critical, particularly for the younger singers. Training Choirs perform their first concert at the end of October, after only about six rehearsals. A theme is often helpful in planning a cohesive program for several choirs: for example, "Autumn and Animals," "Sun, Moon, Earth, and Sky," "Nursery Rhymes," or "Children's Games and Stories." Each choir sings three pieces related to the theme, and then all choirs join to perform two pieces that all the children must learn in order to graduate into the next choir. Three or four children may read thematic poems as one choir leaves the stage and another is entering—reading poetry expressively is an excellent way for children to develop poise onstage and projection of the speaking voice, two necessities for singers. Three children from each choir who are doing well on an instrument such as the piano or violin play their instruments between each choir's performance.

The Training Choirs sing with the Main Choir and Alumni Choir (former members of the chorus), at the Christmas Concert each December. They also present their own concert in February, where each choir sings three pieces alone and two combined pieces in the first half and then performs a tasteful musical such as Jonathan Willcocks's *The Pied Piper* or a collection of songs such as Ronald Corp's *Cornucopia*. The Training Choirs then sing with the Main Choir in the Spring Concert in May. This concert, performed twice, is often built loosely around a theme.

The Main Choir gives four concerts a year, at the end of October or the first week in November, on the last Sunday afternoon before Christmas, in early March, and in early May. Themes are an excellent way of focusing the concert and of marketing it. We often have a guest choir or guest artist with us at our first concert and try to expand our audience base this way. Themes can revolve around composers, countries, time periods, social concerns, ethnic groups, and/or multicultural ideas and often incorporate other disciplines such as dance and visual art. At Christmas, the Main Choir always sings a feature work, such as Britten's "Ceremony of Carols," William Mathias's "Salvator Mundi," Ruth Watson Henderson's "The Last Straw," or John Rutter's "Dancing Day" or "Brother Heinrich's Christmas." These are great pieces that all choir members should sing at least once during their choir membership. Just as Handel's oratorio *Messiah* is often sung every year, so these pieces deserve a frequent hearing. It is wise to perform the major work at the beginning of the concert. The Training Choirs sit in the hall and listen; this is an important part of their training. The second half of the concert can have audience participation. Having the audience stand, stretch, and sing gives the performers opportunities for stage movement without the interminable gaps that can occur without audience participation. The Training Choirs and Alumni Choir present their own three pieces with an audience carol sung between the choirs. All choirs sing together in the final set.

When I start to rehearse the music for this concert in late October, I always spend a few minutes explaining that Christmas music is sung because of its timelessness and its beauty, not just for its religious significance. For those choristers and families who are uncomfortable with the text, I invite them to think of the Christmas theme as being a fairy tale or a "once upon a time" story. Many members of great orchestras and choirs who are not of the Christian faith perform *Messiah* each year and are quite comfortable doing so. At other times during the year, it is important to recognize other religious festivals with concerts that celebrate the work of Jewish composers, the Chinese New Year, Native Americans, or other members of your community. (Sample programs can be found in appendix 3.)

As soon as the concert season is organized by January, the music must be ordered immediately to ensure that the librarian has received it by May. All music to be performed by the Main Choir is listed on a repertoire sheet for the season; any music that will be started at the August Music Camp is asterisked. Every chorister receives a copy of this list for his or her music bag. Because each singer is responsible for sixty or seventy octavos each year, it is essential that a system be developed for organizing and handling the music. We have found it most helpful to use a series of colored file folders with music organized by the composers' last names; A to C red, D to G blue, et cetera. This system enables a chorister to find music quickly, thereby allowing for more rehearsal time. (Sample repertoire lists can be found in appendix 4B.)

Choristers in the Main Choir are expected to have developed or be developing the skill of watching the conductor while reading the score and marking it appropriately. This enables an artistic rehearsal to take place where choristers mark phrasing, dynamics, and articulation. This, I feel, is a more beneficial way of training artists than having them memorize the score, watch the conductor, and have the tempo, style, phrasing, dynamics, and articulation drilled into them. This traditional way I compare to training seals or painting by numbers—it gets the job done in a mechanical sort of way but leaves precious little room for art to flourish. Great conductors and performers never give the same performance twice. This is one of the true joys of the choral art.

Effective organizational skills, personal time-management skills, and strategic long-term planning skills need to be developed and improved continually by every conductor. Only then will your singers maximize their musical potential by working in a stable, healthy, and productive environment, and only then will your concerts be a source of delight and joy for the children, for the audience, and for you.

# CHAPTER SEVEN

# The Audition Process

*Know Your Children, Your Parents, and Your Community*

## Your Children

The more knowledge you have about the children you teach, the more effective you will be. Whether you are teaching a class of thirty singers or training a large choir of a hundred and thirty, the time spent getting to know each child will be well invested. It is important to know each one by name. It is important to know who the leaders are and where the musical strength lies. It is important for the students to know that you always have their best interests at heart and everything you are trying to do is for their benefit. You will gain their respect and trust initially by getting to know each of them.

The photographic seating chart mentioned earlier will enable you to call each child by name at the first rehearsal. Nothing makes a child feel more special than to be called by his or her first name.

Set up a file folder for every child and staple the second photo beside the name. The file folders should be used to keep all references about the children, personal notes from parents, and a "Personal Profile" sheet that contains important information— the children's names, addresses, and birthdays (very important; these must be recognized), parents' names and phone numbers, and the children's heights (for the purpose of the seating plan). You also need to know if the children study piano or another instrument. The children should list any songs they know and what they like about these songs. It is helpful for the children to list the last three books they have read and what they liked about these books. I also like to know what the children do on Saturdays and how they like to spend their free time, if they have any! Many other questions can follow: "When are you happiest?" "Whom do you admire?" "What would you like to be?" "If you could have a conversation with anyone, living or dead, who would it be?" "What would you ask him or her?" This information helps you to understand who you are training and what realistic expectations you can develop. It also helps you discover troubled children who may face many difficulties. The information should not be used to create bias but rather to create an awareness of the child's environment. Knowing "what makes people tick" helps motivate them, and motivation is the basis of all learning.

It is essential for any music teacher or choir conductor to know the individual voices: to know who has a voice that blends easily, who has a voice that is potentially big and unwieldy, and who sings in the center of the pitch and who sings slightly sharp or flat. In a school or church choir where it may not have been possible to hear the students individually, and before you have developed their trust, walk around the room as they are singing. As they are singing the national anthem, discreetly listen for individual strengths and weaknesses. Base your seating plan on this information. Placing children strategically after the second or third class or rehearsal is essential for routines, for discipline, and for creating the ideal sound. In a choir with a mixture of ages, have older children sit next to younger ones to act as role models. Have two boys sit together, but place a girl on either side. Have two children with strong voices sit together with a child with a weak voice on either side. Having those children with less secure voices sitting between those with more secure voices is not fair to those children with the better voices. Have two children who sing in tune sit together. On either side place those who do not sing in tune. Ideally, there will be children with good ears who can sit on either side of these children. Try not to make two children who have weak ears sit next to each other. The seating plan will change often during the first few months. Play with it until you get as close to the ideal as you can. The importance of an effective seating plan cannot be overemphasized.

## Auditions and the Art of Discovering Each Child's Potential

One of the most fascinating and rewarding aspects of a community children's choir conductor's job is auditioning new children each spring. It is fascinating because no two children are exactly alike. All children have different strengths and weaknesses. Discovering what these are and finding the program and choir that fit each child's needs is most rewarding. The audition must be done with great skill, tact, and warmth and always be a very positive experience for the child. Auditions carried out effectively lay the foundation for successful choir work during the year.

As with all aspects of successful children's choir work, the planning and organization are essential. What is done before the child's audition actually takes place is of paramount importance. This planning and organization can be divided into three sections: advertising and recruitment, parent information booklets, and registration.

Brochures that tell about the choir can be sent to places where children go: schools, churches, synagogues, libraries, day-care centers, camps. Brochures can also be sent to venues where people go to enrich their artistic souls: concert halls, museums, art galleries, and theaters. Parents of current choir members can post the brochures in their workplaces. The brochures should be eye-catching without going overboard. They should not be too detailed and wordy, since nobody will have time to read them properly. The brochures should be focused on the benefits that singing in a choir has in children's lives and possibly contain quotes from the choir members. It might even contain quotes from parents of former members who were transformed by the positive experiences their children received from this choir. The brochures need to be ready in the January of the current year, since the audition process takes about six months to complete. On the brochure there should be a phone number or E-mail address where parents can call for further information and inquire about bringing their child to an open rehearsal. Parents and children can learn much about the positive choir experience by attending a rehearsal together. In February, around Valentine's Day, the current choir members can have a "Bring a Friend to Choir Day," when the children themselves show their friends how great the choir experience is. To keep the venture controlled, the friends would have to informally preregister and a new seating plan would be set up for that rehearsal. A social time could be organized afterward with simply cookies and juice. If time permits, the artistic director can visit schools and take a choir rehearsal for the school music teacher. There must be a happy liaison between the schools and the children's community choir. This might also involve taking the community choir into the schools once or twice a year to provide in-service workshops and inviting teachers to the community children's choir rehearsals to observe.

In a community-based children's choir, a great deal of important information is gleaned before and during the audition process. A volunteer registrar, who is given a list of interested families from the office, calls and sets up the audition. He or she fills out an initial form with the parents' names and phone numbers, and the child's school and musical background, so I have an idea of what I might expect during the audition. In the Toronto Children's Chorus, I am looking for children who are very eager to sing in the choir and willing to put the necessary work into it and have a good musical ear and a good basic voice. I am looking for children who I think will work well in a group and try to get along with others. If they show these qualities, I can teach them most other things they will need to know to be successful in the chorus. I am not necessarily looking for great voices. The ear is more important than the voice. I am always saddened when a child has a very good voice but a poor ear. Often a child has a very good ear and a modest instrument. Unfortunately, great ears and great voices are not necessarily found in the same person.

The audition takes about a half an hour. Ten to fifteen minutes of this time is with me. I hear individually anyone who wishes to audition. Current choristers, with adult supervision, help at the audition at the sign-in desk, with marking theory papers, meeting and greeting, and making the children feel comfortable. The new parents also have a short briefing session with the choir manager and during this interview are given an opportunity to find out about the choir, to ask questions, and to begin to understand the time commitment required to be part of the organization. During the audition with me, the child, the registrar, and a current member of the chorus are present. This is the only time the parent is not present when the child is working with me since all rehearsals are open to parents. The following is the audition procedure:

The children have been asked by the registrar to prepare a song to sing or to sing "O Canada" and to bring an instrument to play or piano music if they study piano. They are also asked to bring three passport-size photographs and (optional) a letter of recommendation from their school music teacher or school principal. They also bring in a form they have filled out at the sign-in desk. (The audition form can be found in appendix 2.)

Before they sing a note, several aspects of the children's personality are revealed. Do they show up? Do they arrive on time? How do they walk into the room? Do they seem interested or bored? Are they tired or alert? Have they forgotten their instrument or the piano music? Do they know any songs? Often well-organized children have Post-it notes in their songbook or piano book. Some bring a second copy of the song for the accompaniment. Some of these traits reflect the organization of the family rather than the child and likely won't influence a decision, but everything begins to paint a picture of this child. Every child is unique! Every child's audition is slightly different.

I call the children by name and make brief small talk to help them feel comfortable. If a child is overly confident, I try to make the audition challenging. If a child is shy or nervous, I try to give the child opportunities for immediate success. I ask the child what he or she wishes to sing and often the answer is, "I don't know." I might play "O Canada" to see if the child recognizes it and can sing along with it. I often use the first eight measures of "Twinkle, Twinkle," going from E-flat major through all the keys up to A or B flat. Sometimes the children will sing a piece they have learned from a recording, imitating a low chest sound. At that point I need to demonstrate two kinds of singing with my voice, chest and head, and ask them if they can hear a difference. Nine times out of ten, they will then be able to sing in a head voice.

This aspect of the audition tells me a few things: the child's school music program, involvement with a church or synagogue choir, and background and taste, the color of the voice, and the child's range ("Twinkle"). It doesn't tell me about the child's ear or tonal memory. Sometimes children will do well in the "singing a song" part because they have learned the song well, but this is only the beginning. With children, one must keep continually digging for further information, since some have had absolutely no background but have the talent yet undiscovered. Others have modest talent but are fortunate in having been exposed to a strong music program in school, private study, or rich cultural experiences.

The ear test and tonal memory exercises are the most important part of the audition. All children can improve their ear or tonal memory with practice and perseverance, but initially the musical ear and tonal memory are precious gifts and indicate innate talent. I begin with very simple tone-matching exercises so that all children will experience success. With six- and seven-year-olds I do it with my voice. With older children, I usually do it with the piano. If the older children cannot match the pitch from the piano, I use my voice. It is important that all children learn to match pitch during the audition. They all must leave the audition feeling they have learned something and it has been a worthwhile experience. During the audition, the ear test becomes gradually more and more complex. If children are overly confident I may take them to a point where they make a mistake. It is unwise to accept a child whose self-confidence is overbearing. I want all children to feel good about themselves after the audition regardless of the outcome, but I do not want any of them to develop an attitude of self-importance, which is unhealthy for them and for the choir. All the children need to be able to work together and respect and appreciate one another's abilities.

Some children have a good ear when they have to repeat only three or four notes back, but a good musician also has a good tonal memory. A good way of testing this is to have two-measure phrases with melodic leaps and strong rhythms. If they are successful with the first, have them try the second.

I likely would not take an older child who has a weak ear and poor tonal memory into the Toronto Children's Chorus. On my checklist I classify the ear and tonal memory into four categories: excellent, good, fair, and poor. The good and fair can certainly improve with practice, but the poor will improve only minimally. The children certainly get the benefit of the doubt during the audition, and I work hard to have them succeed. I always finish with something the child CAN do well, however, even if it is merely clapping four quarter notes. It is important that the children feel good after the audition and, more important, that they have learned something.

In order to decide whether a child goes into one of the three Training Choirs or into the Main Choir, the next thing I would have the child do is name notes, clap simple rhythms, and sight-read. I always begin with something they can do and then progress to things they cannot do. If I feel they are ready for the Main Choir, I also need to determine in which of the six sight-reading groups they belong. Rarely are children accepted directly into the Main Choir, unless they are older and can get private help during the summer months. All children who go into the Main Choir must understand keys and counting and have worked their way through the first three Oxford sight-singing books, where they have begun to master tonic solfa.

The next part of the audition requires the child to read from a novel or a book of poetry that is appropriate for his or her age and grade. This gives me an idea of how expressive the child is, and often there is a strong correlation between how well a child reads words and how well he or she will read music. Understanding what has been read is also important, and often we will engage in a lively discussion afterward.

If the child plays an instrument, I will ask him or her to play at this time. If a child does not play rhythmically or musically, it sometimes indicates poor teaching. As well as listening to the child play, this gives me some time to make notes about the earlier part of the audition with this particular child that will help me recall important information. This is particularly useful if you are auditioning forty or fifty children on consecutive Saturdays.

If I still am having difficulty assessing the child's ability I will try to engage the child in discussion about something that excites or interests him or her. I have often asked them such questions as, "Why do you want to be in the chorus?"; "What do you enjoy doing most at school?"; "Who is your best friend and why?"; and "What do you think is the world's most serious problem and how would you go about solving it?" These questions can be highly revealing about a child's character. As the children make their way through the chorus to the Chamber Choir, which tours, it is important for all concerned that those children get along with others. It is important that they function well in a group. Extensive touring can be stressful and requires that the children be able to cope cheerfully with new and different situations.

The final part of the audition requires the children to take a basic written theory test and to write a story about something that interests them. The written test ensures me that they have been placed in the choir that will challenge but not frustrate them. The story helps me to get to know the children better and gives me something other than music to talk to them about the next time we meet. The six- and seven-year-olds can draw a picture and dictate a story rather than write a story, if they prefer.

## Choir Structure

The 300-voice Toronto Children's Chorus is made up of three Training Choruses of about 60 voices each. I conduct Training Choirs I and II; my assistant conducts Training Choir III. The Main Choir of about 120 singers is made up of a 60-voice Chamber Choir that tours and records and Cantare, for children who are developing the skills necessary for Chamber Choir. The Chamber Choir has a 30-voice Acappella Choir and there is a Choral Scholars Choir of 18 voices, six first sopranos, six second sopranos, and six altos. There is a curriculum to follow before the child graduates to the next choir at the end of the year. The annual compulsory re-audition includes three or four chosen pieces from that season's repertoire, a theory test, and a sight-singing test. The re-audition enables me to hear how each child's voice is developing and to place the child in the appropriate choir for the following season.

The Main Choir of about 120 singers attends a week-long music camp at the end of August. Four fifty-minute rehearsals are held each day; one of the rehearsals has the Chamber Choir separated from Cantare. In addition to the rehearsals, each child takes a one-hour sight-singing and ear-training class. These classes are divided into six levels, with a seventh level called the Independent Sight-Singing Class. Each class contains about twelve students, so there are several classes at each level, more at the lower level than the upper. The Independent Level has about twenty singers. In order to get into the Independent Level, a position all choristers covet, the singers must be able to sight-read anything. The singers in this level have no adult working with them. I appoint a student director and four section leaders for Sopranos I and II and Altos I and II. Levels 1, 2, and 3 are taught by camp counselors who are former choristers, and Levels 4, 5, and 6 are taught by myself and other highly qualified musician/teachers.

An enormous amount of new music for the following season is covered at camp, and a one-hour-and-fifteen-minute concert is given at the end of the week of music the choir has never performed before. The Independent Sight-Singing Class sings two or three a cappella motets alone. The age range in this group is from twelve to fifteen. There is no greater joy for me than to hear these works performed by singers who five years earlier had limited musical skill and now have taught themselves. The new music is given to the Independent Sight-Singing Class at the beginning of camp, and a week later they are expected to perform it at the concert. Generally the pieces are in tune, with careful attention paid to diction, phrasing, blend, and balance. These experiences prove that there are no ceilings for children, except those that are imposed by adults.

The Main Choir singers, in addition to being made up of Cantare, Chamber, Acappella, and Choral Scholars, also contains about twenty apprentices. The apprentices are usually in their first year with the Main Choir, although not all first-year members are apprentices. During the audition process I may feel that the child will need a helping hand beside him/her, and so he/she is assigned an apprentice-trainer. The apprentice-trainer, another highly coveted position in the choir, sits beside the apprentice during rehearsals. The apprentice-trainers' responsibilities are extensive. They must help the apprentice organize the music before the rehearsal begins to make sure everything is in rehearsal order (from the list on the blackboard). They help the apprentice find the line on the page in particularly complex scores. They make sure the apprentice has a pencil before the rehearsal begins and help him or her mark the score properly. They call the apprentice on the telephone and help with memory work and foreign languages. During the first term, the apprentice-trainers write up a report on each apprentice to let me know how he/she is doing and if they think he/she is ready for promotion. Each apprentice also writes a report on his/her apprentice-trainer to let me know how often he/she is calling and helping and if the apprentice thinks the apprentice-trainer is doing a good job. Because this system has been going on successfully for many years now, the apprentice-trainers are mentoring future apprentice-trainers. The children are mentoring and teaching each other. The choristers are all assuming ownership, and the discipline and tone of the choir, as it were, is coming from within the ranks instead of from an adult.

In addition to apprentices and apprentice-trainers, there are fifteen section leaders, one or two head choristers, and a conductor's student assistant who is also the student director of the Independent Sight-Singing Class. The section leaders' work is not music-related, but they make up, with the head choristers, the Chorus Council, which meets with me once a month to discuss problems or concerns that anyone in their section might have. Members of the Chorus Council are invited to bring up all sorts of ideas regarding any aspect of chorus life.

The choir manager and I choose the head choristers and section leaders at the beginning of each new season. These children are thoroughly dedicated choristers who have shown strong leadership skills. All children in the Main Chorus love going to camp. They look up to their counselors who are former choristers. The children all aspire to be apprentice-trainers, section leaders, head choristers, and counselors. There is a very healthy atmosphere in the chorus, where virtues such as responsibility, hard work, mutual respect, caring, sharing, and humility are honored and passed down to the "next generation."

The Training Choruses meet once a week for an hour. The Main Chorus meets twice a week, once for two hours and once for an hour and a half. The Training Choruses give four concerts a year, two alone and two with the main chorus. The Main Chorus has between ten and twenty services a year, depending on how frequently they perform with other professional arts organizations such as the Amadeus Choir, the Elmer Iseler Singers, and the Toronto Symphony Orchestra.

## Know Your Parents

Parents can play a critical role in their child's progress. Parents also can help enormously in a school choir program and with a community children's chorus.

In both the school and community chorus, the parents need to get to know you, your program, your plans, and your expectations of their children. You need to develop the parents' trust and their respect. Most parents want the best for their children. Most parents are willing to assist in some way with whatever talents and time they have if it is clear what your expectations are and if they are doing something that brings them some degree of personal satisfaction. It also must be understood, as with all board members, that decisions are made in the best interests of the program, not of any one individual.

Early in the year, send home a brief outline of your plans for the year. Include in the outline a form that outlines your needs. Parents are very busy people. They need time to plan. The form might include such things as supervising on choir trips, helping at rehearsals (with things like attendance, not accompanying, unless you have worked with them before in a professional situation), and helping with choir uniforms, computer skills, photography, or baking. Leave a few lines at the bottom for other comments. The assistance you ask for must be developed from your plan. Programs need long-range plans. Parents must see that you are organized, that you have a yearly plan outlined, and that their children are going to receive enormous benefits from singing in the choir. The form needs to specify a return date, preferably within five to ten days. The forms, when and if they return, reveal a great deal. If they don't come back, it may be that the parents are not interested or have lost the form or it is not very high on their list of priorities and they haven't had time to deal with it. If you are trying to set up a new program you must have patience. It takes time to convince people.

Knowing your parents and community well can help you understand potential problems and concerns, as the following anecdote reveals. During my early days of teaching, in the late sixties, the choir had sung very well and had won a prize at what was then a board-wide choir competition. (Despite the fact that school sports teams continued to compete against one another, the choir competitions were disbanded in the seventies.) Because my choir had won a competition, we were invited to sing at Massey Hall, at that time the finest concert hall in the city, for the Toronto Board of Education Maytime Music Festival Concert. This was a very prestigious event indeed. Despite the fact that tickets were very inexpensive, very few, if any, tickets were bought by the parents of my choir members. I had to hire a bus to take the children to the hall. When we returned to the school parking lot that evening at 10:15, several parents were not there to pick up their children. After a few telephone calls from a pay phone that I used since I could not get into the school and cell phones had not yet been invented, the last parent arrived at 10:45! I was twenty-two years old and I thought this was normal. Many years later, when I was teaching in a different community, the school choir again was asked to sing at this special May Festival concert. I ran out of my allotted tickets and parents were angry since tickets for grandparents were not also available. I did not need to hire a bus, since the parents all drove the children to the hall, Roy Thomson Hall, this time. The parents often went to this hall, because many had subscription series tickets to the Toronto Symphony Orchestra concerts. The parents were thrilled that their children had been selected to sing at this prestigious concert. The important thing to remember about all of this is that the choir from the very modest community sang just as well as the choir from the solid middle-class neighborhood. The children from the modest community had a unique experience that they treasured. The children from the solid middle-class community had enriching experiences frequently. Singing at Roy Thomson Hall was just one of them.

When the parent forms are returned it is important to act straightaway. Perhaps there is a parent who seems very helpful and could coordinate this for you. Having a "sixth" sense about people is very important. Knowing who might do what well takes some wisdom and people sense. Matching the right person with the right job is critical. Thanking people appropriately is also extremely important. If you can manage it, inviting parents over to your home for some food and fun at the end of the season is appreciated.

## Your Community

Understanding the community and society in which you are training children's choirs will help you become a more enlightened and effective teacher/conductor. While children throughout the world are very similar in many ways and music is the international language that can unite us in unique ways, societies have different expectations of their children. Motivational teaching strategies that may work in a rural area in Nebraska won't necessarily work in inner cities in North America. Expectations from children in Asia are often different from those in North America. I found the children I trained in Jerusalem and Hong Kong were self-motivated and this made my work easier. Children who live in small fishing villages in Nova Scotia bring to the rehearsal very different ideas about life from those of children who live in a wealthy area of Calgary. Superb teachers have to adapt to their environment, understand it, start from there, and make it work for them. Teacher/conductors should not try to imitate someone they feel is successful at training children's choirs and then beat up on themselves when they aren't getting the results they feel they should get. Understanding both the uniqueness of your environment and your own strengths and shortcomings can bring you and your children satisfaction rather than frustration.

The vital thing to remember, however, is this: All children everywhere can be touched by the profound beauty of the choral art. They all can learn how to sing great choral music. The means of getting there are not the same, but the children can get there. A wise teacher/conductor will always find a way. The human spirit is universal. The child's spirit must be nurtured and guided. Music is one of the greatest ways to guide and nurture this spirit.

In one of my darkest earliest days in teaching I taught a boy whose name, let's say, was John. John was twelve years old. I never met his parents. They never came to concerts or to any parent/teacher evenings. John was always in trouble and spent much of his time in the office getting counseling. He had few friends and was known as the school bully. Bullying and petty theft were a way of life for him. He was a troubled child, to say the least, and did not have much going for him. He did, however, have a fine voice. I ran into him in the school hallway the third or fourth week in September and asked him why he hadn't signed up for choir this year, since he had been in it the previous year. With body language that could challenge, frustrate, and anger the most highly experienced teacher John replied, "Oh, I dunno. I guess I might join if we sing "Bist du bei mir." This is a true story, and as I write this I can hear John say it as if this encounter occurred yesterday, yet it happened nearly thirty years ago. This child was touched by the music of Bach. For brief moments John's mind and heart were influenced by the power and mystery of great art. The satisfaction a teacher receives from reaching children like this cannot be measured. Its value cannot be understood in human terms.


## Conclusion

The wise teacher/conductor takes the time to know and understand the children, the parents, and the community. The answers to many of the challenges our work presents are not found in a prescription or a one-size-fits-all formula but in the hearts of our children, our parents, and our communities.

# CHAPTER EIGHT

# Things They Didn't Teach You at Music School

It is one of life's little ironies that a music director can spend a disproportionate amount of time on aspects of the program that have nothing directly to do with rehearsing, teaching, conducting, and performing the music—aspects of the program we were not particularly trained to handle. So many things we need to know have not been taught to us formally, and yet our programs will suffer if we fail to recognize their importance or learn how to deal with them with skill, tact, warmth, and humor.

## Making Your School Choir a Vital Part of School Life

The young woman who succeeded me in my teaching job when I retired is a superb singer, pianist, and oboist. She sang in the Toronto Children's Chorus for five years and in her church choir for three years previously. She excelled in college and won several awards. She is a computer wizard. She is extremely intelligent, personable, and likable. When I told her about this book, she asked if I would write about all the things she wished someone had taught her before she began a career in teaching music in school. These things have less to do with teaching the music than they have with developing a successful program.

One would hope that all the children sitting in front of the teacher who is eager to share a lifelong passion for music would be just as excited about singing great music. One would hope that every child in the choir wanted to sing. One would hope that every staff member, parent, and administrator would see the enormous benefits of the program and would support it without reservation. Sadly, such is rarely the case. How does one deal with these issues?

The issues are complex. Each person reading this book has a unique personality, has various strengths and weaknesses, and is in different circumstances. Each teacher must find his or her own way eventually, but I would hope it will be helpful to share with you some ideas, thoughts, and experiences from my years in teaching.

Everything emanates from the heart, mind, and spirit of the teacher. There must be an enthusiasm and passion for the art that approaches missionary zeal. There must be indefatigable optimism. There must be a charisma that genuinely inspires others. There must be a rock-solid belief that great art touches every human soul and that every child who experiences great art will be forever changed. There must be a willingness to take risks without feeling discouraged when ideas do not work out. There must be strong leadership skills. Without these attributes, even a conductor with great musical knowledge, skill, and technique will not produce an active, satisfying, exciting, and artistically successful music program.

A great teacher/conductor must have the philosophy that children can discover and appreciate great art by performing great art. While teachers may not necessarily motivate inexperienced singers by conducting Bach initially, they will never develop a music program that enriches the lives of students, parents, staff, administrators, and members of the community by having their students sing junk. Why have sixty seven-year-olds scream, "All I want for Christmas is my two front teeth," when they could have been taught meaningful pieces such as the familiar Czech "Rocking Carol" in F-sharp major or "I Have a Little Dreydl" in E-flat major, both wonderful pieces that develop a child's natural head voice. Parents would not dream of giving their children chocolate bars for breakfast, lunch, and dinner. English teachers would not dream of giving their students comic books to read all day. Why do some music teachers feel they have to give the equivalent of chocolate bars and comic books to motivate their students? Once children experience the thrill of singing great music with a glorious sound, they will never look back. Children rapidly develop discriminating taste. To arrive at this juncture takes patience, tact, and Olympian energy, combined with a single-mindedness of purpose.

Initially, the class or choirs need goals and activities to look forward to in order to be motivated to sing well:

1. Begin with three or four songs they can sing at a seniors' home or a hospital. Have one child or a trio with a particularly beautiful sound sing something alone. (If you have thirty children, you will always find two or three who have a beautiful natural timbre.) This could be Handel's "Where E'er You Walk," or Rodgers and Hammerstein's "The Sound of Music." This will make these children feel special without making the others feel inadequate. It will give everyone an opportunity to hear what the ideal sound is. These children can be taught during recess or before or after school. It could encourage the others to improve their own singing and develop their musical taste.

2. Because the children need to hear what a great children's choir sounds like, take them to a festival where several children's choirs are singing the same piece.

Organize a festival where three or four schools come together to sing a common piece with a highly skilled conductor.

3. Organize a music evening early in the school year where you teach the parents, staff, and school administrators to sing. One ideal piece is "Haida," arranged by Henry Leck, since people who are uncomfortable with their own singing become so involved with the body movements that they lose their inhibitions. Another piece to teach parents is a simple four-part round such as "Ars longa vita breva," which means, "Art is long, but life is short." After they have learned the round in unison, have them stand in circles in four sections of the room. Let the parents experience the joy of singing in harmony as the round is sung. At the end of the evening, hand out a one-page bulletin that outlines the tremendous benefits of teaching children to sing. This evening could be part of the school's curriculum night or parents' night held early in the fall.

4. Set up an exchange with a choir that is a few hours' bus drive away. Prepare four combined pieces and four separate pieces, possibly around a common theme: nature, animals, nursery rhymes, colors, et cetera. Perhaps enhance the program with poetry readings. Have the children sing solos, duets, trios, and quartets and invite children who play instruments well to perform one or two contrasting pieces. Hold the concert in the other choir's school and in yours.

5. If your music program just cannot seem to get off the ground, write down a list of obstacles and begin chipping away at them one by one, starting with the easier ones. If you have a large Sunday school, and your church choir has few members, ask yourself why more children are not involved. Perhaps you need to call all church parents early in September or take flyers around the neighborhood. Perhaps you could direct a thirty-minute musical in early November with simple costumes and acting. I have yet to encounter parents anywhere who do not want their children to participate in worthwhile activities. Most problems have solutions. A strong, charismatic leader will find the solutions. If after years of struggle no solution is forthcoming, quit and move on. Stop banging your head against a brick wall!

6. Encourage boys to sing by starting them as early as age six and seven. When they are eight, nine, and ten, it is important that they rehearse without the girls. The boys need fifteen or twenty minutes during rehearsal to play active games. They need to sing songs that are appropriate for boys' voices. They need to be told about the uniqueness of the boy's voice. They need to hear recordings of such great boy sopranos as Aled Jones. (The Three Tenors, Carreras, Domingo, and Pavarotti, have done wonderful things for the masses, and some boys may be motivated to sing by hearing one of their recordings or watching one of their videos.) Having all the boys in Grades 4 and 5 or 6 and 7 sing together to form a choir is highly effective. Then it is not a matter of choice but an expectation. Taking all the boys in the school to hear a performance by a superb boys' choir in your area may be logistically challenging, but it will be well worth the effort. For a list of pieces appropriate for community and school boys' choirs, please see appendix 9.

7. Building strong relationships with the adults with whom you work and the parents of the students you teach is of paramount importance. Parents can and

should play a very effective role in a healthy music program. In addition, music teachers need to get involved with the nonmusical aspects of the school's program. You need to be helpful on ski day if you have expertise in that area; you need to work on the school social committee or any committee that will give you an opportunity to interact with and help the staff. You need to see things from your colleagues' perspective, not just your own. Because of the performing nature of the music program, a music teacher's profile is often highly visible. By contrast, the classroom teacher, while working diligently, does not always get the recognition or visibility he or she deserves. The music teacher needs to be sensitive to this dichotomy.

8. Finding adequate funds to purchase music and supplies seems to be a persistent problem. While music is costly and a budget is necessary, I do feel that financial constraints cannot be blamed for all our ills. Some of the finest work I have seen was done by conductors who did not have adequate budgets.

9. If you feel that you need more financial assistance from the school than you are getting, make an appointment to see your principal and take the music representative of the parent/teacher organization with you. Have a business plan in writing. Go over your program for the year and present your budget in great detail. If money is available for computers, basketballs, and math textbooks, there should also be funds to purchase octavo scores for a vocal music program. Give your principal some time to work this out, but be prepared to write a letter to him or her, with copies for the school superintendent if you still don't get anywhere. Don't be cowed, but don't be anything less than professional. Ultimately administrators and parents want the best for their children. If all of this proves fruitless and you are unable to get money to purchase music, there are many imaginative ways to accomplish your goal:

- Hold bake sales, garage sales, and car washes.
- Have a free-will collection at malls where the children perform.
- Use proceeds from tickets sold at concerts.
- Use prize money, won at festivals, to purchase music.
- With music that is not copyrighted, such as folk songs and Christmas carols that have not been arranged, write your own arrangements or write out the melodies using blank rhythms and tonic-solfa syllables.
- Ask composers to write something for you (Both less-experienced and well-known composers are often delighted to write a piece for a school choir if it will be sung frequently. If it turns out to be a good piece, arrange for it to be published. Further ideas on commissioning new works can be found in chapter 11.)
- Scrounge: find schools that are closing, teachers who are retiring, publishing companies that are merging and having clearance sales, and churches that are amalgamating and discarding music no one uses anymore.
- In cooperation with administrators and parents, collect a dollar a month or ten dollars a year from each child for the purchase of music that he or she will keep at the end of the year.

Whatever you do, do not photocopy copyrighted scores or music you have downloaded from the Internet. It is not only illegal, but if it continues to be done, eventually there will be no scores published for anyone. There are ways and means to secure printed music. Find them.

There is no question that many problems continue to plague our school music education programs. Perhaps the greatest is the general apathy of many school administrators and the communities. But we cannot throw up our hands and give up. I have experienced how painful it is to have no funds, no support, and not even an adequate room. I, too, felt despair frequently. Without becoming too personal or too maudlin, I began my teaching career in a school portable. I had thirty copies of one piece of music that the senior school music teacher had loaned me—an old Novello publication—titled "A Wet Sheet and a Flowing Sea." The rehearsal was after school. Dozens of children playing in the schoolyard banged on the windows and then ran away. The repertoire, the room, and the timing were hopelessly inadequate, but the good thing was, there was nowhere to go but up!

Throughout the years, I always had the children and I never gave up on them. I always had paper, pencils, and an imagination. And most important of all, I always had one of the most powerful tools imaginable, the power of music. Despite the conditions in which we may find ourselves, music will continue to be one of the greatest gifts to humanity, perhaps *the* greatest. We must never sell it short.

## Serving as the Artistic Director of a Community Children's Chorus

### Creating a Nurturing Environment at the Choral Conductors' Symposium

Every other year, the Toronto Children's Chorus hosts a week-long conducting seminar in which six conductors conduct the chorus each day and prepare for a concert at the end of the week. Many other conductors observe. All conductors also attend sessions on rehearsal technique, conducting gesture, rehearsal preparation, teaching strategies, long-range planning, preparing for recording sessions, commissioning new works, administrations, touring board structure, fund-raising, et cetera. At the beginning of the week I give a one-hour introductory session that sets the week-long symposium in its proper context and fosters, I hope, a spirit of congeniality and caring among all of the conductors. What I say in that hour has nothing to do with the music per se but everything to do with how productive and satisfying the week is going to be for everyone. I try to set a tone or create an atmosphere that is healthy, supportive, and positive, since none of us learns well in a hostile environment. All of us have strengths and weaknesses. None of us knows everything there is to know about choral music. We are each on our own learning curve, and all of us have the ability to grow and to develop our skills. In order to learn more about our craft, I feel that we must let ourselves become vulnerable.

Often growth involves pain and struggle, not to mention an enormous amount of work. We can learn much from one another—egos have no place in a seminar such as this. Some of the most brilliant musicians I have ever had the privilege of working with have been humble to a fault. Because the music is much more significant than we are, a spirit of humility and nurturing is essential. Mentoring in this profession is crucial. Experienced choral directors need to find opportunities to share their expertise with others.

## Working with Management and a Board of Directors

Building effective and genuine relationships with the people you come in contact with is the most important aspect of the job. An artistic director works with an administrative staff, a board of directors, volunteers, committees, and parents. It is a symbiotic relationship; nothing can exist for very long without the other partners. Building these relationships takes not only a great deal of time and tact but also the wisdom of Solomon and the kindness of Mother Teresa. The artistic director must always try to see and understand the perspectives of others.

Such effective and meaningful relationships will be enhanced by the following:

1. A mission statement that outlines long-term and short-term objectives and is thoughtfully developed by the board members, the artistic director and the general manager: Organizations, including children's choirs, without a mission statement will likely flounder. The mission statement must not be something that the artistic director dreams up with the expectation that everyone else will fall in line. It has to be something that board members and staff work on together so that it will be meaningful to all. It can't be thrown together in a quick board meeting but needs to develop over time so that everyone is comfortable with it. There is no question that, depending upon the background of the board and staff, the artistic director needs to guide with tact and wisdom, but the final statement has to be one in which everyone feels they have played a role and made a contribution. From this mission statement objectives evolve. Long-term goals need to be set for a five- to ten-year period. Short-term goals need to be made for the current season.

2. An understanding on the part of all participants in the organization that decisions are made in the best interests of the organization and not a particular individual: Whenever a choir grapples with a problem, the question must be asked: "What solution is in the best interests of the choir?" Solutions cannot be developed if they are going to benefit one individual or family or one committee. The choir collectively is the music, the singers, and the art. Maintaining the integrity of the choir must be the reason that board, staff, parents, and volunteers become involved with the organization in the first place.

3. Clear job descriptions and responsibilities of board, staff, and volunteers written and articulated effectively: All staff and volunteers must have clear expectations of jobs and responsibilities. There must be open and honest communication among all parties. The board chair, the artistic director, and the choir manager must work together with honest and open communication to develop

clear goals for committees and clear job descriptions for themselves. Annual reviews need to take place between the board chair and the artistic director and the board chair and choir manager to assess what is being done, to find more effective ways of doing what they are doing, and to see if the goals are being met. Handbooks need to be developed for the choristers, the board members, the volunteers, and the parents to clarify the expectations and responsibilities of all those concerned.

4. An annual appraisal of people's work, volunteers and staff members alike, with praise and visible recognition: All volunteers and staff members need to be recognized annually for their contribution to the organization. Informal gatherings such as a barbecue at the end of the season with certificates awarded are deeply appreciated.

5. Clear lines of demarcation that outline who is responsible to whom: All staff should know to whom they are responsible. The board of directors ultimately is responsible for the organization's financial well-being. The artistic director and the choir manager work with the board to ensure financial stability. Just as the board of directors of a hospital would not tell a surgeon how to operate, the board of directors of a choir does not tell the artistic director how to train the choir or what pieces the choir should sing. If the artistic director, however, decides to program several concerts of the same type of music and to hire an orchestra that might bankrupt the organization, the board has every right to step in and recommend changes.

6. Effective committees, with the chairs of the committee sitting on the board: There has to be a time frame for each committee to function with a specific purpose and sufficient feedback and assistance from other board members. Committees are struck depending on the needs of the choir. Generally there is a fund-raising committee, a financial committee, a development committee, an outreach committee, a program committee, and a nominating committee. It is wise for the artistic director to be on the nominating committee, since board membership and the chair play critical roles in the organization. Parents are often the most motivated adults in the organization, and some of them who worked well on small parents' committees should eventually be on the board. It is important, however, for the organization to have other strong members of the community on the board to broaden the board's base and to prevent the organization from becoming too inward-looking. Volunteers need to have a clear job description of what it is they have been asked to do. They need to know how long it will take them to do it. Volunteers need to be matched with jobs that will suit their interests and talents. The chair of volunteers could be a board position.

7. A safety net for staff, with genuine concern and respect for all parties involved: Successful people in any area are never "too big" to roll up their sleeves and do the menial stuff. Artistic directors and general managers need to develop an atmosphere that embraces teamwork and mutual respect for all the various components that make up the "big family."

## Health and Well-Being and Personal Grooming on the Podium

The creative artist's life is one that requires much self-discipline. The demands placed on us by our families, our jobs, and society are seemingly impossible. No one can do it all. Sacrifices have to be made. But we do have choices, and the choices we make are our responsibility. (See chapter 6 for a fuller discussion of organization and time management.)

Most conductors are aware of the great need for good health. Countless articles and books outline the benefits of exercise and healthy eating. No one can cope effectively with this job year after year without a proper exercise regime and good eating habits.

Exercise is essential. Daily stretching and two-mile walks three times a week are a good start. A one-hour aerobic program three times a week would be a further goal. Aerobic exercise strengthens the heart and oxygenates the blood, enabling you to work more efficiently and productively. It also gives you a wonderful sense of accomplishment and well-being, improves your sleep, and helps you metabolize your food.

Eating healthy food is also crucial. Three balanced meals each day that contain grains, carbohydrates, fresh fruit and vegetables, protein, and dairy products are necessary. Foods loaded with fats and sugar should be avoided. Constantly running off to rehearsal with a coffee and doughnut for breakfast is a disservice to the body and over years will have severe consequences. High blood pressure and heart disease, diabetes, and other diseases are often the result of poor eating habits and lack of exercise.

Creative artists need time for rest and relaxation. The mind needs to be free. Whether this relaxation is in the form of prayer, meditation, yoga, or the practices of other belief systems is up to the individual, but it is essential and must not be overlooked. A creative mind cannot function well if it is constantly bombarded with noise and interruptions. If this means getting up an hour earlier when the house is quiet, then so be it. Extended periods of time for rest need to be taken in summer or at holiday times. The creative artist often experiences extended periods of adrenaline rush during peak performance times and extended tours. There has to be a time for the body to rest afterward.

The creative artist needs to develop friendships with people in other areas and to read as widely as possible. Conductors can become dull, uninspiring, inward-looking, and narrow if conversations with friends are limited only to the last concert one gave or the perfectly tuned G major chord one achieved in the last rehearsal. One becomes a better artist when one has a wide perspective and global thinking.

For years now, I have thought that someone needs to write about personal grooming for the conductor. I offer these suggestions.

The podium and all its trappings should be respected. When standing on it at rehearsal, one is always faced with a daunting task. Everything one does on that podium should be devoted to making great music, not detracting from it. There is a line of communication that flows between the conductor and all members of the ensemble. If the conductor is thoroughly prepared in every way, the respect for the music, the conductor, and the art will flow back from the singers.

There should be nothing visible about the conductor that will distract members of the ensemble from focusing on creating great music. The conductor needs to be comfortable, wearing clothes that breathe, such as a long-sleeve cotton blouse or shirt with slacks or a skirt that is loose-fitting and made of fabric that drapes well or hangs loosely. Tank tops and revealing necklines should be left at home. I am not particularly in favor of wearing blue jeans to rehearsal, although from time to time I have worn them with a long-sleeved blouse and a jacket. Clothes, for better or worse, say something about the person who wears them and the job he or she has. Trying to "get down to the kids' level" is pedagogy that failed in the seventies. Members of the ensemble spend a whole evening watching the conductor. Do not wear anything that will distract them from making the music. Give them something that reflects your good taste and your respect for them.

It seems to me that over the past twenty years female conductors have run the gamut from wearing elegant sequined evening gowns to wearing tuxedos. At some concerts, I have been so distracted by watching the bow bobbing on the conductor's back that I never heard the music. At others, some outfits were so tight and clingy that members of the audience could see the outline of the conductor's underwear. All conductors can dress tastefully, so that a sense of occasion arises and a satisfying whole emerges from an elegant evening of glorious music making.

## For All Conductors

- Black is best.
- Tuxedos should fit properly and be pressed. A size too big or a size too small is not flattering to the conductor and can be distracting to the audience and performers. Pant legs should be off the floor and not baggy around the ankles. The pant leg at the back should just touch the shoe.
- Wear comfortable, clean shoes that allow you to walk across the stage gracefully and quietly.
- Walk across the stage with your shoulders back and low. Take steps small enough that your head does not bob up and down as you walk. Smile at the audience. Bow before you stand on the podium. The podium is reserved for the music.

## For Women

- Full jersey skirts and pleated crepe skirts and pants hang well and look elegant on the podium.
- Jackets are attractive, but care must be taken with the sleeve length and width. The sleeves must be long enough to be comfortable when the arms

are raised and narrow enough not to be flailing in the air. The front must be done up or it is distracting to watch. A tasteful gold or silver thread in the jacket or a jacket in a subdued color can also look attractive. Gold or silver tailored jackets look attractive as long as they are not distracting.

- For special grand occasions, a green, blue, or red velvet dress or two-piece outfit can look elegant onstage, as long as it is not distracting for the audience or the ensemble.
- The outfit must suit the occasion—one would wear one type of outfit to conduct the *War Requiem* and another for a Christmas gala.
- Always make sure the outfit hangs well from the back. The type of fabric is very important. Take a female friend with you when you plan to purchase a conducting outfit. Have her view each outfit in a variety of lighting and from all angles.
- Tasteful makeup is important. Lipstick, rouge, and a light powder to remove the shine are important because of stage lighting.
- Your hairstyle should be discreet and controlled. If your hair is long, it needs to be held back and off the face. The singers need to communicate with your face and eyes. This is impossible if your hair is hanging over your eyes.
- Discreet jewelry, such as gold stud earrings, can enhance an outfit, but leave the dangly earrings and the baubles and rhinestone necklaces at home.
- Wear black hose if the outfit is black and neutral hose if it is another color.
- Wear a full-length slip if wearing an unlined skirt.
- Wear neutral nail polish. Wild colors on the fingernails are distracting.
- Leave the stiletto heels and four-inch platform shoes at home.

It is hoped that the following limericks shed some levity on this rather sensitive topic and at the same time reinforce the need for us to be critical of our stage appearance:

*There was a conductor from Stack*
*Who wore colorful things on her back,*
   *Blue bows that were frilly,*
   *Red sequins looked silly,*
*'Twould be better if she had worn black.*

*There was a conductor from Reading*
*Whose tux always needed a pressing,*
   *His shoes they were grimy,*
   *Not once have been shiny,*
*He needed some help with his dressing.*

*There was a conductor whose earring*
*Had the audience constantly peering,*
   *The light was so strong,*
   *It just blinded the throng,*
*And the choir was silently jeering.*

*There was a conductor whose gown*
*Made her look like the talk of the town,*
> *The slit up her thigh*
> *Made some gasp and some sigh,*
*While her husband just sat with a frown.*

*There was a conductor from Maine*
*Who dressed elegantly time and again,*
> *Long sleeves that were graceful*
> *And hemlines so tasteful,*
*The choir sang well, not in vain.*

Good taste is never out of fashion. How you appear in public speaks volumes about the respect you have for yourself and those people with whom you are working. It can also add to, detract from, or nullify the audience's pleasure in hearing a fine performance!

# CHAPTER NINE

# Conducting an Orchestra

Conducting an orchestra that is accompanying a children's chorus is a thrilling experience. For a choral conductor it also can be a daunting experience. Regardless of whether it is a professional, community, or student orchestra, the choral conductor must take full responsibility for the success of rehearsals and performances. The following suggestions and ideas may be beneficial as you prepare for this role.

## Understanding Orchestral Players

A failure to understand orchestral players and their needs can be devastating for a choral conductor. Orchestral players are different from choral singers. Orchestral players often make their living playing and are used to working with many different conductors. Singers in a choir may rehearse once a week with the conductor, with whom they often have developed a special bond. Singers may spend several months preparing a score, whereas instrumentalists, particularly the top professional players, sight-read the score at the first rehearsal, fine-tune it at the second rehearsal, and then play the concert. Singers may be used to choral conductors who change their minds about such things as tempi, subdivided beats, phrase lengths, and articulation. Orchestral players need to see clear, concise, and consistent conducting patterns that are the same in the initial rehearsal and final performance. Orchestral players do not have to think about "word coloring" as singers do, but they are deeply concerned about such things as dynamics, fermatas, correct tempi, and changes of tempi. Ideally, orchestral players will understand and be sensitive to the words that are being sung. Conductors need to explain the text to them.

For a choral conductor with limited knowledge of the various instruments, it is perhaps easier to conduct a professional orchestra rather than a student orchestra. The wise choral conductor would not dream of telling a professional orchestral player "how" to play a passage—these players have spent a lifetime developing technique that the choral conductor can never hope to master. You can sing a passage to the players the way you would like to hear it, but let them decide how best to play it. (Telling brass players, for example, not to split notes will cause you to lose the respect of the entire orchestra!) When conducting a student orchestra, a conductor needs to understand instrumental technique and be able to help the players. It goes without saying that the more knowledge one has about all the instruments, the better. (Early in a conductor's career, the knowledge and experience the conductor gains from spending some apprentice time for several years working with a student orchestra would be invaluable. He or she would learn many valuable things "on the job.")

## Thorough Score Preparation

Your success in the first rehearsal is dependent on your level of preparation. This involves endless hours of score study, and analysis, as well as thorough understanding of the stylistic elements of the music of the period. Ideally, after this lengthy preparation you could conduct the score by memory.

You must have studied the parts that the players have in front of them and have checked them thoroughly to make sure there are no errors. Time with an orchestra is always at a premium. A player whose part is marked with eight measures' rest instead of nine could cost you precious—and expensive—rehearsal time. Make absolutely sure that your score and the orchestra parts have the same letters or bar numbers. The conductor's preparations of the score and parts beforehand should make their working environment easier for the players. In all orchestral parts, you should mark whether they are conducting in two or four or, for example, where the two and three groupings are in mixed meter. If there are many measures where an instrumentalist has nothing to play, a chorus text cue could be added. Players appreciate any practical help that will make their job easier and enable them to play their best.

String players will appreciate it if the concertmaster, after consultation with you, has marked the bowings beforehand. To avoid confusion and lost rehearsal time, make sure all parts have the same bowings marked or show none at all. This is especially important when rental scores are used. Do not insert your own bowings if your knowledge of bowings is minimal; rather, before the first rehearsal work hand in glove with the concertmaster, whose job it is to make sure the parts are bowed properly. If you are working with a very small group, which children's choir directors often do (e.g., four first violins, three seconds, three violas, two celli, and a string bass), it would be safer to start with clean copies. String players are used to marking their scores on the fly.

## The Orchestral Score

Use the full orchestral score at all your choir rehearsals and imagine the color of the various instruments as you hear their parts played on the piano. Mark important entries and get used to cueing those "imaginary" instruments. Learn which orchestral passages double the choral parts and which solo instrumental lines can be heard. Get a sense of the texture you want to hear and consider the balance problems you may encounter. Transitions from one section to the next are vitally important. You must have these changes of tempo, articulation, and dynamics thoroughly in your arms and in your baton so the players are never confused or unsure.

## Transposing Instruments

You must know the orchestral instruments which transpose and which do not. (Please see appendix 13.) If you are a novice, always give pitch clarification in concert pitch, rather than trying to figure out, for example, what note the French horn should be playing. You need to be able to read the alto clef for the viola and often the tenor clef for the trombone at the same speed that you read the treble and bass clefs.

## Orchestral Language

You must understand the language orchestral players are accustomed to hearing in rehearsal and learn to use it. (Orchestral language is different from the language a conductor uses in choral rehearsals.) Imagery is very effective in choral rehearsals but usually not in orchestral rehearsals. Telling players that the opening movement of a work should have the splendor and majesty of a sunrise often does nothing for them. Telling them instead that a movement is in two, not four, starts *pianissimo,* and builds to a *forte* over eight measures, with a *sforzando* and *tenuto* on the final chord, likely has a much better chance of giving you what you want to hear.

String players are used to being asked to play with more bow or less bow or close to the tip or close to the frog. Be able to sing a passage with the articulation or phrasing that you want. The players are usually quite good at imitating you! Wind players are used to being asked to play short or long, more mellow, make it sing, louder/softer (brass hardly ever louder!). Understand their terminology and become comfortable with it. Rather than telling brass players to play softer, since you still want, for example, Brahms to sound like Brahms, tell them it is too heavy and let them decide how to fix it. In rehearsal, orchestral players are used to shorter, more precise commands than are the singers.

It is often important to specify articulation to orchestral players. It is helpful for you to realize the nature of the different instruments and their varying colors, articulations, and attacks. For instance, a conductor will often clarify articulations by the use of "ta," "da," and "daaa" to show different attacks and lengths of notes. Realizing that wind players attack notes by using their tongues, brass players with vibrations of their embouchures, and string players by using their bows will make it possible to clarify how you wish them to articulate.

Orchestral players are used to rehearsing lengthy passages before the conductor stops to correct several different things at the same time. This is a great challenge for most of us, who have to remember a great deal more in an orchestral rehearsal than a choral rehearsal. Whatever you do, do not stop the players every few measures the way choral conductors often stop and correct their choirs for one thing at a time. Learn to give verbal directions as you conduct. It saves a lot of time and is greatly appreciated by the players. Anticipate problem passages and remind the players just before the passage begins and as they play. Conductors also must be careful not to turn an orchestral rehearsal into a string rehearsal. Wind and brass players despise this! The choral/orchestral rehearsal must be just that; the conductor needs to work with the entire ensemble.

If you are conducting in a country where the native language is different from yours, learn some phrases in their language such as, "Good evening; I'm very pleased to be here"; "Very good. Now play it again only softer from measure . . .";  "Try not to rush from measure . . ."; "Be sure you are absolutely together at measure . . ."; and "We need more . . . at measure . . ." If necessary, have all measure numbers translated on a sheet of paper or learn the numbers by heart. In countries such as Australia and the United Kingdom, where a semibreve is a whole note, a minim is a half note, a crotchet is a quarter note, a quaver is an eighth note, and a semiquaver is a sixteenth note, you should use their terminology—do not expect them to change to yours.

## Your Ears

As in choral conducting, your ears are your most important asset. If you know the score thoroughly, with experience you will begin to hear everything in the rehearsal. An orchestral score is infinitely more complex than most choral scores and the colors and timbres far more challenging to achieve. You will gain the respect of the players if you know the score thoroughly and can hear if they play incorrect notes. They may even test you. If you make a mistake, admit it, apologize briefly, and then get on with it. Don't bluff your way through. Orchestral players can sense incompetence instantly.

## The Baton

Your conducting technique must be clear, concise, and consistent. The players' ability to play their best depends on it. Use a baton. It gives your beat focus, and the players will be used to following one. Don't conduct rhythms! This is confusing and demoralizing for orchestral players. Tell the players whether they play *on* the stick or *behind* the stick and on the *top* of the beat or at the *bottom* of the beat. Most often instrumentalists play *on* the stick at the *bottom* of the beat. (Many great European orchestras are now playing *behind* the stick. It apparently gives the players a greater sense of momentum and a split second to plan and execute what they are going to do.) Orchestral musicians want clarity from the beat, but it is not necessary to overbeat or use the baton as a whip! Too much beating often results in difficulties for the players, since the natural delay of orchestral attacks (that subtle lag between baton and orchestra) is inherent in the players' listening to one another. If the baton is too insistently beaten, the musicians will not know whether to follow the orchestra ensemble or the baton, which may be milliseconds earlier. "Let the orchestra play" is a useful concept as long as the work is progressing according to the conductor's vision.

Cueing is vitally important for orchestral players. Given little rehearsal time available, the potential for counting errors is tremendous. The less experience the players have, the more cues you will need to give them. Cue with your left hand or give them a nod. Do look at them! Eye contact is helpful. As with choral conducting, your facial expression is very important. It should be inviting rather than intimidating and reflect the style of the music you are conducting.

## The Student Orchestra

If you are working with a student orchestra that has already prepared the music with its conductor, go to the last two or three rehearsals and observe how the conductor works with the players. Insist that their conductor attend your first orchestral rehearsal and the first choral/orchestral rehearsal to listen and to assist the players if they are having technical difficulties. If you do not have thorough knowledge of instrumental technique do not attempt to correct the players—you could thoroughly confuse the students and end up with worse results than if you said nothing.

## Percussion

Children's choir conductors often have some of the children accompany the choir on percussion instruments or work with professional players. The conductor needs to be wary of several things.

If, for example, the choir is performing, "Children's Crusade," by Benjamin Britten, which demands six professional solo players and a large body of tutti players on a huge battery of tuned, rhythmic, and clashed instruments, the choral conductor needs to consult the lead player to learn about the complexities and intricacies of the instruments. If the children are to be involved in the tutti sections, the professional should train them. The choral conductor should not assume the children will know how to hold and play a wood block or triangle properly.

When the children are using percussion instruments, make sure that the instruments are of high quality and in good repair. Several common problems must be avoided:

- claves being held improperly, resulting in a poor sound
- use of the wrong kind of drum
- improper tuning of the drum
- muted triangle sound due to its not being suspended properly
- striking the triangle with an improper beater
- noisy placement of the instruments on the table or floor
- holding the tambourines incorrectly and striking them in the wrong place

The most common problems with adult professional percussion players are balance, rhythmic precision, and tuning. Children's choir conductors need to be aware of these problems and address them during the rehearsal. The timpani are tuned instruments that often need retuning during a rehearsal or performance. If they are played too loudly, they can overpower the children and spoil the balance. Hard sticks and sometimes brushes are used with the snare drum. If you are concerned about balance when mallets are used on the timpani or hard sticks on the snare drum, ask the percussion player to let you hear sticks of other weights and sizes. With cymbals, the problem often concerns the length of time that a tone is sustained. You may have to suggest that the sound be sustained longer or shorter depending on the context. The final problem relates to the bass drum, which tends to be behind the beat. Make sure your ictus is very clear. Since the bass drum can be heard above the orchestra and children, it must be absolutely rhythmic and precise.

The percussion players, perhaps more than any other members of the orchestra, given their lengthy passages of silence, need cues from your baton and eye contact. Anticipate their entries, look right at them, and cue precisely.

## The Rehearsals

Orchestras have long-standing traditions that are sacrosanct. They start precisely on time and finish precisely on time. Before you stand on the podium give them the time they need to tune to the oboe's A. Shake the concertmaster's hand and when the concertmaster sits down stand on the podium. Find out beforehand from the personnel manager when and how long the breaks are.

It is essential to have at least one rehearsal with the orchestra before the choral/orchestral rehearsal. If you are rehearsing several short pieces, make sure the players have a list of music in the order you are rehearsing. Read through the entire piece or movement and let the players get a sense of how it fits together. Do not be dismayed when the players start to discuss the music as soon as you stop. Concertmasters need to tell the string players what they want to hear and often will show them. This verbal interruption is not a sign of disrespect but, rather, how orchestra players work. Cover all of the music in this rehearsal before spending time on detail. Many technical errors will be fixed by the players before the second rehearsal. If you have time for detailed work, rehearse difficult tempi changes and address balance problems and ensemble playing—all aspects that the instrumentalists cannot fix on their own time.

At the first choral/orchestral rehearsal, begin with a pleasantry that lasts no longer than five seconds. Welcome any guest soloists and introduce the choir to the orchestra or orchestra to choir, depending on the relationship and the occasion. Then name the composer, the work, and the movement, if necessary tell the orchestra if you are in two or four, and *begin.* Do not use podium time for telling them stories, anecdotes, and your life story. Always speak loudly and clearly, since there are often players far away from the podium.

The timing of the rehearsal must be planned very carefully. Respect each musician's time and abilities. If you are rehearsing several shorter pieces, start with those that involve all the instruments and work down to those that involve the least number of instruments. (A tuba player who plays only in the last piece will not appreciate sitting around for an hour and a half waiting for his or her turn to play.) Always have a starting point in mind when you do stop—a measure number or letter number. Directions must be clear and precise. Talk as little as possible; the musicians want to play. Do not shorten a rehearsal to curry favor. Professionals want to do as good a job as possible, and they know when rehearsal time is necessary.

Let the choir members fend for themselves in the first choral/orchestral rehearsal. They should not need to be spoon-fed at this stage. They must be responsible for their own entries and cutoffs while you work primarily with the orchestral players. Have a trusted colleague sit out in the hall with a score to check for balance. It is often very difficult to judge balance problems from the podium. Insist on balance. The children's chorus needs to be large enough, with a strong vocal technique, to carry them above the orchestra without the orchestral players having to play substantially softer than the dynamics on the page. Placement of the children's chorus onstage is vitally important, but more often than not, it is not ideal.

Always shake the concertmaster's hand and recognize individual players with a bow during the applause. Orchestral musicians' names (particularly in choral concerts with a pickup orchestra) should be listed in the program.

There is no need to be intimidated at the prospects of conducting an orchestra if you have done your homework. The players are not concerned that your background is choral conducting—they just want to play in an environment where they can play well. This environment occurs

- when the conductor knows the score thoroughly and knows exactly what he or she wants
- when the parts are readable and clearly marked

- when the conductor lets the musicians play
- when the conductor's conducting pattern is clear, concise, and consistent

## Conclusion

Conducting an orchestra takes a lifetime of study. The suggestions in this chapter do not begin to cover in depth the work involved, but I hope the suggestions given here will assist the conductors of children's choirs to approach the job with greater skill and confidence.

# CHAPTER TEN

# Preparing the Children to Sing a Major Work with Orchestra

Singing a choral masterpiece with an adult choir, professional soloists, and a symphony orchestra is one of the most thrilling and memorable experiences a young chorister can have. For the children's choir conductor, however, preparing such a massive work can be a daunting task. This chapter outlines the problems he or she may encounter in six specific works and offers suggestions for overcoming them through thorough preparation and organization. These problems generally fall into three major categories: the number of children needed and their location in the hall, the acoustics of the hall, and the balance of orchestra, adult choir, and children's chorus.

If one is fortunate, the orchestral conductor will take the time to share his or her ideas about the complete score with the children's choir director. This, of course, helps enormously with score preparation. Failing this collaboration, the children's choir director must do the preparation alone or with the assistance of an experienced and knowledgeable colleague.

A week or two before the performances, the orchestral conductor must come and work with the children in a piano rehearsal in their own rehearsal home, before the first choral/orchestral rehearsal takes place. This gives the children an opportunity to become accustomed to his or her conducting; the children may find this awkward if they are used to being spoon-fed by their own conductor. It also enables the orchestral conductor to make suggestions while hearing the children in a smaller space. The children's choir director should take detailed notes during this rehearsal and conduct a subsequent piano/choral rehearsal before the children's choir works with the orchestra, in order to implement the orchestral conductor's ideas. Giving the children a written reminder of suggestions that should be drilled during warm-ups is often helpful at this stage.

In all music with foreign-language texts, the children must have translations of what they are singing. They should be taught the story and background of the work. They should also be taught about the composer and how he or she fits into the historical musical context. At the performance they must not stand up like trained seals without any knowledge of what they are doing and why they are doing it. To be worthy professional artists, they must be thoroughly prepared.

In most of the works discussed here, treble voice sections were intended for boys' voices. The contemporary children's chorus—an instrument of considerable beauty, flexibility, and sophistication—was unknown when these pieces were written. (I am certain that if these composers could hear the children's chorus of today, they would be very pleased indeed!)

In each of the following six works, background information is given to assist the children in becoming familiar with the composer and the work; a text and a good translation are also included. Ideas are given to help the conductor teach children particular parts and overcome obstacles in the score, and a list of highly recommended compact discs is included at the end of each section.

## Gustav Mahler: Third Symphony
*Timing: 1 hour 35 minutes*

### Background Notes for Choristers

Gustav Mahler was born in the village of Kaliste on the border of Bohemia and Moravia in 1860; he died in Vienna in 1911. His childhood was not a very happy one. Of the twelve children born in his family, five died at birth. His younger brother Ernst died at thirteen; his older brother Otto committed suicide at twenty-five. His parents did not have a happy marriage, and there were many family arguments. During one family row, Mahler heard a hurdy-gurdy out in the street, playing a popular Viennese song; the sound of this hurdy-gurdy found its way into some of Mahler's music, as did the sound of marches and reveilles reminiscent of the military barracks close to his home.

Mahler studied at the Vienna Conservatory and the University of Vienna. Composition students had to conduct the student orchestra, and Mahler eventually made his living as a conductor, composing only during the summer months. He conducted at many opera houses, including the famous Vienna Opera House. He received great praise for his conducting skill from such luminaries as Brahms and Tchaikovsky. Toward the end of Mahler's life, he came to the United States, where he conducted the Metropolitan Opera and the New York Symphony Orchestra. In the maestro's dressing room at Carnegie Hall there is a bust of Mahler, and the framed letter on the wall thanks the Carnegie staff for their kindness.

In his lifetime, Mahler composed nine symphonies and a tenth that he never finished. His Third Symphony, written between 1893 and 1896 at a summer home in Steinbach-am-Attersee in northern Austria, was first performed in Krefeld in

1902, with Mahler conducting. The symphony has six movements, unlike the usual four, and lasts for an hour and a half. Two of the movements contain vocal parts: the fourth features a mezzo-soprano, and the fifth is for mezzo-soprano, women's chorus, and boys' chorus. The symphony can be divided into two parts: the first movement, which lasts for just over half an hour, and the rest of the symphony. The children sing for only five minutes in the fifth movement, so it is critical that they have an understanding of the rest of the work to make their listening more informed and their appreciation of the symphony more meaningful.

Mahler has given us titles for each movement to indicate the varying moods. The first is "The Introduction: Pan Awakes. Summer Marches In." This movement, which introduces all the themes and is very much the exposition, is quite solemn. The final part of the exposition is a brighter section, with horns and trumpets and a boisterous march before the development section and sonata form principals take place. The movement ends in a lengthy coda in F major, the relative major of the home key of D minor. The second movement, "What the Wild Flowers Tell Me" is a minuet in binary form with each section again divided into two subsections. The third movement, "What the Animals in the Forest Tell Me," is a scherzo, and the trio, or middle section, is a post horn solo that the children should listen for, as it is played offstage. The fourth movement, "What Man Tells Me," is very slow and mysterious and contains material from the first movement. It is a setting for mezzo-soprano that uses the text of Nietzsche's "Zarathustra's Midnight Song." "O Mensch, gib Acht!" ("O man, take heed!"). The fifth movement, "What the Angels Tell Me," is merry in tempo and bold in expression. The text, from *Das knaben Wunderhorn,* is German folklore. The sixth movement, "What Love Tells Me," is a slow sonata-rondo movement and contains one of the most lyrical and poignant melodies ever written. The B and C sections of the rondo contain material from the fourth movement with the words "Tief ist ihr Weh" ("Deep is his woe"). The movement builds to a great climax that ends the symphony.

## Text

The angelic children's chorus represents bells and sings "bimm, bamm" until measure 85 and again at the coda, from 110 to the end. It is important that the "b" is explosive, the "i" vowel of short duration, and the "mm" elongated and sung as strongly as possible. The children's chorus sings its final four phrases in German. The consonants must be explosive throughout or the text will never be heard.

The women's chorus sings "Es sungen drei Engel" from the folk-poetry collection *Das knaben Wunderhorn.* It is the "Amer Kinder Bettlerlied" ("Poor Children's Begging Song"). The translation is as follows:

> Three angels sang a sweet song and with blessed joy it sounded in heaven.
> They shouted joyously there for Peter was free from sin.
> And as the Lord Jesus sat at the table eating the evening meal with his twelve
> disciples

The Lord Jesus said, "Why are you staying here? When I look at you, you are weeping for me."

"I should not weep, gracious God." "You need not weep."

"I have broken the ten commandments, I will go and weep bitterly."

"You need not weep." "Ah, come and take pity on me."

"If you have broken the ten commandments

Then fall on your knees and pray to God."

[The following four lines of text are also used with the children's chorus.]

Love only God forever so you will attain heavenly joy.

Heavenly joy is a blessed city; heavenly joy knows no end.

Heavenly joy was given by Jesus to Peter

For us and for our eternal happiness.

## Musical Challenges

Since the children begin on a unison F without any introduction from the orchestra, the first difficulty is finding the pitch. The previous movement ends on the dominant of D major, played by the celli and basses. The children must listen for this A and silently sing down a major third. It is wise to have several dependable children use tuning forks to make sure the first pitch is accurate. Make sure that in the piano/choral rehearsals the accompanist plays from figure 9 of the fourth movement. The soloist will give the children a very strong sense of D major, which they should try to retain in order to find the F major tonality of their fifth movement. Make sure the upper voices sing a bright major second at the outset. The G often tends to be flat.

Since much of the tessitura lies around middle C and low B flat, the children must use chest voice in order to be heard. Ideally, the children should be placed near the percussion section, since the glockenspiel often doubles the "bimm, bamm." I would suggest a minimum number of sixty children, with a dozen or so twelve- and thirteen-year-old boys who have the ideal timbre for those middle C's and B flats. Two-thirds of the choir should sing the upper notes, which do not carry as well as the repeated whole notes in the lower voice.

At measure 88, the children enter with "Liebe nur Gott" ("Love only God") on an ascending E major scale marked *forte* with accents. These two measures often tend to sharpen if the children have not been told to be wary of that. The entry at 92 gives the main theme to the trebles. Again it is marked *fortissimo* and must be sung very strongly. The best way to get this is through *marcato* singing with explosive consonants. Pay particular attention to the middle C pickup note to 100. It must be sung in the chest voice or it will never be heard.

The performance will be greatly enhanced if the children sing the piece from memory. Because of the repetition of the "bimm, bamm," this is not as easy as one might expect. Memory work is achieved by going through the various tonalities by section: Section 1 to measure 10, Section 2 to measure 33, Section 3 from measure

43 to measure 50, Section 4 only measures 55 and 56 (choirs often have trouble finding the B flat; if they think of the mezzo word "bitterlich" as a descending E-flat major scale, their entry should not be as difficult), Section 5 from 63 to 77, Section 6 from 82 to 90, Section 7 from 92 to 106, and Section 8 from 110 to the end.

## Recommended Recordings

| Georg Solti | Chicago Symphony Orchestra and Chorus | London | 1982 |
| | Helga Dernesch, Glen Ellyn Children's Chorus | | |
| Klaus Tennstedt | London Philharmonic Orchestra Ortrun Wenkel, the London Philharmonic Choir, the Southend Boys' Choir | EMI CZS 574296-2(2) | 1979 |
| Neeme Jarvi | Royal Scottish Orchestra Royal Scottish Orchestra Chorus and Junior Chorus | Chandos 9117/18 | 1985 |

## Gustav Mahler: Eighth Symphony
*Timing: approximately one and a half hours*

### Background Notes for Choristers

The Eighth Symphony was composed in only nine weeks during the summer of 1906. Mahler himself conducted the first performance in Munich on September 12, 1910, with massive forces—858 singers and 171 instrumentalists. Ever since this grand performance, it has always been known as the "Symphony of a Thousand." Unlike other symphonies, such as his Third and Fourth and the Beethoven Ninth, which use choral and solo forces sparingly, Mahler's Eighth uses eight soloists, two large adult choirs, and treble choir throughout. The premiere was an overwhelming success and certainly one of the most spectacular events to take place in Europe in the decade that preceded the First World War. Mahler regarded it as the peak of his public career, but it also proved to be his final triumph; he died the following year, on May 18, 1911.

The work is set in two parts. The first part, sung in Latin, is based on the great ninth-century Pentecostal hymn "Veni, Creator Spiritus," a celebration of the descent of the Holy Spirit. The second part, sung in German, is based on the final scene of Goethe's *Faust,* which outlines Faust's sudden and unearned salvation. In the presence of the Virgin Mary (Mater Gloriosa), he is able to glimpse the truths for which he had been searching. The juxtaposition of these two texts enabled Mahler to grapple with two distinct ages of thought, premodern and modern, and to bring these thoughts into a unified whole where principal agents of healing are developed—spiritual and physical love, eternal love, unearned grace, and eventual forgiveness.

## Text and Translation for the Treble Chorus

### Part One—Hymnus: Veni, Creator Spiritus (Treble Chorus Section Italicized)

a) Veni, Creator Spiritus,
Mentes tuorum visita.
Imple superna gratia,
Quae tu creasti pectora.

b) Qui diceris Paraclitus,
Altissimi donum Dei,
Fons vivus, ignis, caritas
Et spiritalis unctio.

c) Infirma nostri corporis
Virtute firmans perpeti;
*Accende lumen sensibus;*
*Infunde amorem cordibus.*

d) *Hostem repellas longius*
Pacemque dones protinus.
Ductore sic te praevio
Vitemus omne pessimum.

e) Tu septiformis munere,
Digitus paternae dexterae . . .

f) Per te sciamus da Patrem,

Noscamus . . . Filium,
. . . Spiritum
Credamus omni tempore.

g) Da gaudiorum praemia.
Da gratiarum munera.
Dissolve litis vincula;
Adstringe pacis foedera.

h) *Gloria (sit) Patri Domino,*
*Natoque (ac Filio) qui a mortuis*
*Surrexit, ac Paraclito,*
*In saeculorum saecula*

a) Come, O creator Spirit,
Visit the souls of thy people.
Fill with grace from on high
The hearts which thou hast created.

b) Thou who art called the Comforter,
The gift of God most high,
The well of life, fire, love
And the anointing of the soul.

c) Strengthen the weakness of our bodies
With thine unfailing power;
*Kindle light within our senses;*
*Pour love into our hearts.*

d) *Do thou drive the enemy far away*
And grant us peace right early.
Thus with thee to guide us
May we avoid every great ill.

e) Thou who art sevenfold in thy gifts,
Finger of the Father's right hand . . .

f) Grant us to know the Father through thee,
. . . To come to know the Son,
To believe always . . .
[In] the Spirit.

g) Give us the rewards of joy.
Give us the gifts of grace.
Loosen the chains of strife;
Tighten the pacts of peace.

h) *Glory be to the Father, the Lord,*
*And to the Son, who from the dead*
*Is risen, and to the Comforter,*
*World without end.*

circa ninth century (with additions)

### Part Two—Chorus of Blessed Boys

Hände verschlinget euch
Freudig zum Ringverein!

Join your hands
Joyfully in a circle!

| | |
|---|---|
| Regt euch und singet | Move and sing |
| Heil'ge Gefühle drein! | Of your holy feelings! |
| Göttlich belehret, | Divinely instructed, |
| Dürft ihr vertrauen; | Dare to trust; |
| Den ihr verehret | Whom ye worshiped |
| Werdet ihr schauen. | Shall be revealed to you. |

*The Blessed Boys (continued)*

| | |
|---|---|
| Freudig empfangen wir | Gladly we receive |
| Diesen im Puppenstand; | Him in chrysalis state; |
| Also erlangen wir | Thus we redeem |
| Englisches Unterpfand. | The angels' pledge. |
| Löset die Flocken los | Loosen the cocoon |
| Die ihn umgeben! | That envelops him! |
| Schon ist er schön und gross | Already he is fair and tall |
| Von heiligem Leben. | Through holy life. |

*The Blessed Boys (continued)*

| | |
|---|---|
| Er überwächst uns schon | He is outgrowing us already |
| An mächtigen Gliedern, | With mighty limbs, |
| Wird treuer Pflege Lohn | And faithful care he will |
| Reichlich erwidern. | Amply repay. |
| Wir würden früh entfernt | We were early removed |
| Von Lebechören: | From life's chorus; |
| Doch dieser hat gelernt; | But he has learned; |
| Er wird uns lehren. | He will teach us. |

*Chorus Mysticus*

| | |
|---|---|
| Alles Vergängliche | Everything transitory |
| Ist nur ein Gleichnis; | Is but a symbol; |
| Das Unzulängliche | The inadequate |
| Hier wird's Ereignis; | Here becomes the fulfillment; |
| Das Unbeschreibliche | The indescribable |
| Hier ist's getan; | Here is done; |
| Das Ewig-Weibliche | The eternal feminine |
| Zieht uns hinan. | Leads us aloft. |

Johann Wolfgang von Goethe (1749–1832)

## Musical Challenges for the Treble Chorus

The children's choir conductor would be wise to get a list of tempi markings from the orchestral conductor before starting to rehearse. The children sing sporadically throughout the work, and much time will be saved at the first rehearsal with the orchestral conductor if the children have become used to the different tempi.

Since the children probably will be using the Knabenchor score published by Universal Edition and not have the benefit of a full choral score, it is important for them to know approximately how much time lapses between their entries. The children should write these approximate times in their scores:

### Part One

> Before figure 38 there are twelve minutes.
> Between figures 68 and 79 there are three minutes.
> Between figures 79 and 80 there are three minutes.

### Part Two

> Before figure 58 there are nineteen minutes.
> Between figures 60 and 84 there are five and a half minutes.
> Between figures 88 and 155 there are fourteen minutes.
> Between figures 164 and 182 there are five minutes.
> Between figures 185 and 213 there are seven minutes.

The greatest challenge in this work is for the children to be heard. It is helpful to know when the children are doubled and when adult chorus parts do not double them. One needs to be particularly concerned with hearing them when their part is not doubled.

In Part One, they are not doubled in the following sections:

> From figure 40 to five measures after 41
> From two measures before figure 45
> From figure 49 to one measure after figure 50
> Two measures before figure 53
> The second, third, and fourth measures after figure 53
> The third, fourth, and fifth measures after figure 83
> From figure 88 to figure 89
> From figure 91 to figure 92

As long as each child has a substantial sound to begin with and there is room to seat them, the more children who sing this work the better. (Mahler used 350 children at the first performance.) They need to have a chest voice that will carry. Everything in the first movement needs to be sung *marcato* and *fortissimo,* with exaggerated consonants that project. The material at figure 40 is very important, since the treble chorus carries the melodic line alone. Particular attention has to be given to the pickup note on the pitch B. This low pitch must be sung in the chest voice. Even a raucous sound will do as long as it is in tune and is projected. The trombones, bassoons, and strings and the bass section of the adult choir are all at a *fortissimo* dynamic, so the trebles must work very hard to be heard. The four measures that begin at figure 83 are the most important measures in Part One, since the treble choir, singing alone, heralds the new key of D-flat major and must blast forth like trumpets. (They are actually doubled by the trumpets, whose parts are marked *forte,* and accompanied by low strings and winds, whose parts are marked *mezzo forte.* You might consider asking the orchestral conductor to have the trumpets play *mezzo forte.* These four measures can never be too loud, and the children must sing at least three hard G consonants on the Glorias so they will be heard. In the final E-flat major chord, I always have the chorus sing a unison top E flat that will carry, since the root, third, and fifth of the chord cannot be heard in the midst of the thick texture.

In Part Two, the children (or Blessed Boys, as Mahler calls them) represent souls who have died too soon to experience sin. They are never doubled, except at figure 183 for two measures and from figure 213 to the end. It is in Part Two where the children's chorus is most exposed. The only doubling is at the end from figure 183 for two measures and from figure 213 to two measures after 214. There are four distinct sections where the children's choir has important musical material of its own, and it is here that most rehearsal time should be spent:

1. At figure 58 the children's entry is six measures after all women from Choirs I and II begin; this lovely contrapuntal duet continues until figure 60.
2. From figure 85 to four measures after 88, the children sing a duet with Dr. Marianus, one of the most challenging tenor roles in the repertoire. Because of the tessitura of the vocal writing and the relatively light orchestration, the children's choir can be heard quite distinctly.
3. From one measure before 155 to four measures after figure 160, the children sing alone in one of the most beautiful sections of the entire symphony. The chest voice must be used for the three pickup notes before 155 or they will not be heard. At figure 160, in the only two-part divisi written for the children, I would revoice the parts and put two-thirds on the lower part; the upper part will be heard because it lies in that part of the child's voice that will carry. Ignore the *piano* marking four measures after figure 156, since the four horn parts and three bassoon parts are marked *forte* and the children are singing in their middle register. Figure 160 also needs to be *fortissimo* since the children are singing in their lower register and, for four measures, the adult sopranos of Choir II enter in their high register.
4. From one measure after figure 161 to four measures after 164, the children sing alone, but this time the orchestration becomes very thick. The children need to sing as loudly as possible using explosive consonants in order to project the text.

These four sections should be memorized so the children's full attention can be given to the conductor. During early choral rehearsals, after notes and words have been learned, the children need to get used to hearing the material that is going on before they sing. An expert accompanist is needed and, if you are not comfortable singing the solo parts yourself, in any octave, bring in someone who can sing them or play a compact disc. (The former is preferable.)

Be very fussy with the tuning. The two measures before figure 59, as well as the six measures after figure 59, tend to flatten, and the G sharp four measures before figure 60 is never high enough. The C four measures after figure 157, which is the only whole step after three half steps, is never high enough. The A natural three measures after figure 163 tends to flatten, as does the A natural at figure 185.

The children must be very still in the *tacet bis* section just after figure 185. The adult choirs introduce "Alles vergangliche," one of the most breathtaking passages ever composed, by singing triple *piano* in E-flat major. The children then join in at figure 213, with the same musical motif and text in the key of A-flat major with soloists added and this time singing *fortissimo*. The *subito piano* at figure 214, another breathtaking moment, must be strictly observed by the children.

The children must be comfortable with the stand and sit requirements before the first orchestral rehearsal. The orchestral conductor has much to think about and would, I know, be grateful not to have to cue the children. The following are customary: Stand at figure 37 and sit at 68. Stand from 80 until the end of Part One. In Part Two stand six measures before 58 and sit at 60. Stand at 84 and sit four measures after 88. Stand at 153 and sit at four measures after 164. Stand at 182 and sit five measures after 185. Stand at 212 until the end.

After much hard work, in both preparation and performance, this extraordinary work of genius will provide the children with one of the greatest experiences of their lives.

## Recommended Recordings

| | | | |
|---|---|---|---|
| Giuseppe Sinopoli | Philharmonia Orchestra and Chorus<br>The Southend Boys' Choir | Deutsche Grammophone, 459406-2 | 1992 |
| Leonard Bernstein | Vienna Philharmonic<br><br>Vienna State Opera Chorus and Vienna Choirboys | Deutsche Grammophone, 2 459406-2 | 1991 |
| Robert Shaw | Atlanta Symphony Orchestra and Chorus<br>Ohio State University Chorale, Ohio State University Symphonic Choir, Master Chorale of Tampa Bay, University of South Florida Chorus, Atlanta Boychoir | Telarc 80267 | 1991 |
| Sir Colin Davis | Bavarian Radio Orchestra<br><br>Berlin Radio Choir and Tolzer Boys' Choir | RCA Victor 09026-63348-2 Recorded live | 1996 |

# Carl Orff: Carmina Burana

*Timing: approximately 55 minutes*

## Background Notes for Choristers

Carl Orff was born in Munich in 1895 into an old Bavarian military family. He studied piano, organ, and cello as a child, but rather than practice in the traditional way, he preferred to improvise. Sadly, though he wrote many songs while still a young child, he destroyed many of his early compositions. Orff graduated from the Munich Academy of Music in 1914; his compositions were greatly influenced by Debussy, Schoenberg, and Strauss. In 1924, Orff began teaching and, with Dorothee Gunther, founded the Guntherschule for gymnastics, music, and drama. The seeds of his life's work in music education were planted here, and he eventually opened a summer school in Salzburg to train music teachers from all over the world. His philosophy of music education, the Orff-Schulwerk method, assumed that all children can develop an understanding of rhythm, pitch, and musical form through creative group improvisation. In the music education classes for young children, primitive musical elements such as ostinati, drone basses, and triads that moved in parallel lines were sung and played on simple instruments and accompanied by movement. Many of these musical elements can be heard in his compositions for adults.

His first important original composition was *Carmina Burana,* completed in 1935. Its premiere in the Municipal Theater in Frankfurt included elaborate staging with dancers and mime, and it was an immediate success, perhaps because of its simple harmonies and driving rhythms. The text is taken from the *Songs of Benediktbeuern,* a thirteenth-century manuscript found in the monastery at Benediktbeuern in southern Bavaria and published in 1847. The secular poems are mostly in Latin; a few are in German. The anonymous writers were scholars, many in religious orders. The subject matter covers fortune and fate, sensuality, drinking and making merry, and the joys and tribulations of love. The work is divided into three sections; Spring, In the Tavern, and The Court of Love. Although children sing only in the third section, it is important for them to know what they are listening to in the first two sections.

## Translation and Explanation

The following information could be given to the children as a handout:

- *Carmina Burana* is written for a huge orchestra, an adult choir, soprano, tenor, and baritone soloists, and a children's choir.
- The orchestral part contains much work for the percussion family—you will frequently hear glockenspiels, xylophones, large and small cymbals, timpani, and many types of drums. (Many of you use Orff instruments at school—the instruments were named after the composer, Carl Orff, who was very fond of strong percussive and rhythmic effects.)

• You will hear twenty-five songs; all have great rhythmic energy—some are drinking songs; some sound like the chanting used in church services; some even sound like beautiful Italian opera melodies.

Where does the children's chorus begin? When do you stand up to sing? What are you singing about? Read on!

## Part One: Spring

| | | |
|---|---|---|
| 1. | Fortuna Imperatrix Mundi | (Fortune, Empress of the World)<br>(Sometimes we have good luck, sometimes bad luck— it is the way of the world)<br>2.5 minutes: Adult choir |
| 2. | Fortune plango vulnera | (Bad luck is sad)<br>3 verses: men's part begins; then ladies join them.<br>2.5 minutes |
| 3. | Primo vere<br>Veris leta facies | (Springtime)<br>(The joyous face of spring)<br>Adult choir: sounds like chanting—very soft and quite slow.<br>2.5 minutes |
| 4. | Omnia sol temperat | (The sun is good to all things)<br>Baritone solo (man's low voice), sounds somewhat like the chanting in Number 3.<br>2.5 minutes |
| 5. | Ecce gratum | (Finally spring has arrived. We rejoice!)<br>Adult choir sings very loudly; tenors begin.<br>1 minute |
| 6. | Uf dem anger | (On the green)<br>This is a dance and the orchestra plays without the choir; listen to the syncopation/time:<br>$\frac{4}{4} \frac{3}{8} \frac{4}{4} \frac{3}{8} \cdot$<br>1 minute |
| 7. | Floret sylva nobilis | (The noble forest)<br>Adult choir ends in, "Ah!"<br>3 minutes |
| 8. | Chramer, gip die warwe mir | (Salesman, give me colored paints; if I can have red paint, I will color my cheeks and make them more attractive.) This is not Latin but old-fashioned German, just to make things more complicated for you!<br>Ladies in adult choir sing only three verses in unison, ending with humming.<br>2.5 minutes |

9. Reie
   A dance, again played by the orchestra.
   1.5 minutes

   Swaz hie gat umbe
   (They who here go dancing around)
   A loud drinking song sung by adult choir; lots
      of cymbals.
   .5 minute

   Chume, chum' geselle min
   (Come, dear heart of mine)
   Adult choir, very, very soft. Listen for the
   flute solo.
   1 minute

   Repeat of 9b
10. Were diu werlt alle min
   (If the whole world were mine . . .)
   Adult choir. Listen for the trumpet fanfare and
      a loud "hey" at the end.
   1 minute

*Part Two: In the Tavern*

11. Estuans interius
   (Woe is me! Seething inside with violent anger)
   Baritone solo; listen to the dotted-eighth/
      sixteenth-note rhythm.
   2 minutes

12. Olim lacus colueram
   (The roasted swan sings, "Once I had a beauti-
      ful home by the lake.")
   A very high tenor solo at first (often sung in
      falsetto, or the very high part of a man's
      voice produced with the high position of the
      vocal cords, in a range above the more
      natural tones).
   Three verses with all tenors coming in.
   5 minutes

13. Ego sum abbas
   (I am the abbot of Cockaigne, and I like to
      drink with my friends . . .)
   Baritone solo/cymbals/baritone solo.
   Adult choir ends in, "Ha! Ha!"
   3 minutes

14. In taberna quando sumus
   (When we are in the tavern)
   Seven verses—men in adult choir, very loud—
      end with "io, io, io (yo)" (men only—this is
      your cue).
   6 minutes
   When they finish singing, stand immediately!

15. Amor volat undique
   (Love flies everywhere)
   Children's chorus and soprano soloist (she has
      also been waiting all this time to sing!).

1. Bells; 2. Very gentle woodwinds; 3. Children; 4. Soprano soloist; 5. Children.
4 minutes
Sit four bars after "fit res amarissima."

16. Dies, nox et omnia
(Day, night, even all the world is against me!)
(Woe is me, once again)
Baritone solo, very soft and high.
2 minutes

17. Stetit puella
(There stood a young girl)
A beautiful soprano solo.
5 minutes

18. Circa mea pectora
(My heart is filled with sighing)
Baritone solo and adult choir.
3.5 minutes

19. Si puer cum puellula
(If a boy and girl linger together, it is a happy pair)
Men only; no orchestra.
2 minutes

20. Veni, veni, venias
(Come to me, do not let me die)
Piano accompaniment; adult choir, fast and loud.
2.5 minutes

21. In trutina
(I find it very difficult to make up my mind. Do I love him or not?)
Soprano solo; beautiful melody. Listen for the flutes that repeat the soprano melody.
3 minutes

Stand at the end of this song—wait until it is completely over. (Strings hold a long D in unison. Flutes and trumpets have a three-bar tune.)

22. Tempus est iocundum
(The time is very pleasant. All is happy.)
The children sing in this movement.
The tune is repeated nine times, as follows:
a. Full adult choir
b. Baritone solo repeats
c. Full adult choir
d. Soprano soloist and children sing together
e. Full adult choir
f. Baritone solo
g. Full adult choir
h. Soprano soloist and children sing together
i. Full adult choir
j. Soprano soloist and children join the adult choir. Remain standing for soprano solo.
3 minutes

23. Dulcissime                    (Sweetest one . . .)
                                  Soprano solo. Children must sit as adult choir
                                      begins Number 24.
                                  15 seconds
24. Ave formosissima              (Hail to thee, most lovely lady)
                                  Full adult choir.
                                  3 minutes
25. O Fortuna                     (O Fortune . . .)
                                  Adult choir repeats Number 1 as the finale.
                                  2.5 minutes

*Part Three: The Court of Love*

Sadly, the trebles sing only briefly in the third section. Some conductors invite the children to double the sopranos in the first movement, "O Fortuna," from measure 5 to figure 6, and to double the alto line from one measure after figure 6 to the end of the movement. The trebles then repeat this in the final movement.

The trebles sing the fifteenth poem at the beginning of Part Three and the refrain in the twenty-second poem.

Translation 15:
Court of love
(Trebles)
Love flies everywhere,
He is seized by desire.
Lads, lasses,
Are rightly joined together.
(Soprano)
A girl without a lover
Is without every joy;
She holds the darkest hours of night
In the most secret place
Of the heart in custody;
(Trebles)
It is the bitterest fate.
22. Oh, oh, oh, I'm all in bloom;
I'm all on fire now for love of a girl;
It's a new love for which I'm dying.

## Musical Challenges

A great challenge for the children's choir director is to have the children characterize the singing and not sing in bel canto style. This is difficult because directors spend a great deal of time teaching children to sing with a beautiful tone. The performance of *Carmina Burana,* however, is a wonderful opportunity for children to experiment with a more raucous, raw sound.

The children sing four phrases in "Amor volat undique." Since they are all a cappella, balance is not a problem. Rather, the problems lie with the articulation and the dynamic. Despite Orff's *piano* dynamic, the piece is really much better if sung *mezzo forte* and staccato. The fermata should be the length of four eighth notes, and the metronome marking of 112 equals a quarter note strictly observed. There is always a problem in the third phrase, since the children want to breathe after "coniunguntur." The third phrase is much better if the children stagger-breathe. Tell the children to be aware of the nine measures in which the soprano soloist sustains the D just before their final phrase.

In the twenty-second poem, the first and second time the children sing the refrain they are doubled by the soprano soloist and accompanied by piano secondo, which the children must be able to hear. It prevents them from rushing the *accelerando*. The third time they sing the refrain, the baritone and adult choir sing with them. It is impossible to hear them. They must be very still afterward. The soprano soloist sings "Dulcissime" very softly a cappella up to a high B, followed by her florid a cappella passage that takes her into the stratosphere to a high D.

*Carmina Burana* is an excellent work for a children's choir to begin its orchestral/choral experience, since it is the least demanding of all the major works for children's choir, adult choir, and orchestra. As a result, it can be performed well by a less-experienced young choir.

## Recommended Recordings

| | | | |
|---|---|---|---|
| André Previn | London Symphony Orchestra and Chorus<br>St. Clement Danes Grammar School Boys' Choir | EMI 7474112 | 1999 |
| James Levine | Chicago Symphony Orchestra and Chorus<br>Glen Ellyn Children's Chorus | Deutsche Grammophone 15136 | 1985 |
| Herbert Blomstedt | San Francisco Symphony and Chorus<br>San Francisco Girls' Chorus | London Decca 430509-2 | 1991 |

## Benjamin Britten: War Requiem
*Timing: approximately one hour and twenty minutes*

## Background Notes for Choristers

Benjamin Britten is regarded as one of the greatest composers of the twentieth century. Born in 1913 on November 22, Saint Cecelia's Day—Cecelia is the patron saint of music—Britten composed throughout his life and left us a rich legacy of operas, chamber music, solo vocal music, instrumental music, and large-scale works such as the *War Requiem*. Perhaps his greatest gift for children's choirs is the brilliant literature he wrote for boys' choirs. Works such as "Ceremony of Carols," "Missa Brevis," "Friday Afternoons," "Psalm 150," "Children's Crusade," and "Noye's Fludde" represent the greatest works written by any one composer for treble choirs in the twentieth century.

The first performance of Benjamin Britten's *War Requiem* was given on May 30, 1962, to consecrate the restored St. Michael's Cathedral in Coventry, England. (The original medieval cathedral had been bombed during the Second World War, and the new cathedral was built around the ruined shell.) Since Britten was a lifelong pacifist who came to North America during the war, this commission provided him with an opportunity to express his strong antiwar sentiments in a most profound way; and the result is one of the greatest choral masterpieces ever written. It is scored for three soloists, (soprano, tenor, and baritone), two adult choirs, a boys' choir, a large orchestra, and a chamber orchestra. The juxtaposition of the Latin and English texts is ingenious.

Britten uses the text of the Missa pro Defunctis, the Latin Mass for the Dead, for the adult choir and soprano soloist. The poetic text for the tenor and baritone soloists was written by Wilfred Owen, a British soldier killed in action one month before the end of the First World War. The treble choir sings the Latin text, used throughout the work to offer a kind of disembodied commentary on the proceedings. To add to the drama of the first performance, Britten chose as his soloists English tenor Peter Pears, German baritone Dietrich Fischer-Dieskau, and Russian soprano Galina Vishnevskaya. Ironically, Ms. Vishnevskaya was not permitted to travel to England for this performance and English soprano Heather Harper filled in. At the first performance the Coventry Festival Chorus joined forces with the City of Birmingham Symphony Orchestra under the baton of Meredith Davies. The chamber orchestra, the Melos Ensemble, was conducted by Britten himself. The boys' choir was made up of singers from Holy Trinity, Leamington, and Holy Trinity, Stratford.

## Text and Translation for the Treble Chorus

a) Te decet hymnus, Deus in Sion,
   et tibi reddetur votum in Jerusalem.
   Exaudi orationem meam,
   ad te omnis caro veniet.
b) Domine Jesu Christe, Rex gloriae,
   libera animas omnium fidelium
      defunctorum
   de poenis inferni,
   et de profundo lacu:
   Libera eas de ore leonis,
   ne absorbeat eas tartarus,
   ne cadant in obscurum.

a) For you a hymn is proper, God in Zion,
   and to you a vow is made in Jerusalem.
   Hear my prayer,
   for unto you all flesh shall come.
b) Lord Jesus Christ, King of glory,
   free the souls of all the faithful
      dead
   from punishment in the inferno,
   and from the deep pit:
   Deliver them from the lion's mouth,
   lest the abyss swallow them up,
   lest they fall into darkness.

c) Hostias et preces tibi
Domine laudis offerimus;
tu suscipe pro animabus illis
quarum hodie memoriam facimus:
Fac eas, Domine,
de morte transire ad vitam.
Quam olim Abrahae promisisti
et semini ejus.

c) Sacrifices and prayers to you,
Lord, we offer with praise;
receive them for the souls of those
whom today we commemorate:
Make them, Lord,
to pass from death to life.
As once you promised to Abraham
and to his seed.

d) In paradisum deducant te Angeli;
in tuo adventu suscipiant te
Martyres
et perducant te
in civitatem sanctam Jerusalem.
Chorus Angelorum te suscipiat,
et cum Lazaro quondam paupere,
aeternam habeas requiem.

d) May the angels lead you into Paradise;
at your coming may the Martyrs
receive you
and conduct you
into the holy city Jerusalem.
May the chorus of Angels receive you,
and with Lazarus, once a pauper,
eternally may you have rest.

e) Requiem aeternam dona eis,
Domine,
et lux perpetua luceat eis.

e) Rest eternal grant them, Lord,

and may perpetual light shine on them.

## Musical Challenges

Because Britten wanted the treble choir to sound distant he had them sing offstage, accompanied by portativ organ. Depending on the hall, this can present certain problems. First, it may limit the number of children who can participate—a minimum of sixty is desirable in this work. Second, the children may experience less than desirable conditions sitting in the wings. Third, the children's choir director must direct the choir using a monitor or peeking through a door to watch the orchestral conductor. If the orchestral conductor has a clear beat and stands in one place, a monitor can work; if the conductor moves so as to be no longer visible in the monitor, it can be disconcerting, to say the least.

It is very important that the children be able to see and hear everything that is going on. They can learn so much. Work with the orchestral conductor and the hall staff until you locate a place where the children can see the stage and yet produce a distant sound while remaining seated. You will need to conduct the children in all movements except the Offertorium, at which point the children should stand and follow the orchestral conductor. Shadow conducting with the orchestral conductor is very helpful to the ensemble, particularly in the Hostias and In Paradisum movements. The audience should not see you or be distracted by you.

In the Te Decet, the children should be made aware of the central importance of the diminished fifth; it should also be noted that the alto line is the inversion of the soprano line. Careful attention given to the tuning will avoid the pitfalls inherent in the many whole and half steps. In typical Britten fashion, the portativ organ doubles the vocal line throughout to make it easier for the trebles.

The children have thirty minutes to wait before they sing the Offertorium—they should mark this time in their scores. The opening of the Offertorium needs to be well accented and rhythmic. The children need to note the twos and threes in the libera animas—"L"'s and triangles are the most effective markings. (This skill can be taught in rehearsals and warm-ups.) The stress needs to fall on the natural stress of the Latin syllable. The altos in particular need to use their chest voice in order for the sound to carry through the hall.

The Hostias, which follows five minutes later, always sounds "singsongy" if a stress is placed on each beat. This is difficult to avoid when the metronome mark is 60. The children must learn to sing with a long legato line in complete phrases, without any stress on the two beats in the bar. Tuning can also be a problem in this section, because the treble voice part is not doubled by the organ and because of where this passage lies in the child's voice. Keep the repeated A's and D's high and the ascending whole steps wide.

The children have approximately twenty-seven minutes to wait before they sing the Libera Me. The Libera Me tends to flatten on the rising scale. This is curious, since A major is a wonderful key for children's voices. The organ doubles the vocal line, and the children should listen carefully and tune to it. The only major balance problem in the *War Requiem* happens in three measures in the *diminuendo* after figure 132. The children should not get much softer than the entry at figure 132 or they will not be heard. The F sharp five measures after figure 132 is also difficult to sing in tune if the sound becomes too soft. The Libera Me is also challenging for conductors. Some suggest the following strategy: Beat nine twice from the entry, one measure after figure 128. Beat eight once, one measure after figure 129. Beat twelve once, starting on "te" of "suscipiante." Beat nine twice, starting at figure 130. Beat six in the last measure the children sing. In this way, the treble choir conductor prevents any lack of cohesion with the tenor and bass parts.

For the children to appreciate this work fully, they need to be aware of the background and structure of the work. A simple quiz, given out at the first choral rehearsal, will not only encourage the children to research the subject but also, it is hoped, spark their curiosity about musicians and music history in the process. Figure 10.1 illustrates a possible format for such a quiz.

## Recommended Recordings

| | | | |
|---|---|---|---|
| Benjamin Britten | London Symphony Orchestra | London Records 414 383-2 | 1963 |
| | Melos Ensemble, Bach Choir, | | |
| |   and London Symphony Orchestra | | |
| |   Chorus; Highgate School Choir | | |
| | Galina Vishnevskaya, soprano; | | |
| |   Peter Pears, tenor; Dietrich | | |
| |   Fischer-Dieskau, baritone | | |

## Quiz on the *War Requiem* by Benjamin Britten

Our performance will make much more sense to you if you understand what is going on. Find the answers to the quiz on background notes, on CD inserts, in music dictionaries, in music history books, on the Internet, or from your parents.

1. Tell me four things about Benjamin Britten: _____

    _____

2. When and where was the first performance of the *War Requiem*? Why is this important?

    _____

    _____

3. What is a requiem? _____

    _____

4. There are six parts to a requiem. Name them:

    1. _____  4. _____

    2. _____  5. _____

    3. _____  6. _____

5. How many soloists are used in this work? What are their voices? _____

    _____

6. In which sections of the requiem is the Treble Choir involved? What does the Treble Choir

    represent?  _____

    _____

    _____

7. The tenor and baritone soloists do not sing the Latin text of the requiem. What do they

    sing? _____ Who wrote the text? _____

    Tell me something about the poet. _____

8. Who was the first soloist to sing the tenor role? _____

    Who will sing it at our concert? _____

    Who will sing the soprano role? _____

    Who will sing the baritone role? _____

    Name the adult choir. _____

    Name the symphony orchestra. _____

    Name the conductor. _____

Figure 10.1a

9. Practice reading this Latin text out loud. Find an English translation for it and write it out:

a) Te decet hymnus, Deus in Sion, _____

et tibi reddetur votum in Jerusalem._____

Exaudi orationem meam,_____

ad te omnis caro veniet. _____

b) Domine Jesu Christe, Rex gloriae, _____

libera animas omnium fidelium defunctorum _____

de poenis inferni, _____

et de profundo lacu._____

Libera eas de ore leonis, _____

ne absorbeat eas tartarus, _____

ne cadant in obscurum. _____

c) Hostias et preces tibi _____

Domine laudis offerimus; _____

tu suscipe pro animabus illis _____

quarum hodie memoriam facimus: _____

Fac eas, Domine, _____

de morte transire ad vitam. _____

Quam olim Abrahae promisisti _____

et semini ejus. _____

d) In paradisum deducant te Angeli; _____

in tuo adventu suscipiant te Martyres _____

et perducant te _____

in civitatem sanctam Jerusalem. _____

Chorus Angelorum te suscipiat, _____

et cum Lazaro quondam paupere, _____

aeternam habeas requiem. _____

e) Requiem aeternam dona eis, Domine, _____

et lux perpetua luceat eis. _____

Figure 10.1b

| Kurt Masur | New York Philharmonic | Teldec 0630-17115 | 1998 |
| | Westminster Symphonic Choir and American Boychoir | | |
| | Carol Vaness, soprano; Jerry Hadley, tenor; Thomas Hampson, baritone | | |
| Simon Rattle | City of Birmingham Symphony Orchestra | EMI 47034-8 | 1983 |
| | City of Birmingham Symphony Chorus and Boys of Christ Church Cathedral, Oxford | | |
| | Elisabeth Soderstrom, soprano; Robert Tear; tenor; Thomas Allen, baritone | | |
| Robert Shaw | Atlanta Symphony Orchestra and Chorus | Telarc 80157 | 1989 |
| | Atlanta Boychoir | | |
| | Lorna Haywood, soprano; Anthony Rolfe Johnson, tenor; Benjamin Luxon, baritone | | |

## Gustav Holst: The Planets

*Timing: approximately fifty minutes*

### Background Notes for Choristers

Gustav Holst was born in Cheltenham, England, in 1874 and died in London in 1934. He studied piano, organ, trombone, and composition at the Royal College of Music, where he met his lifelong friend Ralph Vaughan Williams. Holst and Vaughan Williams had a mutual interest in English folk songs and often visited remote areas in the countryside to record them. They also sought each other's advice about the first drafts of new compositions.

After graduation, Holst made his living as an orchestral trombonist and later became a teacher at St. Paul's Girls' School and Morley College. His time at St. Paul's produced some great literature for treble choirs, including the eight-part a cappella setting of "Ave Maria" and, accompanied on the harp, the "Choral Hymns from the Rig-Veda."

Holst's idea for *The Planets* grew out of a meeting with Clifford Bax, brother of the English composer Arnold Bax, while on a holiday in Spain in 1913. Holst became fascinated with astrology. He already had an interest in things mystic and studied the philosophy and poetry of the Hindu religion. He even took adult education classes in Sanskrit. *The Planets,* written between 1914 and 1916 in a soundproof room in St. Paul's, consists of seven movements—Holst intentionally did not include the planet Earth; nor, did he include the planet Pluto, which was not discovered until 1930. It was not Holst's intention to write program music, nor is there any connection with the deities of classical mythology who bear the same names as the planets. The subtitle of each piece is merely a guide:

> Mars, the Bringer of War
> Venus, the Bringer of Peace
> Mercury, the Winged Messenger
> Jupiter, the Bringer of Jollity
> Saturn, the Bringer of Old Age
> Uranus, the Magician
> Neptune, the Mystic

This work requires a massive orchestra, and had it not been for Holst's benefactor Balfour Gardiner, its first performance, during the stringent times of the First World War, might never have taken place. The first private performance took place on September 29, 1918, at the Queen's Hall in London, with the London Symphony Orchestra under the direction of Sir Adrian Boult. According to Holst's daughter Imogen, the cleaning ladies working in the building put down their brooms during "Jupiter" and began to dance!

It is important that the children have an opportunity to heat the first six movements before they sing as an offstage chorus. If the orchestral conductor agrees, seat the children in the hall so they are able to see what is going on. They should listen for the following:

1. "Mars" is in five-four time and has driving and relentless ostinati rhythms. The climaxes are played quadruple *forte,* and war is expressed by Holst as a senseless and ugly event.
2. In "Venus," the children can listen to the way the flutes and oboes illustrate the idea of peace, in contrast with what they have heard in "Mars."
3. "Mercury" is a scherzo, but without any particular direction. This winged messenger doesn't seem to know where he is going.
4. Holst's love of folk songs is evident in "Jupiter," and the overall effect is one of calm and happiness. The stirring hymn "I Vow to Thee My Country" is beautifully and powerfully orchestrated, with all strings and horns introducing this expansive theme in unison.
5. "Saturn" is lively and full of different ideas that happen quickly. The children should listen for the regal concluding theme in B minor.
6. "Uranus" has all the effects of a magician with lots of tricks up his sleeve. There is a four-note motif that suggests a magician's spell. The quadruple *forte* suddenly vanishes to a *pianissimo,* and the movement ends on an unresolved note.
7. "Neptune" is a themeless, transparent movement that alternates between two chords, E minor and G-sharp minor. Brilliantly conjuring up the feeling

of the vastness of space, this movement is Holst's awe-inspiring account of the Infinite. The treble chorus begins singing on a *pianissimo* high G six measures after Roman numeral V and concludes with a *diminuendo* so subtle that the audience should not know when it stops.

*The Planets,* one of the most imaginative and sophisticated works of the early twentieth century, firmly established Holst's reputation as a great composer.

## Musical Challenges

The children sing the vowel sound "ah" throughout the final movement. To help maintain the tuning, the vowel must be very bright, with no hint of the vowel sound "aw."

The first great challenge is finding the first pitch entry, a unison *pianissimo* high G. The violins play an E minor chord, but it is often so soft that it is inaudible; it is also in the wrong octave to be of much help to the choir. The celli's G sharp is easier to hear and provides one way of finding the correct pitch. Repeated drills with the piano during choral rehearsals are essential. The best way I have found for the children to secure that high G is to have the children with the best ears use a tuning fork: "Up the octave and down a tone." (After two orchestral rehearsals and a performance, the children do seem to sense where the G is.)

Other major problems are the seven-part divisi, the tuning, the counting, and the tessitura. Drill unison warm-ups using tonic solfa. The children's conductor should write out each vocal part on a separate page or work sheet and teach them the entire piece using tonic solfa. This preparation is laborious but saves time in rehearsal, because the choral score is visually difficult for the children. Once the children have learned their parts, destroy the work sheets and return to the proper choral score. Sectionals are a necessity. Take the Sopranos I and II together and work down the octave. Have them count their parts without any singing at first, since they often sing the same notes in canon. When the count is secure, drill the tonic solfa. Use the same procedure with Altos I and II without singing down the octave. Only when these parts are secure should they be sung together.

Another potential problem is the entry eleven measures before the end. The choir actually comes in on a C minor chord, but it is scored as B sharp, D sharp, and F double sharp. One measure before, the violins play an open fifth on C and the violas play an E flat, so the entrance for the choir is not as difficult as it first appears so long as the children know what to listen for. In addition, the children must maintain a steady rhythm throughout—the eighth-note passages tend to rush, and there is absolutely no room at all for rubato. The whole-step and half-step intervals must be exact—ascending tones need to be wide, and descending tones need to be narrow. The whole effect must be transparent and otherworldly. The timbre of children's voices is ideal for this movement. To achieve the *diminuendo* in the final bars, the children could turn around to face the back of the hall or, if they are offstage, a door could gradually be closed. The children could also put their hands or elbows close to their mouths. However it is achieved, the effect must be magical.

## Recommended Recordings

| | | | |
|---|---|---|---|
| Sir Andrew Davis | Toronto Symphony Orchestra | Seraphim Classics CDR 7243 5 73733 2 6 | 1982 |
| | Toronto Children's Chorus | | |
| Sir Simon Rattle | Philharmonia Orchestra | EMI LC0 464 | 1979 |
| | Ambrosian Singers | | |
| Sir Adrian Boult | Vienna State Opera Orchestra | Classics MA D80099 | 1966 |
| | Chorus Millennium | | |
| John Eliot Gardiner | Philharmonia Orchestra | Deutsche Grammophone 445860-2 | 1991 |
| | Monteverdi Choir | | |

## Felix Mendelssohn: Incidental Music to *A Midsummer Night's Dream,* Opus 61

*Timing: approximately fifty minutes*

## Background Notes for Choristers

Felix Mendelssohn (1809–1847) was one of four children born to Abraham and Lea Mendelssohn in Hamburg, Germany. The children enjoyed the privileges of a well-educated middle-class family and from early childhood were both formally and informally immersed in music, literature, and philosophy. Young Felix and his sister Fanny, who became a superb pianist and composer in her own right, used to put on plays for family and friends. Their favorite play was *A Midsummer Night's Dream,* the twelfth play written by William Shakespeare, in 1595–1596, translated into German by A. W. Schlegel in 1797. The first performance of Shakespeare's play with Mendelssohn's music took place on October 14, 1843, at the Neue Palais in Potsdam.

Mendelssohn wrote the Overture in 1826, when he was seventeen years old, and did not complete the work until 1843. Several themes used in the Overture are utilized as leitmotifs later on. The leitmotifs are used to identify the various characters in the play that depict various levels of the strata of society and, of course, the spirits, elves and fairies. The great works of Bach and Mozart profoundly influenced Mendelssohn, and this work harks back to the classical form of Mozart. The work is easy for the children to listen to and enjoy.

Thirteen movements follow the Overture. The treble choir, as well as an adult soprano and mezzo-soprano, who represent two fairies, sing in the fourth (4'30") and final movements. (4'50")

With choirs whose first language is English, rather than German, it should be sung in English.

## Text

At the opening of the fourth movement, Titania asks, "Come, now a roundel and a fairy song," and the fairies sing her to sleep with "Ye Spotted Snakes with Double Tongue," accompanied by gentle strings and lightly scored woodwinds.

In the Finale, Titania says to the fairies:

"First, rehearse this song by rote:
To each word a warbling note,
Hand in hand with fairy grace
Will we sing and bless this place."

And the fairies reply, singing, "Through this house give glimmering light by the dread and drowsy fire."

## Musical Challenges

There are generally no balance problems for chorus and orchestra in the fourth movement because the orchestral scoring is lightly written. The only problem that may arise is with the balance and blend between the adult voices and the children. It is best if the women can be separate from the children and singing downstage close to the conductor. The children should be on risers at the back so they can be heard as a distinct entity. Their entrance, marked *pianissimo,* is much more effective if sung *mezzo forte.* The children's chorus has a tendency to drag behind the beat if they are not careful. Breaths have to be taken quickly, without any loss of time. When "so good night" is repeated through the voices, great care has to be taken with the final "t." It must come on the quarter rest the first time and on the eighth rest the second time. Great care must also be taken with the vowel sound "u" in "lullaby." It should almost approach "ah." The "l"s are problematic because there are so many of them so quickly. The children must be taught to elongate the vowels without getting behind the beat. An exercise that will help is to have them sing the movement using vowels only. When the desired rhythmic accuracy and uniformity are achieved, the consonants should be added.

In the Finale, all orchestra parts are marked *pianissimo,* so again there should be no balance problem. The major difficulty is getting the words across with the necessary vitality and rhythmic accuracy. In the word "fire," the "f" needs to be exaggerated while the "r" is almost ignored; the "i" vowel needs to sound as "ah." There should be no breath after the word "house." There is only one German word for that whole measure "Feuers," so Mendelssohn was not expecting a breath there. The final "sing and dance it" on a low B needs to be projected in the chest voice or it will never be heard.

## Recommended Recordings

| Claudio Abbado | Berlin Philharmonic | Sony SK62826 | 1996 |
| | Sylvia McNair, Angelika | | |
| | Kirschlager, Women | | |
| | of the Ernst-Senff Chorus | | |
| Seiji Ozawa | Boston Symphony Orchestra | Deutsche Grammophone | 1992 |
| | | 439897-2 | |
| | Kathleen Battle, Frederica | | |
| | von Stade, Judi Dench, | | |
| | Tanglewood Festival Chorus | | |
| André Previn | London Symphony Orchestra | EMI CDC 747163 | 1990 |
| | Lillian Walsh, Delia Wallis, | | |
| | Finchley Children's Music Group | | |

# CHAPTER ELEVEN

# Recording, Commissioning, and Touring

This chapter outlines three important aspects of community children's choir work: recording sessions, commissioning new works, and touring. All are vitally important, not only for the enjoyment of the singers and the musical growth of the choir but also for meeting the organization's responsibility to the greater community.

## Recording Sessions

This summary is not intended to be a technical manual on microphone placement and recording technique. For that kind of detail, it would be advisable to consult a professional music producer or recording engineer, your local library, or the Internet. (The microphone manufacturer Shure has a wealth of information available on its Web site.) Experienced producers/engineers can lend an impartial set of ears to the performance and will follow music scores as the sessions proceed. They will keep a log of which "takes" have been successful and which passages need to be repeated. They will also be able to assess when it is possible to edit between separate performances to achieve a good "composite" performance. Producers/engineers will also have access to better-quality microphones and the technical knowledge and experience to ensure that the allotted time is used in the most efficient manner.

Recordings may be drawn from specially arranged sessions (where the performance can be stopped and started at your discretion) or from live performances of the choir. There are advantages and difficulties with both methods. Formal recording sessions pose a great challenge to children's choir directors. Since no audience is present, it is a formidable task to achieve the commitment, dynamism, sparkle, focus, and tension present in a live performance. In addition, if you are working with professional musicians, four or five takes may be needed for them to get "in the groove"; meanwhile, the children may become vocally tired and frustrated from the repetition. Recording a live performance is best, and if you are touring and presenting the same works in a variety of venues, a professional producer or recording engineer can create a fine recording by choosing only the best performances from the tour. The downside of this, of course, is that one encounters a variety of acoustics, some good and some poor. If you find a good hall, but it is professionally staffed, recordings may not be permitted unless the crew is paid union scale. On tour, you will also have to deal with a variety of pianos, organs, and instrumentalists. It is wise to send a competent staff member on a pretour so that any potential problems can be anticipated and addressed. It is also important to tour with enough repertoire—both accompanied and a cappella works—so that programs can readily be adapted to best suit the venues.

For a formal recording session, the following checklist will be a useful guide:

- Prior to a formal recording session, make a live concert recording for study purposes—examining your own performance with the score in front of you will help clarify ideas and give you greater insight into the music.
- If you make any changes afterward, add a rehearsal so that the choir is comfortable with those alterations.
- Engage the finest recording engineer you can find and make sure he or she is familiar with your ensemble and the optimum sound of the choir—the sound you are constantly striving to achieve. Classical radio stations and university music departments often have experienced personnel.
- Record in the venue where the performance was held so that the singers are working in familiar acoustics. A radical change in environment can lead to difficulties in the blend of parts. Record in the early evening on a Saturday or Sunday, or record after a holiday when the children are fresh. (January and July are ideal.)
- Make sure people are stationed at entrances and exits to avoid interruption. The fewer stops for lawn-mower, construction, and traffic noise, the better. (The Montreal Symphony Orchestra records in a church located in a small village north of Montreal. Signs are placed around the church and traffic is diverted to help ensure that the immediate area is as "noise-free" as possible.) The artistic director and producer/engineer need to take the time to plan for the optimum recording conditions.
- If you are using instrumentalists, give them a forty-minute call before the choir arrives so that you can prepare them for immediate recording. Give them a twenty-minute break while you warm up the choir.
- As the children need to be disciplined, make sure people around you will look after them properly for you. Recording protocol should be outlined to them weeks before the sessions actually take place. (Recording protocol includes everything from arriving at the session rested and healthy, to wearing

loose, comfortable clothing and slippers, to being ready to get on the risers within seconds of being asked for another take.) The children need to arrive with sunny dispositions and be prepared to work extremely hard to be the best they can be. The children must not only sing well; they must also be self-disciplined. Because recording sessions are so taxing, it is essential that the children be extremely motivated, responsible, and hardworking.

- Have water and juice on hand for the singers.
- Always record the first take—you can never predict when you will achieve your best work.
- Remember that three hours is the maximum time that most people can remain productive. A compact disc often requires three such recording sessions, ideally not on consecutive nights unless the sessions are in the summer when the children are not attending school.
- Be loose, relaxed, comfortable, and well rested. Being uptight and on edge does not allow you to produce an inspired recording.
- While recording, use time very carefully. It is wise to begin by recording two or three takes of the first piece or section and then take a ten-minute break to listen to what you have. Make sure the recorded sound achieves the desired balance and blend. Adjustments to the microphone placement may have to be made. The piano may have to be repositioned or the lid removed. You may need to change the positions of certain singers to get a better blend. Recording is stressful for an artistic director because your instrument, the choir, is partly in the hands of the producer/engineer. It is critical that the artistic and technical forces agree on the optimum sound at this juncture.
- Having made the necessary moves and achieved a natural-sounding balance, get another take of the same material and listen to it once more. Ideally, you will now have the sound you want. If not, more changes will have to be made. You should, however, be able to record for the next half hour before calling the next break. At this point, the producer/recording engineer may ask you if there is anything else you want to repeat. His/her role is to listen carefully to the performance for flaws, both artistic and technical, and he/she should be able to assess which imperfections can be corrected through editing and which will require further takes before moving on to the next work. This is where you rely heavily on his/her skill and experience. The producer/engineer may hear false entries or poor cutoffs that ruin an otherwise good take and may ask you to repeat small passages so that a correction can be inserted into the existed material. It is important to remember that listening to music through headphones in the control room often provides a better vantage point than listening from the podium. To get the best recording with maximum efficiency, you must trust the producer/engineer. Together you can achieve a level of artistry with recorded performances that can even surpass the choir's best live performances!

- As you move through the second and third recording sessions, the conductor, the producer/engineer, and the artists will become more and more comfortable with one another and great art has a chance to flourish. This part of the recording session is most exciting and satisfying.

Recordings are permanent examples of your work. How I wish I had been aware of these tips when I started recording compact discs. How I wish I now had an opportunity to rerecord some of them! It is very revealing to listen to a recording of a Beethoven symphony that Herbert Von Karajan made in the middle of his career and compare it to his recording of the same symphony made twenty years later. Conductors do grow, mature, and change their minds about many aspects of interpretation, such as tempi, articulation, dynamics, and phrasing. One of the fascinating things about this job is that there is no end to discovering new and better ideas.

## Commissioning New Works

Commissioning and premiering new works annually should be an integral part of every children's choir program. The choral art rejuvenates itself through the work of living composers, and choristers should be given the opportunity to be a part of this creative process. They must learn that not all composers are men who lived hundreds of years ago.

Composing is a great art as well as a formidable craft. Like all crafts, it can only improve through practice. It is only through performance, however, that the composers' craft can be evaluated and improved. Not all well-known composers' works will be outstanding. It is our responsibility to work with composers so that our period in history will leave its own legacy of great compositions. More and more composers are getting the children's choir sound in their ears and are realizing that its only limitation is a two-octave range.

### Choice of Text

The choice of text is of paramount importance, since choral composers derive their inspiration and musical ideas from the text. The text of a new work must have aesthetic value and superior literary merit and be worth singing. The text should sing even before the notes are written! Many new choral works are found wanting because the text is mediocre. Many fine composers think because they write music beautifully, they can also write prose and poetry beautifully. This is simply not true. Children's choir directors must have a love and understanding of great poetry and prose and should keep a file of such texts that can be shared with a composer. When a new choral work is about to be commissioned, the choice of text is critical.

## Selecting a Composer

Selecting a composer is yet another challenge for the artistic director. Factors that need to be considered include:

- Will you or the composer choose the text? If you already have a text in mind, will this composer be inspired by it?
- The style of piece you envision and whether or not this composer is comfortable in that milieu.
- The composer's folio of choral music written for children's voices.
- What are the composer's strengths?
- The occasion for which the piece is being written and where it is to be performed.
- Whether the piece is to be a four-part a cappella work, a work for piano and unison trebles, or a three-part work with some instruments or full orchestration.
- Whether the piece is to be an original work or an arrangement.

Artistic directors should be encouraged to seek out lesser-known composers for their commissions. (If you are not as delighted with the works presented by an unfamiliar composer as you would like to be, do not give up on him/her; work with the composer and make suggestions.) Often the "hot" composers are so busy that you may have to wait several years for your piece. A much worse scenario occurs if the well-known and highly accomplished composer is working with an unrealistic deadline and is not able to devote the time needed to come up with a piece that is mutually satisfying.

The composer you commission needs to have a recording of the choir in order to get "the sound" in his/her ear. If the composer lives in the vicinity, invite him/her to attend some rehearsals. At the beginning of the commissioning process, the artistic director and the composer need to work closely together. The composer needs to share some preliminary sketches with the artistic director to make sure that the singers are going to be challenged but not frustrated, especially if the composer has previously written mainly for instruments. It may also be helpful for choristers to sing a section of the new work and express their thoughts about the work afterward. (This takes some time and tact, but it is far better than the horrific scenario of having a composer present a work in its entirety six months later and, because of insurmountable problems, the work is never performed. This predicament must be avoided at all costs.) Neither the artistic director nor the choristers should be afraid of new frontiers. The piece, however, must not be so challenging and vocally taxing that the children in the choir need perfect pitch to sing it!

## Funding

Funding a new commission needs to be examined. In Canada, the Canadian League of Composers has set fees, based upon the number of minutes of music and the type of accompaniment. For a cappella choir or choir with piano accompaniment, the 2001 rate was $331 per minute of music. For chorus and orchestral accompaniment with over fifteen parts, the fee was $529 per minute. (These amounts are in Canadian dollars.) If the commission is awarded to a composer whose residence is in the province of Ontario, these fees are paid through the Ontario Arts Council. In addition, the Canada Council has a national Music Commissioning Program with similar rates. The composer is responsible for providing a legible score that can be reproduced. An amount for copy costs will be set aside, to be released to the composer when the arts council has received a copy of the relevant invoice. It is the responsibility of the composer to ensure that the copyist is paid.

If government funds are not available, there are other means of funding new works. Charitable foundations should be approached. Members of the community or choir parents could be invited to commission a work, perhaps to be premiered at a grand occasion such as a wedding, a bar or bat mitzvah, a birthday, or a festival. Children's choir festivals and honor children's choirs are also ideal for commissions, since children from many children's choirs and often other countries will be involved in the project. (If the work is subsequently published, acknowledgment of the commission should appear on the title page.) When three or four children's choirs make a joint commission, the fee is divided three or four ways; perhaps more important, such a joint venture ensures that the work will receive at least three or four performances! Depending on the occasion, the amount of publicity, and possible performance opportunities, the composer may be willing to accept a smaller fee. Arts organizations must realize, however, that composers should be duly compensated for their work.

## Performances

It is vitally important that further performances of commissioned new works be scheduled. Sadly, world premieres are much more frequent than second performances. Artistic directors need to share new works with one another and take advantage of as many opportunities as possible to give composers a vehicle for their art. New music—researching it, performing it, sharing it—is a fundamental responsibility of all of us. A Saturday morning read-through of any new work that a less familiar composer wishes to submit is very helpful to the composer. Feedback from the audience and choir members is appreciated. Composers need to hear their work sung, and our choirs are being seriously shortchanged if they are not given the opportunity to experience the thrill of new music.

All great choral works—including Bach's *St. Matthew Passion,* Handel's *Messiah,* the Mozart Requiem, the Beethoven Missa Solemnis, Mendelssohn's *Elijah,* Elgar's *Dream of Gerontius,* Stravinsky's *Symphony of Psalms,* and the Britten *War Requiem*—once had a world premiere. Many of the anxieties that haunt a modern premiere were doubtless factors when these works were first performed: rehearsal time was too limited, parts were too difficult, the tessitura was too high or too low, the harmonies were unfamiliar and seemingly obscure, the intervals were awkward, the rhythms were unusual, the score was unwieldy, or the language was unfamiliar. Choirs and artistic directors need to lay the groundwork for a successful commission and then dig in and do the work! Creative artistry must be nurtured by all of us who dare to call ourselves artists.

## Touring

Touring is one of the highlights of a choir's life. For the singers, it provides unique opportunities to bond with other members of the choir in deep and meaningful ways, to experience cultures different from their own, to have special responsibilities that encourage them to think for themselves, and to hear choirs and learn new repertoire from all over the world. For the conductor, a tour is a strong motivator for peak performance. Since the choir will be repeating the same repertoire in a variety of venues, the standard of performance often becomes far better "on the road" than it is at home.

### Considerations before Touring

As the conductor, you need to consider what is important to you and your organization before planning a tour:

- great venues
- many performance opportunities
- the choir's exposure
- sight-seeing
- concert fees
- the number of children and adults traveling
- meeting and sharing with many other choirs
- traveling a vast distance
- whether the choir organizes the tour itself or has professional company do it
- how much money the choir can raise in two years
- how much each family can reasonably be expected to pay for the tour
- how many children can be partially or fully subsidized
- whether the children will stay in private homes or hotels
- whether the choir will have opportunities to give or have workshops done with them

You cannot do everything in one tour, and you need to decide what is important to your organization before you decide where, how, when, and why you will tour. The length of the tour needs to be determined; depending on the distance, two weeks is ideal.

There are benefits to organizing the tour yourself. You have more control, it can be cheaper, and homestays can be arranged through colleagues. The downside is that it takes an inordinate amount of work. You must organize every last detail, including the transportation, accommodation, and meals; the daily schedule, including sight-seeing; concert venues and advertising; and transportation of all of the programs. After all this, often concert audiences are small. If you decide to go with a professional tour company, it is important that you verify through trusted colleagues the validity of their tours. (Make sure the company is bonded in the event of a severe accident.) The company should have professional musicians on staff, who understand the needs of children and the importance of professional-quality music making. A highly experienced company staff person must travel with the choir, in addition to a tour guide.

Major tours take between eighteen months and two years to plan. A meeting with the parents must be organized once the preliminary plan has been devised. This plan must include an initial concert schedule, sight-seeing opportunities, and approximate cost for each child. In the Toronto Children's Chorus, the touring choir is usually the Chamber Choir, comprised of children who have achieved the highest musical level and proven themselves to be responsible. Traditionally, the choir has forty-two children, including a minimum of ten boys, and eight adults. One bus is ideal, since if all personnel, including the tour manager, music director, and tour doctor, are on one bus this makes the lines of communication with the children and the chaperons much easier. The parents need to sign a consent form to agree to support the tour in principle. Fund-raising strategies need to be in place, with the parents agreeing to work for the common good. In the Toronto Children's Chorus, fund-raising is an ongoing process and in a tour year it is even more rigorous. All families are expected to help raise funds. However, no child is ever left behind because a family cannot afford to pay. Once parents and choristers are committed to the tour, the following activities should take place before takeoff.

*Twelve Months before Departure*

1. Select concert repertoire. Programs during the year should consist of the music the children will be singing on tour. Ideally, the choir needs to prepare three hours of music if you have solo concerts. The children need to know a minimum of one hour of a cappella repertoire, particularly if the manager cannot inspect all concert sites six months before the tour. A major portion of your repertoire should represent your country's living composers as well as a variety of other works that represent many styles and historical periods. Concert programs must be adaptable to a huge variety of situations: very live acoustics, dead acoustics, poor pianos, no piano, poor sight lines with the organ, indoor and outdoor venues, and formal and informal concerts.

2. If you are organizing the tour yourself, begin the huge volume of correspondence necessary to organize homestays, concerts, and sight-seeing opportunities.

3. Begin to work with a highly reputable travel agency to acquire reasonable airfares if you are organizing the tour yourself.

*Nine Months before Departure*

1. Choose adults who will accompany the chorus (other than chaperons) with great care, as many willing adults simply do not have the flexibility and humane qualities necessary to meet the rigorous challenges of touring. A tour doctor is more beneficial than a nurse, in that he or she can expedite matters should a child need to be taken to hospital. The doctor needs to be familiar with the choir and how it functions. On tour he or she looks after and dispenses any prescription medication that choristers must take and carries a complete first-aid kit for any emergency.

2. Approach your accompanist to take part in the proposed tour—he /she must be flexible and a team player. Not all venues, pianos, and organs will be ideal.

3. Choose suitable chaperons, as this is vital to a successful tour. They must be in first-rate physical health, since much walking and lugging and sometimes sleepless nights occur on tour. They must have that special magic great teachers and parents have that is difficult to define but you know when you see it. They must love the children and be able to discipline them fairly. They must be flexible, have a sense of humor, be team players, and be experienced travelers. If you choose a chaperon who is a parent, then that parent must be able to leave his/her own child in the care of a fellow chaperon without interfering, as all the other parents have done. Each chaperon will be responsible for looking after between eight and ten children. This ratio can vary depending upon the number of places the children are visiting and whether the children stay in hotels or private homes.

4. When the chaperons have been selected, have them meet with the tour director and/or choir manager and music director to discuss their responsibilities. Make sure there are no misunderstandings about job responsibilities, lines of communication, and who has the final say—there is still time to decline the invitation. Make sure the following factors are clear and in writing:

- The health and well-being of the children and the quality of the music must always come first. Many items on the chaperons' personal agenda, such as people and places to visit, may not be met. There will be moments of sheer exhaustion and frustration, but it is hoped these will be balanced with the thrill of glorious concerts, the joy of guiding and caring for extraordinary children, and the rewards of experiencing other cultures.
- As well as caring for the children, chaperons will be asked to do other tasks: looking after belongings during a concert when a locked room is not provided, ironing uniforms, making the final check of rehearsal and concert rooms before departure, selling tapes and tickets, and turning the accompanist's pages.
- The chaperon is responsible for the money that belongs to each chorister in the group. For younger choristers, this means the chaperon carries their money at all times, handing it out as necessary and making sure they have

enough left for required spending for some meals and sight-seeing. For older choristers, money management will be at the discretion of the chaperon, still making sure the children have enough for required spending. The children may use traveler's checks; they should be in the currency of the country you are visiting. They should only be used in retail outlets, to avoid bank charges.

- Chaperons become surrogate parents. Chorister parents expect them to guide, advise, and discipline their children and keep them safe. The safety and happiness of the choristers in their group must be the chaperons' primary concern on tour.
- Chaperons are also entrusted with all passports and airline tickets while the children are touring.
- An entourage of extra parents who may be interested in accompanying the choir should be discouraged unless those parents have a structured and full agenda that is different from that of the choir and the only time they see their children is at a concert.

*Six Months before Departure*

1. Contact the embassy and cultural attaché in the country you will be visiting. Often the cultural attaché can be very helpful in providing a lunch or social event, perhaps in exchange for a brief concert. These contacts, with phone numbers, are essential to have in case of lost passports or other diplomatic issues.
2. Provide the children with detailed memos about passports (new or updated) and vaccinations and a clothing list.
3. Have the choir manager do a pretour of the sites to check concert venues, hotels, and restaurants and meet with choirs they may be visiting. A detailed meeting with the music director must take place afterward and any necessary changes or substitutions made.

*Three Months before Departure*

1. Have each child complete a form that indicates the names of six children in the choir with whom he or she wishes to room. When the rooming lists are made up, it is wise to give children a variety of roommates—even the best of friends need space on a tour.

2. Give the children tour handbooks that outline their responsibilities on tour. A topic covered in the handbook needs to be discussed at each successive rehearsal, and the following should be included:

- The children must be reminded that as they will be their country's ambassadors, it is important that their demeanor and deportment at all times reflect their best efforts to represent their country well.

- Experienced chaperons need to teach the choristers how to do hand laundry and how to pack and repack a suitcase they can easily carry themselves.
- A list of the clothing and other items to be taken on the tour must be provided; emphasize that jewelry, nail polish, and makeup must be left at home.
- Choristers should receive a list of projects or presentations on the countries they will be visiting. Children may choose a topic that interests them, and a list is compiled. The projects are then presented while in that tour location, making sight-seeing experiences even more meaningful. For example, a child's giving a quiz about Versailles while on the tour bus makes the actual trip through Versailles even more meaningful.
- The children also should be given a list of jobs and each asked to choose one that interests him or her. These can include: checking airport lounges, buses, restaurants, and hotel rooms for items left behind, coordinating games at recreation and unexpected times, setting up risers and acting as technical crew, unloading buses, and selling tapes and compact discs after concerts.
- The children should be given the procedure to follow when arriving at a hotel or homestay. For the latter they must learn how to interact with a family, how they can help at mealtimes, making sure they make their beds et cetera. (Experienced choristers enjoy presenting informal skits about the "right" and "wrong" things to do when being billeted.)
- The children need information about jet lag, healthy eating habits, street smarts, and care of money.

3. Plan a tour send-off concert. It gives the home audience, several composers, and chorus families an opportunity to hear the music that will be sung on tour and provides the choir an opportunity to perform. Publicity in local papers is important. Revenue from ticket sales can be used for the tour. The conductor would be wise to have the concert taped for further study.

*Two Months before Departure*

1. Have chaperons arrange a get-together with their choristers to get to know them better. Groups are much more effective if they are mixed in ages, with older ones able to help look after the younger ones.

2. Make sure passports are handed in to the choir office. Two photocopies must be made—one remains in the office, and one is given to the appropriate chaperon. (Chaperons keep the passports with them while on tour and should put the child's name on the front for easy identification. The choristers handle them only at passport security points.)

3. Have completed health forms given to the tour doctor. These forms will list allergies the child may have and any medication the child is taking. Children must be healthy, physically and mentally, to tour. If the tour doctor feels a child is not fit enough to tour, that child cannot go. It is wise for the tour doctor to speak to the children before the tour about common problems that can occur, the value of wash-

ing hands as often as possible, et cetera. The tour doctor must be not only an excellent physician but also an experienced traveler who loves music and children.

4. Make sure power of attorney forms are filled out and given to the tour manager.

5. Assign the billets and give out the names and addresses of homestays.

6. Have each child begin to put together tour information in a three-ring binder. Give out seating plans for two, three, and four rows. This saves time at rehearsals, where only a brief soundcheck should be permitted.

7. Start informal lessons in the language spoken in the country to be visited. Phrases such as "thank you," "please," "how much does it cost?," "we love your country," and "where is the nearest police officer," are not only useful; they are also much appreciated by residents of the host country.

### One Month before Departure

1. Make sure the children and their parents both have a detailed itinerary. The best is a "page a day." In it will be the following: blank spaces they will fill in for their chaperon's hotel room number or telephone number, their own room number, the tour doctor and tour chaperon's room or telephone number, and the names of their roommates; what they wear each day; the concert program and venue; an hour-by-hour list of events as they occur during each day; which tour presentations by the choristers will be given each day; and the address, phone, fax, and E-mail of the hotel.

2. Put in the tour three-ring binder a master list of the names and telephone numbers of everyone involved with the tour: host choirs, tour companies, choir's home base, et cetera. Also include an alphabetical list of all tour music and a checklist of all items that a chorister must remember to put into the suitcase and the location of the next place he/she will stay.

3. As all individuals who have helped with or donated to the tour should receive a postcard from one of the choristers, get small, computerized address labels that can be easily affixed to the cards.

4. Assign each person on the tour a number. It is much easier to see if anyone is missing from a bus if the numbers from 1 to 50 are called out, rather than the names.

5. Make up several performance seating charts for the choir including charts with two, three, and four rows, since you may not be sure how much time the choir has before a performance in the ideal set-up. Some directors have found that several seating charts for the bus is beneficial since it is easy to see who is missing, and it prevents the inevitable cliques and ill feelings that do occur on long and frequent bus journeys.

6. Make sure everything taken on the tour is labeled—clothing, cameras, and so on. Suitcases, music bags, and backpacks must be labeled both inside and out with names, addresses, and phone numbers.

7. Have the choristers buy small gifts for their various host families; particularly appreciated will be gifts that tell something about your country.

## Tips for the Singers While on Tour

- Carry bottled water.
- Never go anywhere without a buddy.
- Do not carry purses. Never take large amounts of money out of your pouch while shopping.
- Wash your hands as often as possible.
- Eat food that is cooked or that can be peeled.
- Write in your journal every day. Take pencils, pens, and Scotch tape with you.
- Take enough film for the entire trip. Carry cards, puzzles, and books. There will be lots of waiting.
- Never use the minibars in hotels. Check with your chaperon about using the telephone. Keep your hotel door locked at all times. Never answer the door unless you know who is there. Never leave your hotel room after lights-out or before breakfast. Always be mindful that there are other guests who deserve quiet and privacy.

## Conclusion

My colleagues and I have developed the preceding suggestions and ideas over twenty years of touring with the Toronto Children's Chorus. The ideas are by no means exhaustive. A well-planned tour can be a life-enhancing experience for all involved, as well as a highlight in the life of the choir.

CHAPTER TWELVE

# *From the Children*

*The fact that children can make beautiful music is perhaps less significant than the fact that music can make beautiful children.*
*—Anonymous*

It is perhaps fitting to conclude with some reflections written by the choristers themselves. Singing in a choir can have a profound impact on children's lives. Their hearts, minds, and spirits are forever enriched by the many experiences they share.

Our work with young people encompasses far more than the music, as these unsolicited letters from former Toronto Children's Chorus members attest:

*From Anna Guglielmin Brown (TCC 1989–1997), February 5, 1997:*

March 4, 1997, is sure to be one of the saddest days of my life. That is the date I will sing my last TCC rehearsal. Over the past seven years, I cannot name another organization that has had such a profound impact on my life.

I can still remember the first time I heard the choir at a school concert. I thought of the whole choir as magicians, as they were able to produce such perfect sounds. I sat mesmerized, not so much as opening my mouth until the final chord. It was that day that music came alive for me. I suddenly saw the reason for all my piano lessons and found the activity that would bring me so much joy. I can picture my audition clearly. I had started preparing months in advance on a song far too difficult for me. I will always remember the day my mother stood waving at the door with my acceptance letter in her hand—it was one of the happiest days of my life.

It was a year later, when I joined the Main Choir, that I was sure this was the organization for me. At my first rehearsal I couldn't even sing, for fear of ruining such perfection. It was then that I met choristers who shaped my goals and morals. Those choristers gave me something to aim for.

I remember, piece after piece, wondering how they knew all the notes so well, so soon. I was amazed at *Ceremony of Carols,* but in shock at *The Children's*

*Crusade*. I practiced night and day to learn that piece and felt so much satisfaction at the concert. That is another of the invaluable things the choir teaches: perseverance.

It's that skill that prevails in my life today. How would I get through math without stubborn determination? Every time I look at a question that seems impossible, I try and try again until it finally comes together.

The chorus has also shaped my musical life. I learned phrasing, tuning and, most importantly, sight-singing. I hope to go into music teaching when I'm older. The choir has influenced every aspect of my life. When I look back I see concerts, not schools or birthdays, and rehearsals (and more rehearsals!). I hope I never lose the skills the choir has taught me. I hope I will have the opportunity to stay closely involved with the choir. My love of music is something I will never lose. I hope that someday, when I have children of my own, they will be able to join the same TCC as I joined in 1990.

*From Andria Bulfon (TCC 1992–1996), April 9, 1993:*

There are many different aspects of the TCC. Not only do I love the singing, but I love the feeling of having a family away from home. Being a new chorister, I was hesitant in the beginning; I did not know if I would adjust to so many new people. I was pleasantly surprised to find how friendly and welcoming the choristers were. I love coming to rehearsals because I have a chance to see everyone. It is also nice that we all basically have something in common—we love music. I also enjoy the challenge of learning new pieces in various languages. The idea of discipline in the choir is wonderful. It's great when you can have fun one moment and yet, when rehearsal begins, you're serious and ready to work. One of the best things about being in the choir is performing with various wonderful musicians.

I wish that all children and young adults could be involved in an organization like this, because the impact the choir has had on my life is amazing. I know I will not forget these years for as long as I live.

*From Hilary Cameron (TCC 1984–1993), June 21, 1993:*

After eight years, I am leaving the TCC. Before I do, I thought I would try to tell you how much this choir has meant to me and how much I have learned. Being a member of the TCC has so many obvious benefits. I have had the privilege of working with the world's best choirs, under the world's best conductors. I have traveled to seven countries (eight, counting the stopover in Fiji!), made many friends, and learned so much beautiful music.

TCC has taught me that I am never in a choir solely for myself. TCC has taught me that ego and surface "fairness" must occasionally be sacrificed to produce a better sound, a nicer blend, or a richer tone. It is a concept that I hope I will always apply to my life.

One of the very best things I have received from the choir is some of the closest friends I will ever have. Many of them have already left the choir and I cannot imagine us soon drifting apart. In fact, it is not at all unusual for a weekend get-together to resemble an Alumni function.

The choir has also taught me many valuable life skills. After eight years of balancing TCC and school, I could not procrastinate effectively if I were paid. I have learned to organize both my time and my work. For the rest of my life, I will most likely show up for meetings ten minutes early. Touring with the choir has also taught me responsible habits, such as healthy eating and sleeping, which will be of great use to me, especially at university.

TCC has even played a major part in the direction I see my life taking. My love of languages has been developed largely through the encouragement I have always received in the choir and, while I doubt that I will choose to pursue music as a career, it will now always be an important part of my life.

*Also from Hilary, May 31, 1999:*

My time in the TCC continues to affect me, years after I sang my last concert. Many of my choir friends who have gone on to study music at university are now professional musicians. Almost all of us continue to sing in some capacity. Without doubt, the love of music that developed during my time in the TCC is one of the greatest gifts I have ever been given.

*From Christina Chabot (TCC 1994–1999), June 2000:*

For the past six years, the choir has essentially been my lifeblood. I've turned to it in times of sadness, anger, loneliness, and even despair. It has been my cornerstone, my steadfast friend. I could always depend on it in times of need and, with that first song, my emotions were released and I could find real joy again.

The TCC has taught me many things—dedication, professionalism, organizational skills, and artistry that I could never learn elsewhere. It has made me the person I am. It continues to shape the person I aspire to be—a responsible, compassionate and life-loving woman who finds joy in beautiful, pure music. The Toronto Children's Chorus will be a golden memory, impossible to forget.

*From Jessica Clague (TCC 1995–2001), June 1, 2001:*

Five years have come and gone so quickly. During these five years I have developed musically and have learned organizational and leadership skills. You've inspired me to reach my goals. The memories of my years in the Toronto Children's Chorus will remain with me always. Thank you for opening many doors to wonderful opportunities. It's been a great journey.

*From Erica Huang (TCC 1990–1998), June 1999:*

The past eight years have been a wonderful experience. I have come to understand the meaning of music and am able to make music with enjoyment and pleasure. Not only have I become more experienced musically, but also a great amount of discipline and maturity have been applied and developed in my life. I will miss you and the choir greatly.

*From Natalia Lobach (TCC 1989–1994), August 1993:*

I really enjoy the TCC because I love music and singing. The choir has exposed me to many forms and styles of music, from classical to contemporary, and has introduced me to many other musical groups. From the choir, I have learned listening skills, posture, stage presence, and projection of my voice. The choir has also taught me to organize myself and work hard.

I also enjoy the fun things that the choir does. Camp at the beginning of the year gives me a chance to meet new people and to see my old friends again. Touring is one of my favorites—it gives me a sense of independence and I have a chance to solve my own problems. It also helps friendships become closer. I will keep my friends from the choir for the rest of my life.

*From Laura Pedersen (TCC 1989–1995), August 4, 1995:*

Besides learning how best to use my voice, I have gained a greater understanding of music, a love of excellence in music, and a wish to share that joy with others. The choir has given me time-management and leadership skills, discipline, and the best friends I have; every minute I spend here teaches me something valuable. Without the choir, I would not have had the chance to tour so extensively. I also would not have the social skills I now have (socializing during breaks only, of course, not during rehearsals!). I will carry the TCC with me always and look forward to listening to all the concerts.

*From Tim Rutledge (TCC 1990–1993), June 1992:*

Q: Why do I stay in the TCC?
A: Even though at some times, I think I might have to leave the choir to do school, family life, and my so-called "social" life, I know that I never will unless there is no choice (voice changing) And here are the reasons why:

1. I love singing. Not only do I get to do that in the TCC, I get to sing pieces that are worth singing.
2. Choir seems to be a better investment than hockey.
3. After I joined I found out that there's not a single person in the choir who can't get along with anyone. (There are lots of nice people.)
4. I never did like hockey anyway.
5. I like touring, especially when we go to big places like Mt. Forest.
6. I like the fact that we do a lot of sitting at the concerts and it doesn't take a lot of physical effort like the twenty-minute hockey game I had each week.
7. My music teacher at school likes me now.
8. It's good to know that there's a place I can go other than Speedy Muffler to be a somebody and be treated that way.

Oh, and did I mention, my parents want me to be in the TCC too?

*From Chelsey Schill (TCC 1992–1996), July 6, 1996:*

The Chorus not only helped my singing and musical abilities, but it also helped me manage my time. The music I have learned is incredible—*The Children's Crusade,* which I learned in my first year, is my absolute favorite!

The years have gone by so fast. I can still remember crying my first day at camp—not because of homesickness, but because I never wanted to leave! I'll feel weird in August when I don't return to camp, and I'm sure when I go to the first concert next season I'll feel out of place. I'll probably be running around looking for white pantyhose and my collar!

I have enjoyed being a part of the TCC for four years. I'm sure that I will also enjoy being a part of the Alumni for the rest of my life.

*From Lauren Simmons (TCC 1994–1999), August 18, 2001:*

I wanted to touch base with you before I leave for university to study Music Education. As I prepare to start this new chapter in my life, I am wistful at leaving behind the TCC and the years of training, friendship, and musical expression that the choir gave me. I will take with me the practical skills, the personal responsibility, and the lifelong friendships so readily fostered by the choir.

*From Giles Tomkins (TCC 1988–1995), June 1995:*

Next to my family, the chorus has been the most important part of my life over the past five years. It has given me the opportunity to experience people and places I would never have known otherwise. On our concert tours, we have visited many different places, from Phoenix, Arizona, to Chartres Cathedral in Paris, and from Fort Myers, Florida, to Tewkesbury Abbey in England, just to name a few. These tours come about through hard work, but there are many benefits—we develop strong friendships and learn to be very organized.

*From Nicholas Wilkinson (TCC 1987–1993), June 1993:*

The one thing everybody misses when they leave the TCC is the friends they've made, but the friendships made here will definitely last a lifetime. In my first year, if someone had asked me, "How can you spend all that time rehearsing?" I probably would have answered, "It's a real pain!" (When a rehearsal was cancelled, I was overcome with joy!) But now, six years later, I would wince and dread not being able to sing or see my friends for a week.

The music we sing is always challenging, pushing us to be that much better. It always takes lots of hard work to get it right but, when we do perform it, the hours of rehearsing seem like nothing.

One of the things I like best about the choir is touring. Most people won't ever go to the places I've been. And nobody will experience the rush of pride after singing in a venue like Chartres Cathedral—it's a feeling I will never, ever forget.

*From a TCC parent, Marie Houghton (1996–present), June 9, 2001:*

It is the end of our family's fifth year with the chorus and naturally we have accumulated numerous memories along the way. Some are of billets staying in our home or of the driveway covered in flats of spring flowers. There are also, of course, the wonderful musical memories.

I was a concert assistant when you recently conducted *Freedom Trilogy.* There were two full choirs massed at either end of the balcony and another with TCC on the main floor. As the sounds of "Amazing Grace" spiraled up among the beating African drums, I looked over at Emily. She was visibly transported in the moment. She was so focused on your hands I was afraid she would tumble forward on the steep balcony steps. Emily was nine years old that day when the sight of your hands allowed her to experience the amazingly powerful sensation of being part of a musical ensemble. It still brings tears to my eyes just to think about that moment!

*And finally from members of the current Training Choirs:*

"I feel good when people like my singing."—Nila Rosborough, age seven

"The Toronto Children's Chorus means standing up at a concert and singing your best, making beautiful music that other people can also enjoy." —Melissa Walter, age eleven

"The Toronto Children's Chorus means the world of music around me. Being in a choir makes me happy and full of joy."—Lusila Mazi, age seven

"The TCC isn't about who can or can't sing; it's about learning and self-fulfilling dreams of artists in the making."—Matthew Quitasol, age twelve

# Warm-up Vocal Exercises

Warm-up exercises are vital for singers and, if used effectively, can be extremely valuable for the voice, the mind, and the ear. They should be used not only to warm up the voice and teach solid vocal pedagogy but also to focus the children's attention and improve inner hearing. Effective warm-ups can also create a nurturing atmosphere for the intense work that will follow.

Warm-up exercises must never be dull or merely routine. They should not be reduced to a series of mindless vocalises sung in exactly the same order each week. The following list could be used with a choir of eight- to fourteen-year-old children:

- Ask a child to sing an A, written on the chalkboard, without hearing it first from the piano. Gradually, as the weeks go by, the child who is asked to sing the A will get closer to the correct pitch. Play an A on the piano after the child has sung it and ask someone to identify the note the child sang (if it was different). Have that note written on the board, beside the original A. The relationship between the two notes may then make an effective exercise.
- Start the rehearsal by having the children hum gently a unison A.
- Make sure the children stand on the balls of their feet, with knees flexible and arms loose. There should be no tension in the neck, shoulders, jaw, or face. If there appears to be any tightness, have the children gently roll their heads from side to side. (See figure A1.1.)
- If the children are very young and have not yet learned to connect the breath with the placement, use the breathing awareness exercises found in chapter 2. Generally speaking, breathing exercises have little value unless linked to actual singing.
- On the breath, on the pitch A, have the children sing the five pure vowels sounds: "mee," "may," "mah," "moh," and "moo." Great care must be taken to ensure that these vowels are pure and uniform, with no hint of diphthong. (See figure A1.2.)
- On the breath and if possible without the piano, have the children repeat the preceding exercise on ascending half steps to a D. The A should then be repeated. On the breath, the children should sing the same vowels on descending half steps to an E. Correct faulty intonation and impure vowels by modeling the desired sound.
- Take great care to ensure that the children are singing "on the breath."
- Try this exercise, which again starts on A and descends a fifth. It is important to warm up the voice in the midrange before any extremities are attempted. There should be a ringing quality to the sound if the children are singing correctly—on the breath and with proper vocal placement.
- Use the preceding exercise, with "flee," "flay," "flah," "flow," and "floo," to remedy the tendency of children, in their attempt to sing well, to try too hard, often resulting in raised tongues. They sound as though they are singing with plums in their mouths.
- Have the children, with Soprano I, Soprano II, and Alto voicing, sing a D major triad using the five primary vowels, gradually ascending in half steps to A major.

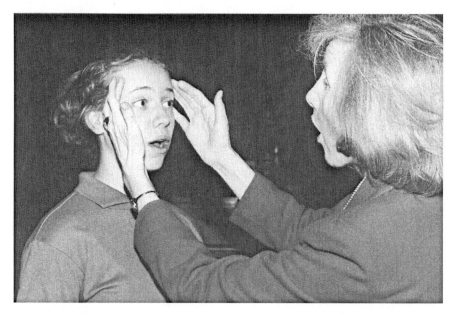

Figure A1.1

Nothing should be sung beyond a *mezzo forte* range. (While sustaining a major triad, advanced choirs, with the conductor requesting specific intervals from the three voice parts, could then be asked to make the triad minor, augmented or diminished.)

- Give the children an exercise that engages the breath but is not vocally taxing. Singing staccato on "ho," beginning on D and ascending in thirds, is very effective. Staccato singing engages the breath, and well-tuned thirds improve the ear. The range is stretched slightly to a tenth but does not go beyond middle C sharp or high E.

- Repeat the same exercise with the children singing *legato* on the repeated sound "mah." Care must be taken that the jaw is relaxed and dropped. (See figure A1.4.)

- Now have the children do several other exercises listed here for flexibility and range extension.

- Before the warm-ups are complete, have the children sing a chromatic scale and a whole-tone scale with note names. This improves the ear greatly. Games can be implemented in which the children sing silently when your fist is closed and out loud when your hand is open. If you wish to hear small groups of singers, invite certain rows, children who had a math test that day, those who have three sisters, or those who have a birthday in May to sing along. Keep them on their toes and make the learning process fun!

- Derive tailor-made exercises on a chalkboard or in a memo from tricky passages in new music that is being studied. These will not only warm up the voice but also enhance the learning of new music.

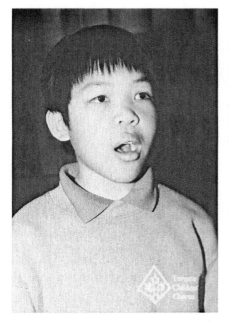

Figure A1.2

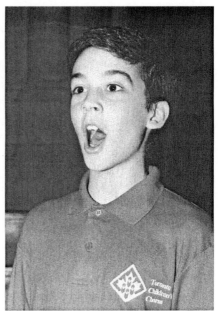

Figure A1.3

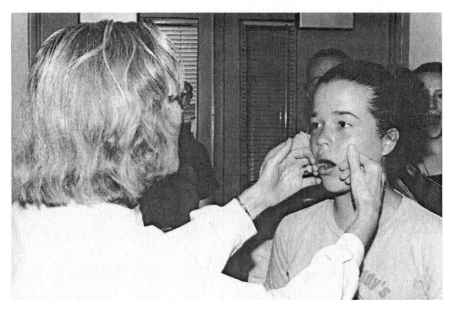

Figure A1.4

The percentage of time spent on warm-ups depends on the age and ability of the singers and the conductor's ability to determine when the choir is ready to rehearse the music. Well-planned warm-ups teach singing skills that will be transferred to the pieces the children sing. When used imaginatively with sound pedagogy, warm-ups are an indispensable tool for the children's choir director.

## Vocalises

The exercises on pages 155 and 156 will help the children develop good singing technique as well as train the ear. Carried over into the repertoire, these skills will vastly improve the standard of the choir.

The vocalises on pages 157 and 158 are highly recommended for ten- to fifteen-year-old children. The scales, sequentials, and intervals sheet is highly recommended for "training" choirs—children's choirs in the first, second, and third years of study, regardless of age. The tonic-solfa syllables encourage a uniform vowel sound. The syllables are invaluable in teaching a child to read music and sing whole steps and half steps in tune. The conductor needs to model each exercise for the children and, after it is mastered, move on to the next.

# THE INTERVAL SONG

# THE ADVANCED INTERVAL SONG

# VOCALISES

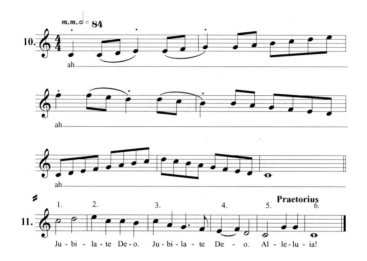

10. _m.m. ♩ = 84_

ah

ah

ah

11. Praetorius

1. 2. 3. 4. 5. 6.

Ju – bi – la – te De – o. Ju – bi – la – te De – o. Al – le – lu – ia!

# *Audition Form*

The following is the audition application form used by the Toronto Children's Chorus:

---

**For office use only   DO NOT FILL IN**

Audition result: Yes_____ No_____

| | |
|---|---|
| Training Choir I _____ | Toronto Children's Chorus _____ |
| Training Choir II _____ | Section: Sop I _____ |
| Training Choir III _____ | Sop II _____ |
| Boy _____ Girl_____ | Alto _____ |

**Audition Application**

** It is very *important* that every section of this form be filled in *accurately* as this form will constitute your permanent office record. Personal information is kept in strictest confidence, with the exception of chorister name, address and telephone number, which is distributed to fellow choristers in June. **

PLEASE PRINT NEATLY: (Please use fine black marker provided)

**Audition Applicant's General Information**      Today's Date _____

Name: _____ Sex:  M _____  F _____

Address: (Apt. #) _____ (Street) _____ (City) _____

Postal Code: _____ Telephone: (_____)_____

Telephone Number to call during the day: (_____)_____
(Occasionally, messages need to be delivered quickly regarding rehearsal schedules, homework, etc.)

Age: (as of Aug. 1/2001) _____ Birth date: (Month) _____/ (Day) _____/ (Year) _____

Any allergies we should be aware of: _____

**Parent Information:** Strictly Confidential

I live with: (Check one ✓)

Both Parents _____ My Mother _____ My Father _____ Other (specify) _____

Father's Name: _____

Father's Address and Phone # (if different from applicant): _____

_____

Father's Occupation/Profession: _____ Position Held: _____

Name of Company: _____

Business Address: _____ Phone: _____

---

Mother's Name: _____

Mother's Address and Phone # (if different from applicant): _____

_____

Mother's Occupation/Profession: _____ Position Held: _____

Name of Company: _____

Business Address: _____ Phone: _____

*Please read and sign below:*

If I pass my audition and am admitted as a 2001–2002 member of one of the choirs in the Toronto Children's Chorus programme, I promise to faithfully attend all rehearsals and performances of the Toronto Children's Chorus in 2001–2002. Only then can the exceptionally high standards, which the Toronto Children's Chorus has reached, be maintained. Concert and rehearsal schedules are given out in advance and family and school planning should be arranged to accommodate the schedule. I realize that severe illness and intense study during the week of exams are the only accepted reasons for rehearsal absences. I realize that missing rehearsals unnecessarily will jeopardize my chances of remaining in the Chorus in the 2001–2002 season. I understand that as part of my acceptance as a **member of the Toronto Children's Chorus**, I must attend a Pre-Camp meeting on August 24, 2001, and complete the residency at Music Camp from August 26 to September 1, 2001. I agree to replace any Chorus music and any Chorus uniform which I have lost or damaged during the season. **Members of the Training Choirs do NOT attend Camp or the Pre-Camp meeting.**

Child's Signature: _____

Parent's Signature: _____ Date: _____

N.B. : Audition results will be mailed to you in June. There will be a meeting for all TCC Parents on June 25, 2001, from 7:00 pm to 9:00 pm at Lawrence Park Community Church.

**School Information:**

School Grade (as of Sept/01) _____ (N.B.: school grade next Sept., not this school year)

Name of School (as of Sept/01) _____

What do you like best at school? _____

_____

What type of student are you? (check one ✓)

Superior ( ) Above Average ( ) Average ( ) Below Average ( )

Have you brought a letter of reference? Yes ( ) No ( ) From whom? _____

**Music Education Information:**

Names of choirs in which you have sung and length of time in each:

1. _____ 2. _____

Names of instruments you play: 1. _____ 2. _____

Have you taken examinations in these instruments? Yes ( ) No ( )

Names of Music Teachers:

Private Teachers: _____

School Music Teacher: _____

Have you studied theory formally? Yes ( ) No ( )

With whom did you study theory? _____

List grades passed: Instrument _____ Theory: _____

Other information about the child's music background which you think would help Mrs. Bartle
assess the child's musical abilities: _____

_____

_____

_____

_____

**Personal Information**: (To be filled in by child, as detailed as possible.)

1. What are your hobbies? _____

_____

_____

2. Name the books you have read this year:   a) _____

b) _____   c) _____

d) _____

3. In what other activities are you involved (gymnastics, skiing, other)? _____

_____

_____

_____

4. Why do you want to be in the Toronto Children's Chorus? _____

_____

_____

_____

_____

_____

_____

_____

_____

_____

# Sample Programs from Toronto Children's Chorus

---

**Autumn and Animals in Canada**
**October 22, 2000**

Training Choir I
    Autumn Fires                  Robert Louis Stevenson
        *Olivia Wetzel, age 8*
Horace was a Hippo            **Arthur Baynon**
    Mother Doesn't Want a Dog     Judith Viorst
        *Molly Gurdon, age 6*
    My Lizard                   Kaye Starbird
        *Alana Chung, age 8*
Elephants                   **Clifford Crawley***
    The Giraffe's Breakfast         Ilo Orleans
        *Alice Stevenson, age 9*
    My Cat, Mrs. Lick-a-Chin      John Ciardi
        *Victoria Smith, age 9*
    Point of View               David McCord
        *Robert Binet, age 9*
The Grasshopper             **Stuart Young**

Training Choir II
    Fall Leaves Fall              Emily Brontë
        *Patrick Sinclair, age 8*
    Avec mes amis             Jacinthe Lavoie
        *Hanna Kaploun, age 7*
Someone                    **Violet Archer***
    October Nights             Harriet Cooper
        *Cara Lew, age 8*
    Grizzly Bear                Mary Austin
        *Nathaniel So, age 8*
Marmotte, Op. 52, No. 7       **Ludwig van Beethoven**
    Action                      Ilo Orleans
        *Andrew Chisholm, age 8*
    Zebra Question            Shel Silverstein
        *Jonathan Szwec, age 8*

Training Choir II
Autumn                                     Dean Blair*
    *Meaghen Glover, Calla Heilbron, Kelsey Heyd & Carmel Prince, quartet*
  Something Told the Wild Geese        Rachel Field
    *Lauren DiPede, age 8*
  Introduction to *Bliss Carmen*
    *Rachael Balchin, age 11*
  A Vagabond Song                      Bliss Carmen
    *Lauren Saunders, age 9*
  Introduction to *William Wilfred Campbell*
    *Allison Browne, age 11*
  Indian Summer                        William W. Campbell
    *Jordyn Taylor, age 9*

Training Choir III
La petite hirondelle                       arr. Healey Willan*
  The Orangutan                        Sheree Fitch
    *James Gagne, age 9*
  If You Should Meet a Crocodile        Anonymous
    *Jonathan Mamalyga, age 11*
The Snail                                  Derek Holman*
  Our Hamster's Life                   Kit Wright
    *Charlotte McGee, age 9*
  The Donkey                           Gertrude Hinds
    *Poornima Narayan, age 11*
Sing a Song of Sixpence                    Michael D. Mendoza

Training Choirs I, II, & III
Autumn Tints                               Norman Gilbert*
All Things Bright and Beautiful            John Rutter

    *Canadian Composer

---

*Northern Passages*
*November 5, 2000*          **MUC**

Toronto Children's Chorus
Six Choruses, Opus 15                      Rachmaninoff (1873–1943)
  I. All Glory to Our People          N. Nekrasov
  II. Night                           V. Ladizhensky
  III. The Pine Tree                  M. Lermontov
    *Nellie Stockhammer & Laura Hartenberger, soloists*
  IV. Now the Waves are Sleeping       K. Romanov
  V. Captivity                        N. Tsiganov
  VI. The Angel                       M. Lermontov

Toronto Children's Chorus: Chamber Choir
On suuri sun rantas autius                      Matti Hyökki (b. 1950)
    *Aleha Aziz, Sarah Hicks, Brynne McLeod, Emily Shepard, Nellie*
    *Stockhammer, & Kate Van Buskirk, soloists*
It is Truly Meet                                Tchaikovsky (1840–1893)
From *Suite de Lorca*                           E. Rautavaara (b. 1928)
El grito
Malagueña

Vesnivka Choir
Alleluia                                        M. Verbytsky
From the *Liturgy of St. John Chrysostom*
    Great Ektenia
    Glory Be Only Begotten Son
We Ask for Your Mercy                           M. Hajvoronsky
Hymn to the Holy Spirit                         arr. A. Levkovich

INTERMISSION

Toronto Children's Chorus
Water Under Snow is Weary                       Harri Wessman (b. 1949)

Toronto Children's Chorus
Suita Grammaticale                              Aulis Sallinen (b. 1935)
    1. Die erste Deklination
    2. Intermezzo
    3. Quelle heure est-il?
        *Janet Sung, soloist*
    4. Etudes
    5. Dialogue
        *Lance Elbeck, Oksana Dmitrik, Norman Hathaway, Julie Savard,*
        *Malou Sobrevinus, Rebecca van der Post & Nicole Zarry, violin*
        *Katherine Rapoport, Ignatio Turrion & David Willms, viola*
        *Dana Glinski & Tom Mueller, cello*
        *Peter Pavlovsky, bass*
        *Susan Hoeppner, flute*
        *Russell Hartenberger & Laura Hartenberger, percussion*
Songs from the Sea                              Aulis Sallinen
    1. Sea Prayer
    2. Sea Danger
    3. Ballad
        *Sarah Hicks, Nellie Stockhammer & Laura Redekop, soloists*

Vesnivka Choir
Springtime Dreams                               arr. I. Syvochina
The Little Cuckoo Bird                          arr. V. Lystopad

| | |
|---|---|
| Return of the Swallow | arr. E. Pip |
| Medley of Lemko Songs | arr. S. Hryca |

Toronto Children's Chorus and Vesnivka Choir

| | |
|---|---|
| Hymn to Freedom | Oscar Peterson (b. 1925)* |
| Song for Canada | Paul Halley (b. 1952)* |

*Canadian Composer

---

*A Chorus Christmas*
*Roy Thomson Hall*
*December 2000*

Toronto Children's Chorus
*Let the Bright Seraphim*                George Frideric Handel
    *Stuart Laughton, trumpet*

Toronto Children's Chorus and Alumni Choir
*Go Where I Send Thee*                arr. Paul Caldwell & Sean Ivory
    *Conlin Delbaere-Sawchuk, bass*

Toronto Children's Chorus and True North Brass
*Nou is the Time of Christemas*            Michael Coghlan*
    *Stuart Laughton, Raymond Tizzard & David Locke, trumpets*
*Sweet Songs of Christmas*            Christopher Dedrick
*The Angel Choir and the Trumpeter*        Christopher Dedrick
*It Came Upon the Midnight Clear*        Sir David Willcocks
*Once in Royal David's City*            Sir David Willcocks
   Verses 1 & 2: Toronto Children's Chorus, Alumni Choir & True North Brass
   Verses 3 & 4: Carol for All
    *Ruth Watson Henderson, organ*

Toronto Children's Chorus
*Brother Heinrich's Christmas*            John Rutter
    *Laura Cameron, narrator*
    *Richard Dorsey, oboe*
    *Bassoon TBA*
    *Ruth Watson Henderson, piano*

---

INTERMISSION

Training Choir I
*Entre le boeuf et l'âne gris*            Sydney Northcote*
*Rocking Carol*                Traditional Czech Carol
*O Hanukkah*                Traditional

Training Choir II
*Come, Jesus, Holy Child*            Healey Willan*

| | |
|---|---|
| *Mid-Winter* | Bob Chilcott |
| *Jesus Child* | John Rutter |

Training Choirs I and II
| | |
|---|---|
| *Haida* | arr. Henry Leck |
| *The Sleigh* | Richard Kountz |

Carol for All
| | |
|---|---|
| *O Come, All Ye Faithful* | attributed to John Francis Wade |
| | arr. David Willcocks |

> *Terry Szwec, conductor*
> *Ruth Watson Henderson, organ*
> *True North Brass*

Training Choir III
| | |
|---|---|
| *The Grey Donkey* | Anthony Royse* |
| *Mary's Cradle Song* | Paul Keene |
| *Jingle Bell Swing* | arr. David Elliott* |

> *Mitch Bondy, conductor*

Carol for All
| | |
|---|---|
| *Hark, the Herald Angels Sing* | arr. David Willcocks |

> *Ruth Watson Henderson, organ*
> *True North Brass*

Alumni Choir
| | |
|---|---|
| *We Wish You a Merry Christmas* | arr. Harry Somers* |
| *Lo, how a rose e'er blooming* | Michael Praetorius |
| *In the Bleak Midwinter* | Harold Darke |

Alumni Choir and True North Brass
| | |
|---|---|
| *Unto Us is Born a Son* | arr. David Willcocks |
| *See Amid the Winter's Snow* | arr. David Willcocks |

> *Ruth Watson Henderson, organ*

Toronto Children's Chorus, Training and Alumni Choirs
| | |
|---|---|
| *Star Carol* | John Rutter |

> *True North Brass with David Locke, trumpet*

| | |
|---|---|
| *Little Drummer Boy* | Katherine Davis |

> *Russell Hartenberger, drum*

| | |
|---|---|
| *Away in a Manger* | arr. Elmer Iseler* |
| *Laudate Dominum* | Arthur Honegger |
| From Une Cantate de Nöel | |

> *Stuart Laughton, trumpet*
> *Ruth Watson Henderson, organ*

*Canadian Composer

## *Music for a Sunday Afternoon*
### *February 25, 2001 MUC*

Training Choir I
Vive la Canadienne                                    arr. Hugh J. McLean*
    *Lauren Simmons, student conductor*
Who Has Seen the Wind?                                Udo Kasemets*
Monkeys                                               W. Herbert Belyea*

Instrumentalists: Training Choir I
Country Dance                                         Franz Hünten
    *Ada Chan, age 8, piano*
The Happy Farmer                                      Robert Schumann
    *Barnett Ludwig, age 8, piano*
Last Rose of Summer                                   Friedrich von Flotow
    *Fiona Wu, age 7, piano*

Training Choir II
Grasshopper Green                                     Colin Taylor
Golden Slumbers                                       arr. Ernest MacMillan*
The Kelligrew Soirée                                  arr. Hugh J. McLean*
    *Rachael Balchin, Allison Browne, Ashley Carter, Calla Heilbron,*
    *Kelsey Heyd, Tiffany Kwok, Maria Lee and Arielle Mida, dancers*

Instrumentalists: Training Choir II
Country Dance                                         Franz Joseph Haydn
    *Jennifer Wu, age 9, piano*
Sonatina in G Major, Op. 151, No. 1    Anton Diabelli
    *Nathaniel So, age 9, piano*

Training Choir III
King of Song                                          Eric Thiman
An Irish Blessing                                     Eleanor Daley*
Gospel Train                                          arr. Stewart Johnson

Instrumentalists: Training Choir III
The Jester                                            Johann Ludwig Krebs
    *Lyndon Lear Kirkley, age 9, piano*
Gabby's Ghost                                         Bruce Chace
    *Sabina Sabaratnam, age 10, violin*
"Gigue" from Sonatina in A, Op. 5, No. 9 Arcangelo Corelli
    *Maxine Byam, age 9, violin*

Boys' Choir
Pie Jesu from *Requiem*                               Gabriel Fauré
Ah! si mon moine voulait danser                       arr. Godfrey Ridout*
    *Devin Campbell, spoons*

INTERMISSION

Training Choirs I, II & III
Rip Van Winkle                          John Bryan
   1. Prologue
       *Olivia Mew, Poornima Narayan & Jillian Whitfield, soloists*
   2. Rip Van Winkle
   3. Lazy Man
       *Frances Dorenbaum, Meg Moran & Sabina Sabaratnam, soloists*
   4. Boys and Girls
   5. Procrastination
       *Rebecca Boucher, Maxine Byam, Nyree Grimes & Sara Ho, soloists*
   6. High on a Hill
   7. The Mountain Men
   8. Waking Up
   9. I've Been to Sleep
       *Christopher Purves, Jeffrey Smith & David Walter, soloists*
   10. Finale
       *Narrators (in order of appearance)*
       *Paige Halam-Andres, Calum Mew, Charlotte Bondy, Charlotte McGee,*
       *Kaie Rosborough, Alice Atell*
       *Mitch Bondy, conductor*
       *Randy Leslie, choreographer*

   *Canadian Composer


*Children Helping Children*
*March 3, 2001*
*Toronto Centre for the Arts*

*Come, Ye Makers of Song*                *Ruth Watson Henderson\**
*A Song of St. Francis*                   *Michael Hurd*
       *Sarah Hicks, soloist*
*Songs of the Lights*                     *Imant Raminsh\**
   *Song of the Stars*
   *The Sower*
   *The Sun is a Luminous Shield*
       *Nellie Stockhammer, soloist*
   *Daybreak Song*
*Carla's Poems*                           *Chan Ka Nin\**
   *Mother's Nighttime Hugs*
   *In a Race*
   *Time*

*Sometimes I Wonder . . .*
*Tomorrow, Today*
*It's Our Choice*
*Move the Cloud*
*I Cannot Go*
    *Laura Cameron, narrator*
    *Heather Hurst, soloist*
    *Susan Hoeppner, flute*
    *Richard Dorsey, oboe*
    *Joaquin Valdepeñas, clarinet*
    *Nadina Jackson, bassoon*

INTERMISSION

| | |
|---|---|
| *Freedom Trilogy* | *Paul Halley\** |

    *Laura Redekop, soloist*
    *Carla Hartenberger, percussion*

| | |
|---|---|
| *The Swallow* | *Nancy Telfer\** |

    *Brynne McLeod and Emily Shepard, soloists*

| | |
|---|---|
| *Ave Verum Corpus* | *Eleanor Daley\** |
| *From Sir Christĕmas: Nay, Ivy, Nay* | *Derek Holman\** |
| *My Heart Soars* | *Ruth Watson Henderson\** |

    *Susan Hoeppner, flute*

| | |
|---|---|
| *Joy is Like the Rain* | *Sr. Miriam Thérèse Winter* |

    *Valerie Conforzi, Elizabeth Convery, Laura Goldsmith and Heather*
    *Wilkie, quartet*
    *In loving memory of Debra Cecile Heinrichs (1965–1975)*

| | |
|---|---|
| *From Psalm Trilogy: Psalm 23* | *Srul Irving Glick\** |
| *Choral Selections from* Oliver | *Lionel Bart* |
|   *Consider Yourself* | *arr. Norman Leyden* |

  *Where is Love?*
    *Michael Saunders, soloist*
  *Oom pah pah*
  *There's a Little Ditty*
    *Emily Shepard, soloist*
  *As Long As He Needs Me*
    *Jennie Morgan, soloist*
    *Aleha Aziz, Sarah Hicks, Laura Redekop and Emily Shepard, quartet*
  *I'd Do Anything*
    *Cassandra Luftspring, soloist*
  *Who Will Buy?*
    *Sarah Hicks, soloist*
  *Reprise*

    \*Canadian composer

*Voices of Women*
*April 28, 2001*
*Toronto Centre for the Arts*

Toronto Children's Chorus

| | |
|---|---|
| O frondens virga | Hildegard von Bingen *(1098–1179)* |
| Aure volanti | Francesca Caccini *(1587–1630)* |

    *Sydney Hodge & Nicholas Delbaere-Sawchuk, violins*

| | |
|---|---|
| Ronde du Crépuscule | Cécile Chaminade *(1857–1944)* |
| Mélodie, Op. 4, No. 2 | Fanny Mendelssohn *(1805–1847)* |

    *Katherine Saccucci, piano*

Andante con sentimento      Clara Schumann *(1819–1896)*

    *Ruth Watson Henderson, piano*

| | |
|---|---|
| March of the Women | Dame Ethel Smyth *(1858–1944)* |
| Les sirènes | Lili Boulanger *(1893–1918)* |

    *Sarah Hicks, soloist*

| | |
|---|---|
| Kyrie | Nancy Telfer* *(b. 1950)* |
| Ave verum corpus | Eleanor Daley* *(b. 1955)* |
| Pippa's Morning Song | Jean Coulthard* *(1908–2000)* |
| *from* Three Philosophical Songs | |

    *String Ensemble*

Adventures in Color§      Ruth Watson Henderson*
  Blue      *(b. 1932)*
  Gold
  Red
  White

    *String Ensemble*

    §*World premiere—commissioned by the Toronto Children's Chorus with the generous assistance of the Ontario Arts Council.*

INTERMISSION

Training Choir I

| | |
|---|---|
| *From* Children Singing | Violet Archer* *(1913–2000)* |

  The Cow
  How Doth the Little Crocodile
  The Yak
  Mes Oreilles, Quelle Merveille

Training Choir II

| | |
|---|---|
| Skye Boat Song | arr. Evelyn Sharpe |
| Sing Me A Song | Nancy Telfer* |
| A Great Big Sea | arr. Lori-Anne Dolloff* |

    *Jordyn Taylor, spoons*

Training Choir III

| | |
|---|---|
| Bless the Lord, O My Soul | Ruth Watson Henderson* |
| Tecolote: Song of the Little Owl | arr. Victoria Ebel-Sabo* |

    *Sabina Sabaratnam, shaker*

| | |
|---|---|
| Stars | Larysa Kuzmenko* |
| An Irish Blessing | arr. Eleanor Daley* |

TCC, Training Choirs I, II & III

| | |
|---|---|
| We Rise Again | arr. Lydia Adams* |

    *Canadian Composer

---

## Roots and Wings
## November 14, 1999
## Beth Tikvah Synagogue

Toronto Children's Chorus & Syracuse Children's Chorus

| | |
|---|---|
| Psalm Trilogy§ | Srul Irving Glick* |

    Psalm 92

        *Alison Armstrong, Rena Ashton, Diana Chisholm, Jessica Clague,*
        *Andrea Grant, Heather Hurst and Emily Shepard, soloists*

    Psalm 47

    Psalm 23

        *Mark Skazinetsky (concertmaster), Virginia Wells, Bridget Hunt,*
        *Paul Meyer, Young Dae Park and Mi Hyon Kim, violin*
        *Kent Teeple and Dan Blackman, viola*
        *Simon Fryer and Marie Gelinas, cello*
        *Joel Quarrington, bass*

    §North American premiere; commissioned by Ian Epstein and Kathy Kacer for the Bat Mitzvah of their daughter, Gabi

Syracuse Children's Chorus

| | |
|---|---|
| V'higad'ta L'vincha | Gerald Cohen |

(*And You Shall Tell Your Child*)

    Avadim Hayinu

    Ha Lachma Anya

    Dayeinu

        *Simon Fryer, cello*
        *Shalom Bard, clarinet*

Toronto Children's Chorus: Chamber Choir

| | |
|---|---|
| I Never Saw Another Butterfly | Joel Hardyk |

    At Terezin

    I'd Like to Go Alone

    The Little Mouse

The Garden
The Butterfly
>    *Laura Cameron, Jennie Morgan and Kate Van Buskirk, soloists*
>    *Gillian Howard, oboe*

Toronto Children's Chorus
Gloria Tibi from *Mass*                      Leonard Bernstein
>    *Aleha Aziz, Heather Hurst and Emily Shepard, soloists*
>    *Laura Hartenberger, percussion*
Canon in 5 Parts from *Kaddish*              Bernstein
>    *Jessica Clague, Andrea Grant, Laura Hanson & Heather Hurst, dancers*
Somewhere from *West Side Story*             Bernstein
>    *Gabi Epstein, soloist*

---

INTERMISSION

Syracuse Children's Chorus
When I Am Silent                             Joan C. Varner
Inscription of Hope                          Z. Randall Stroope
Birdsong                                     Paul Read

Toronto Children's Chorus: Chamber Choir
Keewaydin                                    Harry Freedman*
>    *Alexandra Airhart, Gabi Epstein, Sarah Hicks, Laura*
>    *Kishimoto, Katie Mann and Emily Shepard, soloists*

Toronto Children's Chorus
George Gershwin Medley                       arr. Bill Holcombe

Toronto Children's Chorus & Syracuse Children's Chorus
I Bought Me A Cat                            Aaron Copland
>    *Jennie Morgan and Emily Stairs, soloists*
Simple Gifts                                 Copland
The Little Horses                            Copland
At the River                                 Copland
Ching-a-ring chaw                            Copland

>    *Canadian composer. Tom Rayner, Stage Manager

---

*A Chorus Christmas*
*Roy Thomson Hall*
*Saturday, December 18, 1999*

Toronto Children's Chorus
*Sir Christēmas*                             Derek Holman†
>    1. Proface, welcome!
>    2. Sir Christēmas

3. The Wassail
> *Solo I: Jennie Morgan*
> *Solo II: Diana Chisholm, Carla Hartenberger, Laura Hartenberger, Sarah*
> *Hicks, Laura Kishimoto, Jennie Morgan*
> *David Smith*

4. Omnes gentes plaudite

I. Here comes holly
> *Solo I: Kate Van Buskirk*
> *Solo II: Laura Kishimoto*
> *Solo III: Nellie Stockhammer*
> *Solo IV: Sarah Hicks*

II. Ivy, chief of trees
> *Soloists: Sarah Hicks, Laura Kishimoto, David Smith*

7. Nay, ivy, nay

8. Now have good day!
> *David Hetherington, Cello*
> *Susan Hoepner, Flute*
> *Beverly Johnston, Percussion*
> *Judy Loman, Harp*
> *Ruth Watson Henderson, piano*

## Toronto Children's Chorus and Alumni Choir Women

| | |
|---|---|
| From *A Gospel Christmas* | Daryl Runswick |

> The Virgin Mary had a baby boy
> Children go where I send thee
> *Russell Hartenberger, percussion*

## Toronto Children's Chorus and Alumni Choir

| | |
|---|---|
| *Shepherd's Pipe Carol* | John Rutter |

*Alumni Choir*

| | |
|---|---|
| *The Shepherd's Farewell* | Hector Berlioz |
| *In The Bleak Mid-Winter* | Harold Darke |
| *Jingle Bells* | arr. David Willcocks |

### INTERMISSION

Training Choir I

| | |
|---|---|
| *Entre le boeuf et l'âne gris* | arr. Sydney Northcote[†] |
| *Why do the bells of Christmas ring?* | Margaret Drynan |
| *The Cuckoo Carol* | Edmund Walters |

Training Choir II

| | |
|---|---|
| *Donkey Carol* | John Rutter |
| *Long Long Ago* | Mark Sirett[†] |
| *Eileh Cham'dah Libi* | arr. C. Davidson |

Training Choirs I and II
*The Sleigh*                               Richard Kountz

Carol for All
O Come, All Ye Faithful                    attributed to John Francis Wade,
                                           arr. David Willcocks
                                           (Text: Frederick Oakeley)

Training Choir III
*Can You Count the Stars?*                 Jonathan Willcocks
*The Birds*                                Eleanor Daley[†]
*Hanerot, Halalu*                          Baruch J. Cohon
                                           arr. Blanche Chass

    *Mitch Bondy, Conductor*

Carol for All                              English traditional carol
*The First Nowell*                         arr. David Willcocks

Alumni Choir
*Lo, How A Rose E'er Blooming*             Michael Praetorius
*The Twelve Days of Christmas*             arr. John Rutter

Toronto Children's Chorus, Training and Alumni Choirs
*Star Carol*                               John Rutter
*Little Drummer Boy*                       Katherine Davis
    *Russell Hartenberger, Drum*
*Away in a Manger*                         arr. Elmer Iseler[†]
*Laudate Dominum*                          Arthur Honegger
from Une Cantate de Nöel

    [†]Canadian Composer

---

*International Conductors Concert*
*April 16, 2000*
*St. James' Cathedral*

Toronto Children's Chorus & Los Angeles Children's Chorus
Wir eilen mit schwachen                    J. S. Bach
    *Debra Damron, conductor*
Simple Gifts                               Aaron Copland
    *Jan Goodall, conductor*
Come, Ye Makers of Song                    Ruth Watson Henderson*
    *Ardelle Ries, conductor*

Los Angeles Children's Chorus
To Music                                   Betty Bertaux
    *Anna Lynn Murphy, conductor*

My Heart Soars                                    Ruth Watson Henderson*
  *David Christiani, conductor*
Yo le canto todo eldia                            David Brunner
  *Catherine Glaser-Climie, conductor*
Choose Something like a Star                      Randall Thompson
  *Debra Damron, conductor*
Go Where I Send Thee                              Paul Caldwell
  *Stephen Horning, conductor*

Toronto Children's Chorus: Training Choir III
Can You Count the Stars?                          Jonathan Willcocks
  *Jan Goodall & Stephen Horning, conductors*
Winds                                             Larysa Kuzmenko
  *Catherine Glaser-Climie, conductor*

Toronto Children's Chorus: Training Choir III
Don't Ever Squeeze a Weasel                       Ruth Watson Henderson*
from *Musical Animal Tales*
  *Maria-Emma Meligopoulou, conductor*

Toronto Children's Chorus
Sir Christëmas[†]                                 Derek Holman*
  I. Proface, Welcome
    *Catherine Glaser-Climie, conductor*
  II. Sir Christëmas
    *Debra Damron, conductor*
  III. The Wassail
    *Jan Goodall, conductor*
  IV. Omnes Gentes
    *Maria Meligopoulou, conductor*
  V. Here comes Holly
    *Ardelle Ries, conductor*
  VI. Ivy, chief of trees
    *Anna Lynn Murphy, conductor*
  VII. Nay, ivy, nay
    *Stephen Horning, conductor*
  VIII. Now, have good day!
    *David Christiani, conductor*
Keewaydin                                         Harry Freedman*
  *Ardelle Ries & David Christiani, conductors*
Psalm 23                                          Srul Irving Glick*
from *Psalm Trilogy*
  *David Christiani, conductor*
The Glories of Shakespeare[†]                     Sir David Willcocks
  It was a Lover and His Lass
  Fear No More the Heat of the Sun

Full Fathom Five
Under the Greenwood Tree
Who is Silvia?
>  *Sir David Willcocks, conductor*

\*Canadian composer
†Canadian première

---

## *Awake My Heart*
## *July 24, 2000*

*Liebeslieder, Op. 52*                    Johannes Brahms (1833–1897)
>  *Lesia Mackowycz, soprano*
>  *Ruth Watson Henderson, piano*
>  *Peter MacDonald, piano*

*African Mass*                    Norman Luboff
> *Erica Huang and Christina Chabot, mezzo-sopranos*

*The Vagabond*                    ——Ralph Vaughan Williams (1872–1958)
> *Let Beauty Awake*
> *The Roadside Fire*
> *Linden Lea*
>>  *Alexander Dobson, baritone*

*Five Mystical Songs*                    Ralph Vaughan Williams
>  1. Easter
>  2. I Got Me Flowers
>  3. Love Bade Me Welcome
>  4. The Call
>  5. Antiphon
>>  *Alexander Dobson, baritone*

*All proceeds to the Ann Marie Potton Memorial Bursary Fund*

---

## *Music for a Sunday Afternoon*
## *February 21, 1999 MUC*

Training Choirs I, II & III
Simple Gifts                    trad. Shaker Song
                               arr. Derek Holman†

Four is Wonderful              Ruth Watson Henderson†
>  *Jessica Mealia, soloist*

Instrumentalists
Big Teddy, Little Teddy        Linda Niamath
>  *Jessica Leung, age 7*

| | |
|---|---|
| Ecossaise | Anon. |
| *Sabina Sabaratnam, age 8* | |
| Marche | J. S. Bach |
| *Maxine Byam, age 7* | |
| The Wild Horseman | Robert Schumann |
| *Denise Wong, age 7* | |

Training Choir I

| | |
|---|---|
| The Monkeys & The Crocodile | Udo Kasemets† |
| The Window | trad. Korean folksong |

*Nyree Grimes, Lyndon Kirkley, Adam Koves,*
*Jonathan Mamalyga, Julianne Morin,*
*Magdalena Price and Sabina Sabaratnam, soloists*

| | |
|---|---|
| Vive La Canadienne | trad. French Cdn. |
| *Andria Bulfon, conductor* | *arr. Hugh McLean†* |

*Gillian Adams, Alice Atell, Alexandra Belcastro,*
*Frances Dorenbaum, Adam Koves, Patrick McWilliams,*
*Sasha Mitchell and Raeanne Moore, dancers*

Instrumentalists

| | |
|---|---|
| Mist | Clifford Poole† |
| *Charlotte Bondy, age 8* | |
| Two Grenadiers | Robert Schumann |
| *Bryan Allen, age 8* | |
| Mournful Birds | N. Rudnev |
| *Natasha Luckhardt, age 9* | |
| Humoresque | Antonín Dvořák |
| *Reiko Obokata, age 10* | |

Training Choir II

| | |
|---|---|
| A Pirate Song | William Smith |
| Handsome Butcher | trad. Hungarian, arr. Matyas Seiber |
| The Kelligrew's Soirée | John Burke, arr. Hugh McLean† |

*Bryan Allen, Henry Chen, Julia Nestler, Ronald Ng, Jessica Reznek,*
*Michael Saunders, Faryn Stern and Jacqueline Tsekouras, dancers*

Instrumentalists

| | |
|---|---|
| Sonatina in F major, Op. 36, No. 4 | Muzio Clementi |
| *Eugenie Leung, age 10* | |
| Minuet in D minor | J. S. Bach |
| *Anna Betka, age 8* | |

Training Choir III

| | |
|---|---|
| La Petite Hirondelle | arr. Healey Willan† |
| I Will Make You Brooches | Winifred Bury |
| Little David Play on Your Harp | African-American spiritual |
| | arr. Harry T. Burleigh |

INTERMISSION

Training Choirs I, II & III
North American Premiere of the Cantata
Cornucopia                                    Ronald Corp
    1. Seasonal Songs
       Whether the weather *(anon.)*
       Cows (*James Reeves*)
       The Irish pig 'Twas an evening in November' *(anon.)*
       Winter morning (*Ogden Nash*)
    2. Sadder Songs
       The paint box (*E. V. Rieu*)
       Weep no more sad fountains *(anon.)*
       Lone dog (*Irene McLeod*)
       Sensitive, Seldom and Sad (*Mervyn Peake*)
    3. Sillier Songs
       The ship of Rio (*de la Mare*)
       The modern Hiawatha 'When he killed the Mudjokivis' *(anon.)*
       I've had this shirt (*Michael Rosen*)
       Granny (*Spike Milligan*)
      *Tom Rayner, Stage Manager*
      *Andria Bulfon / Sue Cousland, Training Choir I Assistants*
      *Erica Huang, Training Choir II Assistant*

   [†]Canadian composer

*Chorissima*
*March 5, 1999 MUC*
*March 7, 1999 LPCC*

Toronto Children's Chorus: Chamber Choir
I'se the B'y                                  John Govedas[†]
Keewaydin                                     Harry Freedman[†]
J'entends le moulin                           Donald Patriquin[†]

San Francisco Girls Chorus: Chorissima
Hosanna                                       David Conte
Aglepta                                       Arne Mellnäs
Varázsének                                    József Karai
Let Evening Come                              Brian Holmes
Counting (from *Dreams*)                      Herbert Bielawa

Amabile Youth Singers
Salve Regina                                  Ramona Luengen[†]
In Remembrance                                Eleanor Daley[†]
Ave Maria                                     D. MacIntyre

INTERMISSION

San Francisco Girls Chorus: *Chorissima*
From *Suita de Lorca*                    Einojuhani Rautavaara
  El Grito
  Malagueña
Hoj, hura, hoj (from *Lasské helekacky*)    Otmar Mácha

San Francisco Girls Chorus: Chorissima
Three Meditations                    Peter Schickele
  Mary Queen of Scots, on Her Execution
  The City of Our God
  Most Glorious Lord of Life
Teddy Bear's Picnic                    John W. Bratton
                                         arr. Dwight Okamura

Amabile Youth Singers
Queen Jane                    Stephen Hatfield[†]
The Three Kings               Healey Willan[†]
Las Amarillas                 Stephen Hatfield[†]

Toronto Children's Chorus, San Francisco
Girls Chorus and the Amabile Youth Singers
Ave Maria                     Gustav Holst
A Song of St. Francis         Michael Hurd
Choose Something Like a Star  Randall Thompson
Sing — Sea to Sea             arr. Howard Cable[†]

     [†]Canadian composer

---

*Sing!*
*April 24, 1999*
*April 25, 1999*
*Eastminster United Church*

Combined Choirs
World Music Suite                    Donald Patriquin[†‡]
  1. Cabbage Tree Hat (Australia)
  2. Taivas on sininen ja valkoinen (Finland)
  3. The Stuttering Lovers (Great Britain)
  4. Ach! Synku Synku (Czech Republic)
  5. Deep River (U.S.A.)
  6. I Went to the Market (Canada)
    *David Hetherington, cello (Sunday)*
    *Joaquin Valdepeñas, clarinet (Sunday)*
    *Joan Watson, French horn (Sunday)*

Toronto Children's Chorus
Agnus Dei (from *Mass in C*)          W. A. Mozart
Go Down, Moses                        arr. Mark Hayes

The Alabama Boychoir
O Let the Merry Bells Ring            G. F. Handel
Laus Deo                              John Leavitt
Alabama Jubilee                       George L. Cobb
Stars Fell on Alabama                 arr. Steve Sample
Little David, Play on Your Harp       arr. Robert Harris

Central Children's Choir of Ottawa-Carleton
Evolutions (World Première)           Nancy Telfer[†○]
   Seascape
   Landscape
   Dreams of Space

---

INTERMISSION

TCC Training Choir III (Saturday)
Skye Boat Song                        arr. Evelyn Sharpe
Sweet and Low                         W. H. Anderson[†]
Three Hungarian Folk Songs            arr. Matyas Seiber
   The Handsome Butcher
   Apple, Apple
   The Old Woman

TCC Training Choir I (Sunday)
Some Day                              David Ouchterlony[†]
   *Andria Bulfon, Apprentice Assistant—conductor*
Dragons                               Clifford Crawley[†]
The Teddy Bears' Picnic               John W. Bratton

TCC Training Choir II (Sunday)
All Through the Night (Welsh)         arr. Hugh J. McLean
   *Erica Huang, Apprentice Assistant—conductor*
Eileh Cham'dah Libi (Chassidic)       arr. Charles Davidson
Moon at the Ruined Castle (Japanese)  R. Taki, arr. Audrey Snyder

Prague Philharmonic Children's Choir
Ave Maria                             T. L. di Vittoria
Salve Regina                          Josef Mysliveček
Gaude flore virginali                 Jiří Ropek
Studánka (The Well)                   Ilja Hurník
V neček (Floral Wreath)               Zdeněk Lukáš
Lašská helekačka (Shepherd's Song)    Otmar Mácha
Excerpts from *Moravian Duets*        Antonín Dvořák

Combined Choirs
Freedom Trilogy                          Paul Halley[†]

[†] Canadian Composer
[‡] Commissioned by the TCC in honour of its 20th Anniversary Season
[°] Commissioned for the 40th Anniversary of the Central Children's Choir
  *Jamie McLean, Stage Manager*

# Criteria for Choosing Repertoire Appropriate for Children

Clearly, one of the most important and time-consuming jobs that a conductor of children's choirs must do is choose appropriate repertoire. With worthy repertoire, your choir has the potential of reaching great artistic heights. With poor or modest repertoire, those heights will never be realized. Children's choir repertoire must always have aesthetic value. Zoltan Kodàly said, "Children should be taught with only the most musically valuable material. For the young, only the best is good enough. They should be led to masterpieces by means of masterpieces" (*Selected Writings*). A worthwhile piece will always help the child grow musically and help to develop the beauty of the child's voice. Ideally, it will benefit other areas of growth as well—aesthetic, social, historical, educational, and political.

## Text

Always begin by studying the text. It is the text alone that distinguishes choral music from instrumental music. Children's choir directors must develop an understanding and an appreciation of great poetry.

- The text must be worth learning.
- The text should have aesthetic value.
- As great composers derive their musical ideas and inspiration from the text, the text a composer chooses quite often determines the value of the piece.
- A worthwhile text sings before the notes are written. This is probably why countless composers have set the Psalms and Shakespeare's poetry to music. Consider these examples:

## Psalm 47

> O clap your hands, all ye people;
> shout unto God with the voice of triumph.
> For the Lord most high is terrible;
> he is a great King over all the earth.
> God is gone up with a shout, the Lord with the sound of a trumpet.
> Sing praises to God, sing praises;
> sing praises unto our King.
> For God is the King of all the earth; sing ye praises with understanding.

## Twelfth Night, Act I, Scene I

> If music be the food of love, play on;
> Give me excess of it, that, surfeiting,
> The appetite may sicken, and so die.
> That strain again! it had a dying fall;
> O, it came o'er my ears like the sweet sound
> That breathes upon a bank of violets,
> Stealing and giving odour!

## King Henry VIII, Act 3, Scene 1

> Orpheus with his lute made trees,
> And the mountain tops that freeze,
> Bow themselves, when he did sing:
> To his music plants and flow'rs
> Ever sprung; as sun and show'rs
> There had made a lasting spring.
> Ev'ry thing that heard him play,
> Ev'n the billows of the sea,
> Hung their heads, and then lay by.
> In sweet music is such art,
> Killing care and grief of heart
> Fall asleep, or hearing, die.

## Vocal Line and Interest

Choral music needs notes that a singer should be able to "get into" his or her voice. How has the composer married the text to the main melodic lines? Does the text now sing? Is this vocal writing or instrumental writing? Would the melodic line be more effective played on an instrument? (Not all great composers of instrumental music write equally well for the voice.)

Is the composer sensitive to the needs of the singer and the development of the child's voice? Are the high notes on open vowels? Are there places to breathe logically? Do the contour of the melodic line and the climax of a phrase reflect the poetic line?

## Rhythm, Harmony, Counterpoint, Voice-Leading

The music director who is searching for worthwhile literature must study these components carefully: How is musical interest created? Are the musical ideas original? Is it gimmicky? Could anyone have written this in a harmony class or is there a great creative spark somewhere here? Does the harmony reflect and color the words? Is the climax of a phrase congruent with the harmonic or contrapuntal language? Is the voice-leading awkward or logical? Does the rhythm help create interest and convey the meaning of the text?

## Keys and Modulations

Keys have their own character and flavor. Different keys suit different moods and styles. What key is the piece in? Conductors of children's choirs should try to avoid pieces in the keys of C major (too low) and F major (difficult to sing in tune.) Does the key suit the nature of the piece? Are modulations set up carefully, tastefully, and logically?

## Shape/Structure/Proportion/Form

Do the shape and structure of the piece make musical sense? Has the ending evolved from what has gone on before, or is it just "tacked on"? Does continued analysis of the piece reveal more and more musical treasures? (If you can understand everything at first glance, there likely is not much there.)

## Accompaniment

If there is a piano accompaniment, does it merely double the vocal line or does it have different musical ideas that create more interest? It is much more beneficial to children if the piano accompaniment does not double the vocal line. Even very young children need to sing independently of the piano. If the accompaniment features some instruments or even an orchestra, how has the composer solved the problems of balance? The composer needs to consider many things here, such as the number of players, the types of instruments and the range in which they play, which should not be the same range as that of the children. The composer also needs to consider color, timbre, texture, and the instrumental interludes, which can be well contrasted to the sections that accompany the choir.

## Other Important Considerations

Will the piece last or will the children be tired and bored with it by the fourth rehearsal or its second performance? Make sure the edition of a standard work is based on historical accuracy and scholarly research. Compare different editions of the same work. Ask trusted colleagues for their opinion. With experience, the conductor will find that some publishers are extremely reliable and almost everything they put out in print is worth singing. Commissioning is important. For a detailed discussion on commissioning new works, please see chapter 11.

## The Composer

Has this composer made a lasting substantial contribution to choral literature? Do the finest choirs in the world sing the composer's music? (Always be on the lookout for new talent. Do be wary even of well-known composers. Judge for yourself.)

Composers often write for a specific chorus or event. Alice Parker once told me that composing to her is like cooking a meal—there is no way she is going to cook a meal and then look around to see if someone wants to eat it.

## Age Range of Children/Suitable Repertoire

Repertoire for children can be child-centered without being childish. The music should never talk down to the children. Conductors must not select music with the main criterion being that the children like it! Parents would not dream of giving their children nothing but candy and chips to eat all day but insist that they eat fruits and vegetables. Why do some conductors give their choirs the equivalent of junk food? Surely one of the most important aspects of our job is to develop taste and a passion for great music. Once the members of your choir are "hooked," they will never look back. Candy and chips are fine occasionally, but they certainly do not constitute a healthy diet.

Great musical literature is often not "liked" on first hearing. It will take time to develop discriminating taste in your young singers. Having said that, I fully realize that teaching a class of Grade 8 students in a deprived area who may never have sung anything before poses seemingly insurmountable problems. Great motivational strategies, delivered by a highly skilled teacher, will make the difference between success and failure. A balanced diet is crucial here. Beginning in September with Vaughan Williams's "Orpheus with His Lute" likely won't do it, but "Oh, Happy Day" might. NEVER, NEVER, NEVER sell children short or believe that there are ceilings. NEVER, NEVER, NEVER underestimate the power of great music.

### Six-, Seven-, and Eight-Year-Olds

The key and range for this age group are important. E-flat major is the best key. The range should be from D to F, a tenth. The children can develop this range if they are taught to sing on the breath with a ringing head-tone quality. Don't accept, "Oh, we can't sing that high." They can! My favorite composers for children this age include: Peter Jenkyns, Burton Kurth, Eric Thiman, W. H. Anderson, Edmund Walters, Thomas Dunhill, Hugh Roberton, and Alec Rowley. Suitable repertoire can be found in chapter 1. The following seasonal pieces have always worked well for me with this age group.

### *Christmas*

| | | |
|---|---|---|
| Gloria in Excelsis | Robert B. Anderson | Leslie 2056 |
| The Birth-Night | W H Anderson | Leslie 1008 |

| | | |
|---|---|---|
| Wie schon leuchtet der | J S Bach ed. Rao | Boosey & Hawkes OCTB6418 |
| Mary and Joseph | Keith Bissell | GVT/Warner/Chappell G-244 |
| On Christmas Morn | | |
| Child of Bethlehem | William Bush | Leslie 1152 |
| Joulupuu On Rakennettu | Finn Carol arr. Collins | Boosey & Hawkes — |
| | | 051-46981-9 |
| Heaven Bell-A-Ring | Mary Goetze | Boosey & Hawkes OCTB6185 |
| The Piglets' Christmas | arr. Mary Goetze | Boosey & Hawkes OCUB6402 |
| Little Bull | arr. A H Green | OUP U124 |
| Lullaby for the Christ Child | Ruth Watson | GVT/Warner/Chappell G-162 |
| Candlelight, Burning Bright | Helen Kemp | Choristers Guild CGA919 |
| Haida | Leck/Gerber | Plymouth HL516 |
| The Gentle Donkey | David Ouchterlony | Frederick Harris HC1014 |
| Gloria, Gloria, Gloria Deo | David Ouchterlony | Frederick Harris FH1012 |
| The Donkey Carol | W H Parry | OUP U-118 |
| Wake, O Shepherds | Rameau ed. Nelson | Augsburg T1 300 |
| Tydlidom | Czech carol arr John Rutter | OUP ISBN 0 19 330665 4 |
| (from Carols for Schools) | | |
| Carol of Peace | Eric Thiman | Boosey & Hawkes OCTB6621 |
| Dance, Little Goatling | Edmund Walters | Boosey & Hawkes OCTB6142 |
| The Cuckoo Carol | Edmund Walters | Boosey & Hawkes OCTB5721 |
| Three Christmas Bird Songs | Edmund Walters | Boosey & Hawkes 20494 |
| The First Christmas Night | Ashley Winning and | GVT/Warner/Chappell VA1005 |
| I Like Christmas | Meredith Winning | |

## Seasonal Hebrew Music

| | | |
|---|---|---|
| The Chanukah Story | arr. Samuel Adler | OUP 95.501 |
| S'Vivon | arr. Betty Bertaux | Boosey & Hawkes OCTB6193 |
| Mi Chamocha | Jonathan Dinkin | Boosey & Hawkes — |
| | | 051047213-0 |
| Hanerot Halalu | Cohona rr. Chass | Mark Foster MF877 |
| Candle Lullaby | Srul Irving Glick | GVT/Warner/Chappell VG-254 |
| (from Music for Chanukah) | | |
| Al Shlosha D'Varim | Allan E. Naplan | Boosey & Hawkes OCTB6783 |
| Hine Ma Tov | Allan E. Naplan | Boosey & Hawkes OCTB6782 |
| Shalom Yerushalayim | Laura Shur | Lawson-Gould 52652 |

## Nine-, Ten-, and Eleven-Year-Olds

Do not choose repertoire for this age group because it has a catchy tune or funky rhythm or just because the text is about being good to your dog or cleaning up the environment. At this age children should begin to sing and appreciate the works of the masters: Bach's "Jesu, Joy of Man's Desiring" and "Bist du bei mir," Brahms's "Lullaby," Britten's "Friday Afternoons," and pieces by Schubert and Mozart. They should sing many a cappella rounds such as "Dona Nobis Pacem," and they should be singing in two parts as well as unison.

## Twelve- to Fifteen-Year-Olds

If the children have been trained well since the age of six, the sky is the limit here. They are bound only by two octaves and a bit, from low G to high B flat. They can sing in three and four parts. There should be great variety, and their repertoire should contain a cappella music and a substantial amount of contemporary music written by composers from their own country. They should explore the vast array of multicultural music now available; much of it is very good.

## My Thoughts about Musicals

I have no problem with children's choirs occasionally singing a good arrangement of good tunes from musicals such as *The Sound of Music* and *Oliver.* I strongly object, however, when soloists and choirs belt out "Tomorrow" in a chest voice without any skills in vocal production. How many of us have auditioned children with raspy, broken speaking voices, only to be told, "I had the lead in *Annie* last week and we did fourteen performances"? We are not, I believe, in the entertainment business. We are trying to teach children aesthetics.

Children's choir directors must be fastidious with their selection of repertoire. You will do a great disservice to your choir if you give them music that inhibits their musical growth or undermines their musical integrity. It is what you buy and what you perform that dictate what most composers will write. Make sure you are buying music that is worthy of the children's musical development. (For a list of repertoire suitable for unison and two-part songs listed by school grade and for boys' choirs, please see appendix 9.)

# Repertoire Lists for Toronto Children's Chorus

## 2000–2001 Music Repertoire

### Red file folder

| | | | |
|---|---|---|---|
| 1. Adams, Lydia (arr.) | Micma'q Honour Song | Canon | McGroarty MMP-08 |
| 2. Barron, John | An Amabile Grace | SSAA | Manuscript |
| 3. Bart, Lionel | Oliver [Choral Selections] | SSA | Hollis S9008 |
| 4. Bertaux, Betty (arr.) | To Music | SSA | Boosey & Hawkes M-051-46373-2 |
| 5. Boulanger, Lili | Les Sirènes | SSA | Treble Clef TC-115 |
| 6. Britten, Benjamin | The Missa Brevis in D | SSA | Boosey & Hawkes M-060-01470-3 |
| 7. Byrd, William, arr. Bartle | Non Nobis, Domine | SSA | Hinshaw HMC1161 |
| 8. Caccini, Francesca | Aure volanti | SSA | Broude Bros. MW1 |
| 9. Caldwell, Paul, and Ivory, Sean | Go Where I Send Thee | SSATB | earthsongs |
| 10. Carter, John | Will You Walk a Little Faster? | SA | Belwin-Mills FEC10138 |
| 11. Chaminade, Cécile | Ronde du Crépuscule | SSAA | Treble Clef TC-166 |

### Blue file folder

| | | | |
|---|---|---|---|
| 12. Chan Ka Nin | Carla's Poems | SSAA | Manuscript |
| 13. Coulthard, Jean | Three Philosophical Songs | SA | Hinshaw HMC1259 |
| 14. Daley, Eleanor | And God Shall Wipe Away All Tears | Unison | Hinshaw HMC1284 |
| 15. Daley, Eleanor | Ave Verum Corpus | SSAA | Alliance AMP 0137 |
| 16. Daley, Eleanor | Os Justi | SSAA | Alliance AMP 0018 |
| 17. Dubinsky, Leon, arr. Lydia Adams | We Rise Again | SSAA | GVT VA-2005 |
| 18. Duruflé, Maurice | Tota Pulchra Es | SSA | Durand 13901 |

### Green file folder

| | | | |
|---|---|---|---|
| 19. Fauré, Gabriel, arr. Bartle | Cantique de Jean Racine | SSA | Hinshaw HMC1730 |
| 20. Freedman, Harry | Keewaydin | SSA | GVT/Warner/Chappell VG-334 |

| | | | |
|---|---|---|---|
| 21. Glick, Srul Irving | The Hour Has Come | SATB | GVT VEI-1105 |
| 22. Glick, Srul Irving | Psalm 23 | SA | earthsongs |
| 23. Govedas, John (arr.) | I'se the B'y | SA | GVT/Warner/Chappell VG-267 |
| 24. Halley, Paul | Freedom Trilogy | SSA | Pelagos |
| 25. Halley, Paul | Song for Canada | Unison | E. Henry David 392-02512 |
| 27. Hawkins/Sirvatka | I'm Goin' Up a Yonder | SSAA | Boosey & Hawkes M051-46451-7 |
| 28. Hayes, Mark (arr.) | Go Down, Moses | SSA | Hinshaw HMC1302 |
| 29. Henderson, Ruth Watson | Adventures in Color | SSAA | Canadian Music Centre |
| 30. Henderson, Ruth Watson | Come, Ye Makers of Song | SSA | GVT VG-363 |
| 31. Henderson, Ruth Watson | Popcorn | SSA | GVT VG-338 |
| 32. Henderson, Ruth Watson | Sing Ye Praises | SATB | GVT VG-464 |

## Orange file folder

| | | | |
|---|---|---|---|
| 34. Holman, Derek | Little Birthday Mass | SSA | Boosey & Hawkes M051-32430-9 |
| 35. Holman, Derek | Sir Christēmas | SSA | Novello 07-0517 |
| 36. Holman, Derek | A Song to David | SATB | Manuscript |
| 37. Holst, Gustav | Ave Maria | SSSSAAAA | E. C. Schirmer 1.3121 |
| 38. Hurd, Michael | A Song of St. Francis | SSA | Novello 29 0560 04 |
| 39. Hyokki, Matti | On Suuri Sun Rantas Autius | SSA | Fazer FM 06571-4 |
| 40. Larsen, Libby | Eine kleine Snailmusik | SSA | OUP |
| 41. Larsen, Libby | Today, This Spring | SSAA | OUP ISBN 1-19-386040-6 |
| 42. McTell, Ralph | Streets of London | SSA | Essex S9020 |

## Yellow file folder

| | | | |
|---|---|---|---|
| 43. Naplan, Allan | Al Shlosha D'Varim | SA | Boosey & Hawkes M051-46783-9 |
| 44. Parker, Alice | How Can I Keep from Singing? | SSAA | Hinshaw HMC1749 |
| 45. Parker, Alice | A Play on Numbers | SA | E. C. Schirmer ECS 2817 |
| 46. Patriquin, Donald (arr.) | J'entends le Moulin | SA | earthsongs |

| | | | |
|---|---|---|---|
| 47. Peterson, Oscar | Hymn to Freedom | SSA | Walton WW 1135 |
| 48. Poelinitz, Josephine (arr.) | City Called Heaven | SATB | Plymouth HL-105 |
| 49. Purcell, Henry | Sound the Trumpet | SA | Novello 16 0017 06 |
| 50. Rachmaninoff, S. | *Six Choruses, Opus 15 | SA | E. C. Schirmer ECS 5183 |
| 51. Raminsh, Imant | Songs of the Lights: | | |
| Raminsh, Imant | Song of the Stars | SA | Boosey & Hawkes M051-46270-4 |
| Raminsh, Imant | The Sower | SSA | Boosey & Hawkes M051-46271-1 |
| Raminsh, Imant | The Sun Is a Luminous Shield | SSA | Boosey & Hawkes M051-46272-8 |
| Raminsh, Imant | Daybreak Song | SSA | Boosey & Hawkes M051-46273-5 |

## Beige file folder

| | | | |
|---|---|---|---|
| 52. Rautavaara, Einojuhani | "Suite" de Lorca | SSAA | Fazer FM 06946-8 |
| 53. Rautavaara, Einojuhani | For the Beauty of the Earth | SAHinshaw | HMC469 |
| 54. Sallinen, Aulis | Songs from the Sea: Sea Prayer Shipshape Sea Danger Ballad | SSAA | Novello 007 0463 |
| 55. Sallinen, Aulis | Suita Grammaticale | SSA | Fazer FM 05328-0 |
| 56. Smyth, Ethel | The March of the Women | SSA | Treble Clef TC-101 |
| 57. Somers, Harry | Gloria | SATB | GVT VEI-1030 |
| 58. Tallis, Thomas, arr. Brown | Glory to Thee, My God, This Night | Canon | OUP 40.922 |
| 59. Telfer, Nancy | Missa Brevis | SSA | Lenel LSC 105 |
| 60. Telfer, Nancy | The Swallow | SSAA | Neil A. Kjos Ed.8735 |
| 61. Thompson, Randall | Pueri Hebraeorum | SSA/SSA | E. C. Schirmer ECS 492 |
| 62. Von Bingen, Hildegard | O frondens virga | SA | Treble Clef TC-144 |
| 63. Wessman, Harri | Water under Snow Is Weary | SSAA | Fazer FM 06888-2 |

## Pink file folder

TCC warm-ups and skills
Folk songs for sight-
    singing
Loose sheets

## 1999–2000 Music Repertoire

### Red file folder

| | | | |
|---|---|---|---|
| 1. Adams, Lydia (arr.) | Micma'q Honour Song | Canon | McGroarty MMP-08 |
| 2. Bach, J. S. arr. Stuart Calvert | Bist du bei mir | Unison | GVT VG-183 |
| 3. Bach, J. S. | Wir eilen mit Schwachen | SA | E. C. Schirmer 2506 |
| 4. Barron, John | An Amabile Grace | SSAA | Manuscript |
| 5. Bartle (arr.) | Hand Me Down My Silver Trumpet | SA | Hinshaw HMC1535 |
| 6. Bernstein, Leonard | Canon in Five Parts | Canon | Boosey & Hawkes M051-46345-9 |
| Bernstein, Leonard | Gloria Tibi | SA | Boosey & Hawkes M051-46344-2 |
| 7. Bruckner, Anton | Ave Maria | SATB | |
| 8. Byrd, William, arr. Bartle | Non Nobis, Domine | SSA | Hinshaw HMC1161 |
| 9. Chan Ka Nin | Carla's Poems | SSAA | Manuscript |

### Blue file folder

| | | | |
|---|---|---|---|
| 10. Copland, Aaron (arr.) | At the River | SSA | Boosey & Hawkes M051-45512-6 |
| 11. Copland, Aaron (arr.) | Ching-A-Ring Chaw | Unison | Boosey & Hawkes M051-46609-2 |
| 12. Copland, Aaron (arr.) | I Bought Me a Cat | SSA | Boosey & Hawkes M051-45338-2 |
| 13. Copland, Aaron (arr.) | The Little Horses | SSA | Boosey & Hawkes M051-45509-6 |
| 14. Copland, Aaron (arr.) | Simple Gifts | SA | Boosey & Hawkes M051-41903-6 |
| 15. Daley, Eleanor | Prayer of St. Francis | SATB | Manuscript |
| 16. Davis, Katherine | Little Drummer Boy | SSA | Belwin-Mills 60379 |
| 17. Dubinsky, Leon, arr. Lydia Adams | We Rise Again | SSAA | GVT VA-2005 |
| 18. Duruflé, Maurice | Tota Pulchra Es | SSA | Durand 13901 |
| 19. Fauré, Gabriel, arr. Bartle | Cantique de Jean Racine | SSA | Hinshaw HMC1730 |
| 20. Fauré, Gabriel | Messe Basse | SSA | Novello 03 0136 01 |
| 21. Freedman, Harry | Keewaydin | SSA | GVT/Warner/Chappell VG-334 |

## Green file folder

| | | | |
|---|---|---|---|
| 22. Gibbons, Orlando | Hosanna to the Son of David | SATB | OUP 152 |
| 23. Glick, Srul Irving | Psalm Trilogy | | |
| Glick, Srul Irving | Psalm 92 | SA | earthsongs |
| Glick, Srul Irving | Psalm 47 | SSA | earthsongs |
| Glick, Srul Irving | Psalm 23 | SA | earthsongs |
| 24. Govedas, John (arr.) | I'se the B'y | SA | GVT/Warner/Chappell VG-267 |
| 25. Greer, John | *The Beginning of the World | SA | Manuscript |
| 26. Halley, Paul | Freedom Trilogy | SSA | Pelagos |
| 27. Halley, Paul | Song for Canada | Unison | E. Henry David 392-02512 |
| 28. Hardyk, Joel | *I Never Saw Another Butterfly | SSA | G. Schirmer ED.3242 |
| 29. Hatfield, Stephen | Nukapianguaq | SSAA | Boosey & Hawkes M051-46700-6 |
| 30. Hayes, Mark (arr.) | Go Down, Moses | SSA | Hinshaw HMC1302 |
| 31. Henderson, Ruth Watson | Bless the Lord, O My Soul | Unison | Hinshaw HMC1171 |
| 32. Henderson, Ruth Watson | Come, Ye Makers of Song | SSA | GVT/Warner/Chappell VG-363 |
| 33. Holman, Derek | The Invisible Reality | SATB/ Unison | Manuscript |
| 34. Holman, Derek | Sir Christēmas | SSA | Novello 07-0517 |
| 35. Holst, Gustav | Ave Maria | SSSSAAAA | E. C. Schirmer 1.3121 |
| 36. Honegger, Arthur | Laudate Dominum | SATB | Editions Salabert |
| 37. Hurd, Michael | A Song of St. Francis | SSA | Novello 29 0560 04 |

## Orange file folder

| | | | |
|---|---|---|---|
| 38. Mendelssohn, Felix | Lift Thine Eyes | SSA | E. C. Schirmer 1017 |
| 39. Mozart, W. A. | Laudate Dominum | SSA | OUP ISBN 0-19-342590-4 |
| 40. Mozart, W. A. | Agnus Dei, K. 317, from Mass in C | Unison | Neil A. Kjos Ed. 9836 |
| 41. Naplan, Allan | Al Shlosha D'Varim | SA | Boosey & Hawkes M051-46783-9 |
| 42. Patriquin, Donald (arr.) | J'entends le Moulin | SS | earthsongs |
| 43. Patriquin, Donald (arr.) | 3. Ah! Si mon moine voulait danser! | SSAA | earthsongs |

| Patriquin, Donald (arr.) | 5. Morning Star | SSAA | earthsongs |
|---|---|---|---|
| Patriquin, Donald (arr.) | 6. Savory, Sage, Rosemary and Thyme | SSAA | earthsongs |
| 44. Patriquin, Donald (arr.) | *World Music Suite | SSA | earthsongs |
| 45. Poelinitz, Josephine (arr.) | City Called Heaven | SATB | Plymouth HL-105 |
| 46. Poulenc, Francis | Petites Voix | SSA | Editions Salabert ESA 16124(1) |
| 47. Raminsh, Imant | Songs of the Lights: | | |
| Raminsh, Imant | Song of the Stars | SA | Boosey & Hawkes M051-46270-4 |
| Raminsh, Imant | The Sower | SSA | Boosey & Hawkes M051-46271-1 |
| Raminsh, Imant | The Sun Is a Luminous Shield | SSA | Boosey & Hawkes M051-46272-8 |
| Raminsh, Imant | Daybreak Song | SSA | Boosey & Hawkes M051-46273-5 |

## Yellow file folder

| 48. Rutter, John | A Clare Benediction | SSA | Hinshaw HMC1634 |
|---|---|---|---|
| 49. Tallis, Thomas, arr. Brown | Glory to Thee, My God, This Night | Canon | OUP 40.922 |
| 50. Tindley, Charles, arr. B. Baker | The Storm Is Passing Over | SSA | Boosey & Hawkes M051-46841-6 |
| 51. Tyson, L. Craig, and L. Scott | Feel Good | SSA | Boosey & Hawkes M051-46711-2 |
| 52. Willan, Healey | Gloria Deo | SATB | |
| 53. Willcocks, David | The Glories of Shakespeare | | |
| Willcocks, David | It Was a Lover and His Lass | SSA | OUP ISBN 0-19-324637-4 |
| Willcocks, David | Fear No More the Heat of the Sun | SSA | OUP ISBN 0-19-342638-2 |
| Willcocks, David | Full Fathom Five | SSSAAA | OUP ISBN 0-19-342639-0 |
| Willcocks, David | Under the Greenwood Tree | SSA | OUP ISBN 0-19-342636-6 |
| Willcocks, David | Who Is Silvia? | SSA | OUP ISBN 0-19-342606-4 |

## Beige file folder

| 54. Telfer, Nancy | Successful Sight Singing | | Neil A. Kjos Ed. V77S |
| 55. Willcocks, David | Carols for Choirs 4 | SSAA | OUP ISBN 0-19-353573-4 |

## Pink file folder

Loose sheets

# Senior Choir Repertoire List—1995–1996 Season

## Red file folder

| 1. Archer, Violet | Christmas | SSA | GVT/Warner/E.I. 1014 |
| 2. Armstrong, Kathy | Songs from Gahu | Unison | Boosey & Hawkes OCTB6826 |
| 3. Bart, Katie Moran | Blessing | SSA | Curtis/Kjos C8425 |
| 4. Britten, Benjamin | A Ceremony of Carols | SSA | Boosey & Hawkes 16832 |
| 5. Britten, Benjamin | Old Abram Brown (from *Friday Afternoons*) | SSAA | Boosey & Hawkes OCTB1787 |
| 6. Byrd, William, arr. Bartle | Non Nobis, Domine | SSA | Hinshaw HMC1161 |
| 7. Campbell, Norman, arr. Cable, Howard | Anne of Green Gables | SSA | GVT VG-346 |
| 8. Cable, Howard, (arr.) | D'où viens-tu, bergère? | SSA | Hinshaw HMC1188 |
| 9. Cable, Howard, (arr.) | The Huron Carol | SA | GVT VG-253 |
| 10. Cable, Howard, (arr.) | Nöel Nouvelet (Sing a new Noel) | SSA | Hinshaw HMC1289 |

## Blue file folder

| 11. Caplet, A. | Sanctus (from *Messe à trois voix*) | SSA | Durand S.A. D&F9922 |
| 12. Chen, N., arr. D. Rao | Dodi Li | SA | Boosey & Hawkes OCTB6679 |
| 13. Chilcott, Bob | Mid-Winter | SA | OUP T121 |
| 14. Copland, Aaron (arr.) | At the River | SSA | Boosey & Hawkes M051-4 5517-6 |
| 15. Copland, Aaron (arr.) | Ching-a-Ring Chaw | Unison | Boosey & Hawkes M051-46609-2 |
| 16. Copland, Aaron (arr.) | I Bought Me a Cat | SSA | Boosey & Hawkes M051-45338-2 |

| | | | |
|---|---|---|---|
| 17. Daley, Eleanor | Sweet Was the Song the Virgin Sang | Unison | Hinshaw HMC1461 |
| 18. Daley, Eleanor | The Blooming Bright Star of Belle Isle | SSAA | GVT/Warner/Chappell VG-257 |
| 19. Dawson, William | Ev'ry Time I Feel the Spirit | SSAA | Tuskegee/Kjos T126 |
| 20. Duruflé, Maurice | Tota Pulchra Es | SSA | Durand S.A. 13901 |
| 21. Easthope, Martin | Come to the Fair | SA | Enoch & Sons 6138 |
| 22. Evans, Robert | Pie Jesu | Unison | GVT/Warner/Chappell VG-1010 |
| 23. Fauré, Gabriel | Messe Basse | SA/SSA | Novello NOV03013601 |
| 24. Fauré, Gabriel | Pie Jesu | Unison | Boosey & Hawkes OCTB6631 |
| 25. Franck, arr. Cable | Panis Angelicus | SSA | Hinshaw HMC1378 |
| 26. Freedman, Harry | Keewaydin | SSA | GVT VG-334 |
| 27. Glick, Srul Irving | Moments in Time: | | |
| | Laughter | SSAA | GVT/Warner/Chappell VG-247 |
| | Clouds | SA | GVT/Warner/Chappell VG-248 |
| | Orders | SSAA | GVT/Warner/Chappell VG-249 |
| | A Spider Danced a Cosy Jig | SSAA | GVT/Warner/Chappell VG-250 |
| | Time | SSAA | GVT/Warner/Chappell VG-251 |
| 28. Handel, arr. Bartle | Art Thou Troubled? | Unison | Hinshaw HMC1431 |
| 29. Hatfield, Stephen | African Celebration | SSAA | Boosey & Hawkes OCTB6706 |
| 30. Hawkins, arr. Sirvatka | I'm Goin' Up a Yonder | SSAA | Boosey & Hawkes M051-46451-7 |
| 31. Hayes, M. (arr.) | He's Got the Whole World | SA | Hinshaw HMC1390 |
| 32. Henderson, Ruth Watson | Promptement levez-vous | SSA | GVT/Warner/Chappell VG-342 |
| 33. Henderson, Ruth Watson | The Old Woman and Her Cat | SA | GVT VG-265 |
| 34. Henderson, Ruth Watson | The Robin | Unison | GVT/Warner/Chappell VG-187 |
| 35. Hirsh, Nurit, ed. Leck | Bashana Haba-a | SA | Posthorn Press C1019 |

## Orange file folder

| | | | |
|---|---|---|---|
| 36. Holst, Gustav | Choral Hymns from the Rig-Veda | SSAA | Galaxy 1.5091 |

| | | | |
|---|---|---|---|
| 37. Hugh, Robert | Kenya Melodies | SSA | Boosey & Hawkes OCTB6751 |
| 38. Humperdinck, E. | Evening Prayer | SA | Leslie Music 2003 |
| 39. Kesselman, L. | Mbiri kuna Mwari | SA | Boosey & Hawkes OCTB6792 |
| 40. Gerber, T. (piano accompaniment) Leck, H. (arr.) | Haida | Round | Plymouth HL-516 |
| 41. Leck, H. (arr.) | South African Suite | SSA/SSAA | Plymouth HL-200 |
| 42. MacGillivray, arr. Calvert | Away from the Roll of the Sea | SSA | GVT/Warner/Chappell VG-340 |
| 43. MacGillivray, arr. Calvert | Song for the Mira | SSA | GVT/Warner/Chappell VG-326 |
| 44. Mahler, Gustav | Cuckoo, Nightingale & Donkey | SA | OUP 82.075 |
| 45. Mecham, K. | Barter | SA | Schirmer HL50482303 |
| 46. Mendelssohn, F. | Laudate Pueri | SSA | E. C. Schirmer 1839 |
| 47. Mendelssohn, F. | Lift Thine Eyes (from *Elijah*) | SSA | E. C. Schirmer 1017 |
| 48. Monteverdi, C. | Surgens Jesu (from *Anthems for Choirs* 3) | SSA | OUP |
| 49. Mozart, arr. Cable | Overture to *The Marriage of Figaro* | SSA | Hinshaw HMC1328 |
| 50. Naplan, Allan | Hine Ma Tov | SA | Boosey & Hawkes OCTB6782 |
| 51. Patriquin, D. (arr.) | Five Songs of Early Canada The Wreck of the Steamship Ethie Ah! Si mon moine voulait danser! The False Young Man Morning Star Savory, Sage, Rosemary and Thyme | SSAA | earthsongs |
| 52. Peterson, Oscar | Hymn to Freedom | SSA | Walton WW 1135 |
| 53. Pinkham, D. | Angels are Everywhere | SSA | E. C. Schirmer 4235 |
| 54. Poston, E. | Jesus Christ, the Apple Tree | Unison | E. C. Schirmer 141 |
| 55. Poulenc, F. | Petites Voix | SSA | Editions Salabert ESA 16124(I) |
| 56. Purcell, Henry | Sound the Trumpet | SA | Novello 16 0017 06 |
| 57. Quilter, R. | An Old Carol | Unison | Boosey & Hawkes OCTB6622 |
| 58. Raminsh, I. | Ave Verum Corpus | SSAA | GVT VG-255 |

## Beige file folder

| | | | |
|---|---|---|---|
| 59. Rao, D., arr. | Hashivenu | Round | Boosey & Hawkes OCTB6430 |
| 60. Rutter, John | All Things Bright and Beautiful | SA | Hinshaw HMC663 |
| 61. Rutter, John | For the Beauty of the Earth | SA | Hinshaw HMC469 |
| 62. Rutter, John | The Lord Bless You and Keep You | SA | Hinshaw HMC1169 |
| 63. Sallinen, Aulis | Suita Grammaticale | SSA | Fazer FM 05328-0 |
| 64. Tallis, arr. Brown | Glory to Thee, My God, This Night (Tallis Canon) | SSAA | OUP 40.922 |
| 65. Taylor-Howell, S. (arr.) | I'm Goin' Home on a Cloud | SSAA | Boosey & Hawkes OCTB6389 |
| 66. Telfer, Nancy, arr. Powris | The Blue Eye of God | SSAA | earthsongs |
| 67. Thompson, Randall | Choose Something like a Star | SSAA | E. C. Schirmer 2588 |
| 68. Tippett, Michael | Crown of the Year | SSA | Schott T977 |
| 69. Togni, Peter | When the Dawn Appears | SSA | GVT VG-349 |
| 70. Trant, Brian (arr.) | Steal Away | SSA | OUP/London W46 |
| 71. Vaughan Williams, R. | God Bless the Master (from *Folk Songs of the Four Seasons*) | Unison | OUP ISBN 0-19 3437945 |
| 72. Willcocks, David | Carols for Choirs 4 | | OUP ISBN 0-19- 353573-4 |

## Pink file folder

| | | | |
|---|---|---|---|
| 73. Telfer, Nancy, or Malin, Don | Successful Sight Singing | | Neil Kjos V77S |
| | Songs of the Late Renaissance | | Belwin-Mills SB1027 |
| 74. Warm-up exercises and loose sheets | | | |

# Senior Choir Repertoire List—1994–1995 Season

## Red file folder

| | | | |
|---|---|---|---|
| 1. Bach, J. S., arr. Stuart Calvert | Bist du bei mir | Unison | GVT VG-183 |
| 2. Bach, J. S. | Gloria the World Rejoices | Unison | GVT VG-195 |

| | | | |
|---|---|---|---|
| 3. Bach, J. S. | Schafe Können | Unison | OUP OCS 1631 |
| 4. Bissell, Keith | Mary and Joseph | SA | GVT/Warner/Chappell 9-244 |
| 5. Britten, Benjamin | A Boy Was Born | Unison | OUP 145 |
| 6. Britten, Benjamin | A Ceremony of Carols | SSA | Boosey & Hawkes 16832 |
| 7. Buhr, Glenn | Season of Spring Days | manuscript | |
| 8. Byrd, William, arr. Bartle | Non Nobis, Domine | SSA | Hinshaw HMC1161 |
| 9. Cable, Howard (arr.) | D'où viens-tu, bergère? | SSA | Hinshaw HMC1188 |
| 10. Cable, Howard (arr.) | The Huron Carol | SA | GVT VG-253 |

## Blue file folder

| | | | |
|---|---|---|---|
| 11. Chen, N./Rao, D. | Dodi Li | SA | Boosey & Hawkes OCTB6679 |
| 12. Chilcott, Bob | Farewell! Advent (from Two Carols) | SSA | OUP W117 |
| 13. Chilcott, Bob | Hey! Now (from Two Carols) | SSA | OUP W117 |
| 14. Chilcott, Bob | Mid-Winter | SA | OUP T121 |
| 15. Copland, Aaron (arr.) | At the River | SSA | Boosey & Hawkes M051-45512-6 |
| 16. Copland, Aaron (arr.) | Ching-a-Ring Chaw | Unison | Boosey & Hawkes M051-46609-2 |
| 17. Copland, Aaron (arr.) | I Bought Me a Cat | SSA | Boosey & Hawkes M051-45338-2 |
| 18. Cornelius, arr. R. W. Henderson | Three Kings | SSA & Tenor/ Baritone Solo | GVT/Warner/Chappell VG-359 |
| 19. Fauré, Gabriel | Messe Basse | SSA | Novello 03 0136 01 |
| 20. Freedman, Harry | Keewaydin | SSA | GVT VG-334 |
| 21. Freedman, Harry | Simple Simon | SSA | GVT VG-330 |
| 22. Galuppi, Baldassare | Dixit Dominus | SSAA | Roger Dean PC CMC108 |
| 23. Glick, Srul Irving | Moments in Time: | SA/SSA | |
| | A Spider Danced a Cosy Jig | | GVT /Warner/Chappell VG-250 |
| | Laughter | | GVT/Warner/Chappell VG-247 |
| | Clouds | | GVT/Warner/Chappell VG-248 |

## Green file folder

| 24. Hayes, Mark (arr.) | He's Got the Whole World | SA | Hinshaw |
|---|---|---|---|
| 25. Hayes, Mark (arr.) | This Train Is Bound for Glory | SSA | Hinshaw HMC1301 |
| 26. Henderson, Ruth Watson | Barnyard Carols: | Unison/SA | |
| | The Robin | | GVT VG-187 |
| | The Lamb | | GVT VG-188 |
| | The Duck | | GVT VG-189 |
| | The Barn Owl | | GVT VG-190 |
| 27. Henderson, Ruth Watson | Creation's Praise | SSA/SSAA | GVT VG-241 |
| 28. Henderson, Ruth Watson | The Last Straw | SA/Tenor Solo | GVT VG-347 |
| 29. Henderson, R. W. | Promptement levez-vous | SSA | GVT 342 |
| 30. Henderson, Ruth Watson | The Travelling Musicians | SSA | Cdn Music Centre |
| 31. Hirsh, Nurit, ed. Leck | Bashana Haba-a | SA | Posthorn Press C1019 |
| 32. Holman, Derek (arr.) | Christmas Triptych: Song of the Crib Wexford Carol The Garden of Jesus | SSA/Tenor | Hinshaw HMC1224 |
| 33. Holst, Gustav | Choral Hymns from the Rig-Veda | SSAA | Galaxy 1.5091 |
| 34. Humperdinck, E. | Evening Prayer | SA | Leslie Music 2003 |

## Orange file folder

| 35. Iseler, Elmer (arr.) | Away in a Manager | SATB | GVT/Warner/Chappell |
|---|---|---|---|
| 36. Kodàly, Zoltan | Evening Song | SSA | Boosey & Hawkes OCTB5771 |
| 37. Leck, Henry (arr.)/Gerber | Haida | Round | Plymouth HL-516 |
| 38. Leontovich/ Wilhousky | Carol of the Bells | SSA | Carl Fischer CM5276 |
| 39. Leslie, arr. Calvert | Cape Breton Lullaby | SSA | GVT/Warner/Chappell VG-327 |
| 40. MacGillivray, arr. Calvert | Away from the Roll of the Sea | SSA | GVT/Warner/Chappell VG-340 |
| 41. Mahler, Gustav | The Cuckoo, the Nightingale and the Donkey | SA | OUP 82.075 |

| | | | |
|---|---|---|---|
| 42. Mechem, Kirke | Barter | SA | G. Schirmer |
| 43. Mendelssohn, Felix | Laudate Pueri | SSA | E. C. Schirmer 1839 |
| 44. Mendelssohn, Felix | Lift Thine Eyes | SSA | E. C. Schirmer 1017 |
| 45. Page, Nick (arr.) | Niska Banja | SSAA | Boosey & Hawkes OCTB6517 |
| 46. Pedersen, Laura | Golden Carol | SA | Manuscript |
| 47. Pergolesi | Stabat Mater (excerpts) | SA | Hinshaw HMB209 |
| 48. Peterson, Oscar | Hymn to Freedom | SSA | Walton WW 1135 |

## Yellow file folder

| | | | |
|---|---|---|---|
| 49. Pinkham, Daniel | Angels Are Everywhere | SSA | E. C. Schirmer 4235 |
| 50. Poston, Elizabeth | Jesus Christ the Apple Tree | Unison/SA | E. C. Schirmer 141 |
| 51. Purcell, Henry, arr. Lang | Sound the Trumpet | SA | Novello 16 0017 06 |
| 52. Raminsh, Imant | Ave Verum Corpus | SSAA | GVT VG-255 |
| 53. Raminsh, Imant | Cantate Domino | SSAA | Hinshaw HMC1401 |
| 54. Rao, Doreen (arr.) | Hashivenu | Round | Boosey & Hawkes OCTB6430 |
| 55. Rao, Doreen (arr.) | Siyahamba | SSA | Boosey & Hawkes OCTB6656 |
| 56. Ridout, Godfrey (arr.) | Ah! Si mon moine | Unison | GVT VG-182 |
| 57. Rorem, Ned | What Is Pink? | SSA | Boosey & Hawkes LCB252 |
| 58. Rutter, John | Candlelight Carol | SSAA | Hinshaw HMC894 |
| 59. Rutter, John | Jesus Child | Unison | OUP U156 |

## Beige file folder

| | | | |
|---|---|---|---|
| 60. Rutter, John | Shepherd's Pipe Carol | Unison | OUP U133 |
| 61. Sallinen, Aulis | Suita Grammaticale | SSA | Fazer F.M. 05328-0 |
| 62. Telfer, Nancy | Blue Eye of God | SSAA | earthsongs |
| 63. Telfer, Nancy | Carol | Unison/SA | Waterloo OWAT 122 |
| 64. Thompson, Randall | Choose Something like a Star | SSAA | E. C. Schirmer 2588 |
| 65. Vaughan Williams, Ralph (arr.) | Folk Songs of the Four Seasons To the Ploughboy An Acre of Land John Barleycorn | SSA | OUP ISBN 0-19-339086 |
| 66. Willcocks, David (arr.) | Carols for Choirs 4 | | OUP ISBN 0-19-353573-4 |

## Pink file folders

| | | |
|---|---|---|
| 67. Telfer, Nancy, or Malin, Don | Successful Sight Singing | Neil A. Kjos Ed. V77S |
| | Songs of the Late Renaissance (for Independent sight-singing group only) | Belwin-Mills B1027 |
| Various warm-up exercises and loose sheets | | |

# Concepts to Be Learned by the End of Training Choir I, Training Choir II, and Training Choir III

The purpose of the Training Choirs in a community children's chorus is to prepare the choristers for the Main Choir. In rehearsal and in performance, however, the children will not only develop skills necessary to sing and to read music well but also have many opportunities to sing for the sheer joy of it.

At the end of Training Choir I, children should:

- know how to find their seats and organize their music before a rehearsal
- know how to work their tape recorders effectively
- know eight unison songs by memory and be able to sing them in tune on the breath, with projection appropriate for their age
- know the first four sequentials and be able to sing a descending E-flat major scale in tune, using hand signs
- know how to walk onto risers
- have had four concert performance opportunities
- have completed *Keyboard Theory, Preparatory Book A,* by Grace Vandendool
- know how to read in tonic solfa using "doh," "me," "soh," and "lah" in simple time, using quarter and eighth notes
- know how to write out "Twinkle, Twinkle, Little Star" by memory in C major, sing it in tonic-solfa syllables, and sing-count it
- know how to write out "Baa, Baa, Black Sheep" by memory in F major, sing it in tonic solfa, and sing-count it
- know exercises 1–20 in *The Folk Song Sight Singing Series,* book 1

At the end of Training Choir II, children should:

- know twelve more songs by memory, including rounds and simple two-part songs, and be able to project their voices on the breath with energy and vitality
- know the first four sequentials sung in canon and natural, harmonic, and melodic minor scales
- know "The Interval Song"
- know all major key signatures up to four flats and four sharps and how to sing "doh," "me," and "soh" in each, using hand signs
- have had at least four concert performance opportunities and workshop experiences
- know how to sing count in simple time
- have completed *Keyboard Theory, Preparatory Book B,* by Grace Vandendool
- know all exercises in *The Folk Song Sight Singing Series,* book 1

- know how to write out "Frère Jacques" by memory in G major, sing it in tonic solfa, and sing-count it
- know how to sing-count in simple time
- know how to work well in a one-hour rehearsal, and hand in homework assignments on time, and effectively review pieces being studied on their tape recorders at home

At the end of Training Choir III, children should:

- know fifteen more songs by memory, many of which are in two parts, and have an understanding of breath support and placement that enables them to project the voice with ease and confidence
- know how to sing a harmony part with ease
- know all sequentials, minor scales, "The Interval Song," and "The Advanced Interval Song"
- know all major and minor key signatures and know how to sing "doh," "me," and "soh" in major keys and "lah," "doh," and "me" in minor keys, using hand signs
- have had many concert performance opportunities and workshops and traveled on an overnight trip with the choir
- have completed *Keyboard Theory, Preparatory Book C,* by Grace Vandendool
- have completed the exercises in *The Folk Song Sight Singing Series,* books 1 and 2
- know how to write out several easy songs, such as "The Farmer in the Dell" in F major and F minor, by memory, sing them in tonic-solfa syllables, and sing-count them
- know how to sing-count in simple and compound time
- know how to work well in a seventy-five-minute rehearsal

The children likely will need to be taught many of these nursery rhymes and tape them at rehearsal. The children should sing them together as a group from the chalkboard in both tonic solfa and sing-counting. For the first homework exercise the conductor should write out on staff paper the key and time signature and the first two measures of the nursery rhyme for them. Have the children then sing what they have written at the next rehearsal. Mark the papers to see how each child is progressing. To be successful in writing out on the staff the notes and rhythms of the nursery rhyme, each child needs to be able to sing it by memory in tonic-solfa syllables. Each Training Choir rehearsal must be organized creatively and carefully so each minute is used wisely, with a multifaceted purpose.

# *Memos for the First Four Rehearsals*

The following memos are given to the Toronto Children's Chorus Training Choirs at their first four rehearsals at the beginning of the season. The reader may find them useful since they contain important information that is most helpful in establishing routine and standards.

---

MEMO:    TCI #1
TO:        TRAINING CHOIR I
FROM:   MRS. BARTLE
DATE:    September 11, 2000
Happy Birthday!    to Alice S. who turned 9 on September 8th
                     to Gabriella J. who turns 7 on September 14th and
                     to Claire B. who turns 8 on September 14th

1. Welcome to Training Choir I!!!

   Welcome to Training Choir I. This is a memo. Mrs. Bartle will read it with you. Take it to your seat. When you get home ask your parents to read it, sign it, and put it safely in a duo-tang, or three-ring binder, in your music bag. The MEMOS are very important and will help you stay organised.

   Our helpers today are:

   1. Jennifer K., who was a member of the TCC from 1989–1992; she graduated in May with a Bachelor of Music degree from Queen's University and now works in our office.
   2. Mrs. H., who has taught Primary School for many years and helped with TCI last year.
   3. Lauren S., a recent graduate of the TCC who is beginning Grade OAC at the Etobicoke School of the Arts and who helped with TCI last year.

   Other people you should know:

   Lynda C. is the Parent Coordinator for TCI.

   Beth A. works in the office and will be helping TCI from time to time.

2. Seating

   Please find your seat. It will have your name on it. Today I will explain how the seating plan works and next week you will receive your own copy. Next week the seating plan will be different. When you arrive at a rehearsal you will need to cross your name off the Seating Plan located at the Sign-In Desk; then we will know if anyone is absent. Parents, please sit at the back in the chairs provided.

3. Welcome to Visitors

   We would like to welcome the following observers to our rehearsal tonight . . .

   | | |
   |---|---|
   | Maureen C.: Brown P.S., Toronto | Renata K.: Kingsley Primary, Toronto |
   | Nancy M.: Cherokee P.S., North York | Rachel S.: Brookhaven P.S., North York |
   | Sandra C.: Cherokee P.S., North York | Ella K.: Mississauga Private |

Danielle S.: Sterling Hall School, Toronto      Maureen H.: Mississauga
Ray S.: Winchester P.S., Scarborough

4. Music

Today you have received 2 three-ring binders, a red one and a blue one. You have also received an orange scale sheet. Parents, after today's rehearsal, please put the orange scale sheet in your child's blue duo-tang folder at the front.

RED FILE FOLDER

|   |   |   |
|---|---|---|
| 1. | *Away in a Manger* | Elmer Iseler (arr.) |
| 2. | *The First Nowell* | English traditional |
| 3. | *Gloria in Excelsis* | Robert B. Anderson |
| 4. | *Haida* | Henry H. Leck (arr.) |
| 5. | *Laudate Dominum* | Arthur Honegger |
| 6. | *Little Drummer Boy* | Katherine Davis (arr.) |
| 7. | *O Come, All Ye Faithful* | J. F. Wade arr. David Willcocks |
| 8. | *O Hanukkah* | Hebrew trad. |
| 9. | *Rocking* | Czech Carol |
| 10. | *The Sleigh* | Richard Kountz |
| 11. | *Star Carol* | John Rutter |

BLUE FILE FOLDER

|   |   |   |
|---|---|---|
| 1. | *All Things Bright and Beautiful* | John Rutter |
| 2. | *Autumn Tints* | Norman Gilbert |
| 3. | *Dogs and Cats* | Susan Jones |
| 4. | *The Grasshopper* | Stuart Young |
| 5. | *Horace Was a Hippo* | Arthur Baynon |
| 6. | *Rip Van Winkle* | John Bryan |

**Please put your new Songbooks and new Theory books into your blue music bag. Parents, please make sure that you child's name is on the FRONT of the Songbook. Please look after the bag!!! Please do not leave it on the ground, pull on the handle or hold it by the name tag. (This will cause the name tag to break.)

5. Homework (Depending on what we get done today). For next week please:

   1. Memorize the first verse of *All Things Bright and Beautiful* (blue binder).
   2. Memorize *Elephants* (page 29 of the Brown Introductory Songbook).
   3. Practice with your tape recorders every day for fifteen minutes. Working with the tape recorder takes a lot of practice. Please do the best you can.
   4. Do exercises in your Theory Book on pages 20 and 21. Next week, please leave your theory book open in the pile on the sign-in desk. There will be people there to mark your theory homework. Your books will be returned to you during your theory lesson next week. Please make sure your name and seat # is on the FRONT of your book in large black letters. (You will have a new seat number next week. That's the number you need to write on your book.)

6. Photos

The following children did not submit photos at their auditions. Please see my chart. The following choristers should bring three passport size photos with them next week: Alysha H., Claire B., Aanika G., Jackie Z., Hannah T., Vivian C., Alisa U.,

Matthew D., Victoria S., Sandile M., Robert B., Perin W., Kaitlyn B., Shwayta S. Thank you to all those who did submit photos. This will help me to learn your child's name much faster.

7. Training Choir Handbooks
   Please read the handbooks carefully. The chorister/parent agreement form should be handed in at the sign-in desk if not today, then next week at the latest.

8. Parental Observation
   I think it is essential that parents observe their child in a learning situation, so they can see how well their child is progressing, and assist at home. It is important that the following rules be adhered to . . .

   1. Please stay in your seat and do not talk to each other after the rehearsal has started. It is very distracting.
   2. Unfortunately, we cannot accommodate either younger siblings who run around the rehearsal room or crying babies.
   3. If you see your child struggling in the chorus, please do not assist. Talk to your child at home afterwards.
   4. Please make sure your child's tape recorder is in working order before the rehearsal begins. Check the batteries each week. Please have 2 extra tapes in the bag and extra batteries.

9. Uniforms
   We will begin to fit the TCC t-shirts next Monday during rehearsal. Please bring $12.00 in an envelope with child's name on the front marked "Uniforms." Choristers who already have a t-shirt do not need to be fitted for a new one. Please note TCC t-shirts are part of the Training Choir Uniform and should only be worn at concerts.

10. Rehearsal/Concert Assistants
    A meeting will be held for all parents who volunteered to be rehearsal/concert assistants on Monday, September 25th, during the rehearsal. This is an important meeting at which time we will review your role and responsibilities. The Parent Co-ordinator and TCC staff will attend the meeting.

11. Chorister Lists
    Next week we will issue an updated choir list to each chorister.

Reminders . . .

    1) Please call Mrs. Bartle at home if your child is ill and will miss a rehearsal.

    2) Please place this memo in a three-ring binder in your child's bag for next week.

Parent's signature: _____ Date: _____

Please print name: _____

---

MEMO:    TCI #2
TO:       TRAINING CHOIR I
FROM:    MRS. BARTLE
DATE:    September 18, 2000

1. Homework for September 25th
   i) Memorize *The Grasshopper*
   ii) Review *Elephants* (page 29—brown book)

   iii) Practise with your tape recorders
        *Horace Was a Hippo*
        *Autumn Tints*
        *All Things Bright and Beautiful*
2. Absences
   Please Note: (Chorister Handbook—page 4, second last paragraph)
   "Choristers who have been absent should *phone the parent co-ordinator to get any
   instructions from announcements or memos.* Whenever possible, the parent should
   arrange for someone to record the rehearsal (or borrow another child's tape) and
   make sure the chorister listens to the tape before the next rehearsal."
3. Theory Books
   Please open your theory book and put it on Lauren's desk. (The card table next to
   the piano.) Mrs. H. will help here. (Parents too, please!) Mrs. C. will have extra
   black markers on hand at the Sign-in Desk so you can put your child's new seat #
   and full name on the *front* of the theory book. (This makes handing it out at the end
   of rehearsal much easier.)
4. Heights
   Sandile, and Hannah, please get your heights measured tonight. See Mrs. H.
5. Parents Signature Check
   Mrs. H. and Jennifer will be checking your binders during the rehearsal tonight to
   make sure your parents signed Memo #1.
6. Welcome Visitors
   Today we welcome the following observers to our rehearsal.
   Maureen C.; Brown P.S.                    Sarah T.; Steelesview P.S.
   Maureen H.; Toronto Catholic District     Ray S.; Winchester P.S.
      School Board                           Danielle S.; Sterling Hall School
   Ella K.; Mississauga Private School        Renata Z.; Kingsley Primary
   Marion R.; Russell D. Barber P.S.
7. Tape Recorders
   It is essential that your child's name is on his/her tape recorder!!! Please tape tonight's
   rehearsal with a new tape and next week you will be able to tape over last week's
   rehearsal. We will rotate the tapes every two weeks.
8. New Seating Plan
   Tonight you have received a new seating plan which is organized by height. Please
   remember that Row A is closest to me and Row D is the farthest away from me. The
   smallest numbers are closest to the stage. Always begin counting from the stage side.
   For the next two weeks your names will be on the seats. Please try your best to remember your seat number and know how to find it. If you can't remember, please
   look on the seating plan.
9. Readers
   For our October 22$^{nd}$ concert I would like some of you to read a poem about either
   Autumn *or* Animals. If you have one at home that you'd like to read, please bring it
   and read it for me after next week's rehearsal. If you want to read one, and don't
   have one, I'll have one for you.

10. Uniform Reminder

Choristers are being fitted for their uniforms tonight. Please make sure that you hand in your $12 at the Sign-in Desk tonight!

11. Ticket Reminder

Just a reminder to parents that the early subscription deadline of September 30th is quickly approaching. In order to receive the discount on early subscription tickets all orders must be received by midnight on September 30th. Any orders received after that date will be charged full price. If you have already ordered tickets, they will be sent out towards the end of September. As the new season has just started, the office has been busy with preparations for the beginning of rehearsals. If you have any concerns regarding your orders, please call Jennifer at ext. 111. Also, please note that the Autumn 'n' Animals concert on October 22nd is already 50% sold out. If you wish to purchase tickets for this concert and have not already done so, please submit your order form or call Jennifer at ext. 111.

12. Singing Before Rehearsal

If you arrive in plenty of time for rehearsal and have i) signed in ii) handed in your theory book iii) put your blue TCC bag by the right side leg of your chair, please bring to the piano one of the songs we're working on, so you can sing it by yourself for me, and I can hear how you are progressing. This can start at 4:25. (If you'd prefer to sing with a friend, rather than alone, that's OK too.)

13. Rehearsal/Concert Assistants Meeting

A reminder that next Monday, September 25th, a meeting will be held for all parents who have volunteered as Rehearsal/Concert Assistants during rehearsal. The meeting will be held in rooms 1 & 2 in the basement.

Reminder . . .

Please call Mrs. Bartle at home if your child is ill and will miss a rehearsal.

Parent's signature: _____ Date: _____

Please print name: _____

---

MEMO:    TCI #3

TO:        TRAINING CHOIR I

FROM:    MRS. BARTLE

DATE:    September 25, 2000

Happy Birthday!    to Scarlet L. who turns 7 on September 28th,

to Andrew G. who turns 10 on September 29th and

to Perin W. who turns 8 on October 1st!

1. Before the Rehearsal Begins

Even though the rehearsal officially starts at 4:45, it is important for everyone to try and get here at least ten minutes beforehand so that we are prepared to start on time. I would also like to hear children sing individually each week, on a very informal basis to see how they are doing. So, after you have:

• Handed in your theory books to be marked.

• Signed in and picked up your memos.

• Organized your music.

Come over to the piano with one of your own Songbooks. Even though I may not ask you to sing a song from your songbook, I will record it on the inside cover. You may sing any of the five songs you are preparing for this October 22nd concert.

2. Homework for October 2nd:

   1. Memorize *Horace Was a Hippo*
   2. Memorize *Autumn Tints*
   3. Memorize *All Things Bright and Beautiful*
   4. Practice *Elephants* (page 29—brown book) and *The Grasshopper*

3. Theory

   Page 9, #9, a, b, c, and page 10.

   No theory was assigned on last week's memo.

4. Today at 5:45–6:00

   I will hear any children read their poems about Autumn or Animals.

5. Could the following families contact the office *before* September 30th please! Speak to Heather W. at ext. 113:

   Adrienne and Ivanna B.

6. Welcome Visitors

   Today we welcome the following observers to our rehearsal:

   | | |
   |---|---|
   | Sandra C.; Cherokee Public School | Donna M.; Steelesview P.S. |
   | Maureen C.; Brown P.S. | Ray S.; Winchester P.S. |
   | Gini G.; Whitney P.S. | Danielle S.; Sterling Hall School |
   | Maureen H.; Toronto Catholic District School Board | Renata Z.; Kingsley Primary |
   | Ella K.; Mississauga Private School | |

7. Parent Chorister Agreements

   Thank you to everyone who handed in his or her Parent/Chorister Agreement on time! There were a couple received that had illegible signatures. Please tell the rehearsal assistants if your name is on the list below but you are SURE that you handed in your form. The following is a list of all Choristers who have not handed in their Parent Chorister Agreements:

   | | | | |
   |---|---|---|---|
   | Adrienne B. | Gabriella J. | Sandile M. | Molly G. |
   | Ivanna B. | Jennifer L. | Deryn J. | Hayley G. |
   | Sarah G. | Amita M. | Fiona W. | |

   Please hand your forms in at the Sign-in Desk tonight!

8. Memos

   PLEASE read and SIGN the memo each week. Lauren will have seating plans today to check the memos. Thank you for doing your best.

   At the Parents meeting on June 16, I stressed the importance of parents helping their children. In the past, this assistance has contributed considerably to the success the child has in the chorus. This is particularly true for the first few years as routines are beginning to be established.

   It only takes a few minutes each week to:

   • Read the memo.

- Make sure the tape recorder is working and there are extra tapes and batteries in the bag.
- See that all homework—music and theory—has been done.
- See that your Choristers have all their STUFF each week. (Music books, Tape recorder, Memos in a duo-tang)

Thank you!!!

9. POINSETTIA CAMPAIGN LAUNCH—October 2, 2000

The Poinsettia Campaign meeting next week is a MANDATORY meeting for ALL TCI parents to launch the 2000 Poinsettia Campaign. The meeting will be held on October 2nd at 5:00, downstairs in Rooms 1 & 2. If this meeting is absolutely impossible for you to attend (i.e., both parents are out of town), please let the office know by fax (932-8669) or email (singtcc@interlog.com) immediately!

10. Toronto Children's Chorus Holiday CD Card

A Message from David C., Board Member of the TCC . . .

"The Board of Directors is currently offering to the business community an opportunity to send TCC Holiday CD greetings cards to their special clients. The Company's name and seasonal greetings will be customized. Orders of up to 500 will cost $10.00 per card; or just $6.50 per card for a 1000 unit order."

If you think your company might be interested in this special opportunity, further information can be obtained by calling our General Manager, Heather W. (932-8666, ext. 113).

Reminder . . .

Please call Mrs. Bartle at home if your child is ill and will miss a rehearsal.

Parent's signature: _____ Date: _____

Please print name: _____

---

MEMO:     TCI #4
TO:           TRAINING CHOIR I
FROM:     MRS. BARTLE
DATE:      October 2, 2000

Happy Birthday!     to Ping F. who turns 8 on October 8th,
                              to Ellen S. who turns 8 on October 10th,
                              to Nicole Z. who turns 8 on October 11th,
                              to Mackenzie S. who turns 10 on October 14th,
                              to Tesha B. who turns 9 on October 15th and
                              to Hannah T. who turns 10 on October 15th!

1. Programme for the October 22nd Concert

Please find enclosed the programme for the October 22nd concert. Thank you to *all* children who auditioned for poems and solos. Don't be discouraged if you were not selected this time!

a) If the *author* is missing from your poem, please fax it to Beth A. (932-8669).

b) If you brought your own poem, please make me a copy for the October 16th rehearsal.

c) If you are reading a poem, or an introduction, please try to memorize it for October 16th.

d) If I chose a poem for you, please come and get your copy from me today, before you leave.

e) Those reading poems need to come at the following times on October 16th so I can hear them.

4:30–4:40 and 5:45–5:55

TCI

| Olivia W. | *Autumn Fires* | |
| Molly G. | *My Mother Doesn't Want a Dog* | |
| Alana C. | *My Lizard* | |
| *Elephants* | Clifford Crawley | |
| Alice S. | *The Giraffe's Breakfast* | Ilo Orleans |
| Victoria S. | *My Cat, Mrs. Lick-a-Chin* | John Ciardi |
| Robert B. | *Point of View* | David McCord |
| *The Grasshopper* | Stuart Young | |

TC II

TC III

TC I, II and III

| *Autumn Tints* | Norman Gilbert |
| *All Things Bright and Beautiful* | John Rutter |

2. Homework for October 16th
   1. Memorize all 5 songs for the October 22nd concert. Practice regularly with your tape recorders.
   2. Theory—page 13, page 15, page 17 and page 19.
3. Happy Thanksgiving!
   No rehearsal next Monday, October 9th!
4. Calling any or all clarinet players!
   If there are any parents who play the clarinet, and would like to accompany a piece the TCIII is singing, please call Mr. Bondy.

Reminder . . .

Please call Mrs. Bartle at home if your child is ill and will miss a rehearsal.

Parent's signature: _____ Date: _____

Please print name: _____

---

MEMO:    TCI #4 OFFICE
TO:        TRAINING CHOIR I
FROM:    HEATHER W.
DATE:     October 2, 2000

1. New Memo Format
   Starting tonight, we are implementing a new format for memos. The first memo, in yellow, will include all of the music-related items for the choristers from Mrs. Bartle.

The second memo will be in orange and will cover all of the business items from Heather W. in the office. It is very important that parents sign both memos so that we can be sure that everyone has read all of the information.

2. POINSETTIA CAMPAIGN LAUNCH MEETING TONIGHT!

Parents, today you have received in your folder the annual Poinsettia Fundraising Package. Please bring this with you to the mandatory Poinsettia Campaign Meeting to be held in rooms 1 & 2 in the basement at 4:45 today! (Note: Poinsettia Campaign Packages are distributed to the oldest sibling from each family. If you did not receive your package tonight, you will receive it at your other child's rehearsal.)

The annual Poinsettia Campaign is a crucial source of revenue for the operations of and world-class training provided by the Toronto Children's Chorus. Your participation in this well respected Toronto-area fundraiser not only helps to raise funds for the TCC, but directly enhances the resources that are available to your children, such as bursaries, new music and performance opportunities. Your cooperation and attendance at this important meeting would be appreciated.

3. Parent/Chorister Agreements

Thank you to everyone who handed in his or her Parent/Chorister Agreement on time! There were a couple received that had illegible signatures. Please tell the rehearsal assistants if your name is on the list below but you are SURE that you handed in your form. Parents—It is very important that you read the handbook with your child and hand in the agreement! Please hand your forms in at the Sign-in Desk tonight!

4. Thank you!

Thank you to all of the people who helped out in September!

| Rehearsal Assistants: | Lynda C. | Lynn G. | |
|---|---|---|---|
| | Sari G. | John C. | |
| | Lisa B. | Svetlana Z. | |
| | Sylva K. | | |
| Theory Marker: | Dorothy L. | | |
| Uniform Fittings: | Beth F. | Haley F. | Elodie M. |

Reminder . . .

Please call Mrs. Bartle at home if your child is ill and will miss a rehearsal.

Parent's signature: _____ Date: _____

Please print name: _____

---

MEMO:    TCC #1

TO:       TORONTO CHILDREN'S CHORUS

FROM:   MRS. BARTLE

DATE:    September 12, 2000

Welcome Back !!!

I hope you had a great week at school! Please read your memo all the way through *before* you socialize. Then organize your music for tonight's rehearsal from the list on the blackboard.

We would like to wish Happy Birthday to:

September 12—Ashley T. (14)

September 14—Alexandra P. (12) & Aleha A. (15)

September 17—Sandra S. (13)

1. Reminder

   There is no rehearsal this Friday, September 15, 2000.

2. Homework for Tuesday, September 19th

   i) Section leaders are to see me regarding homework before the rehearsal begins.

   ii) On manuscript paper write out all of the notes to *Happy Birthday* in Bb major (from your head, not the piano). Put the tonic-solfa syllables underneath. Put your *full name* and chorister number at the top. Please leave it ON MY MUSIC STAND on September 19th, before the rehearsal begins.

   iii) Memorize *Let the Bright Seraphim*

   iv) Depending on how much we cover tonight, please work on the following with your tape recorders (20 minutes a day, minimum). Apprentices Trainers, please work with your Apprentices.

      i. Yellow—*Sound the Trumpet*

      ii. Red—*Missa Brevis*—*Sanctus and Benedictus*

      iii. Beige—*Songs from the Sea*—#2 & #3

      iv. Yellow—Rachmaninoff—page 14—*The Pine Tree*

      v. Beige—*Water Under Snow Is Weary*

      vi. Orange—*George Gershwin Medley*

      vii. Yellow—*Hymn to Freedom*

      viii. Beige—*Glory to Thee, My God*

      *Chamber*

      1. Yellow—*Ivan at the Coffin of Anastasia* (Prokofiev)

3. Washrooms

   Please use the washrooms in the basement only, not the office hall. Please use washrooms before the rehearsal begins and at break.

4. Break times

   The break will be staggered. 7:15–7:45 for Cantare and 7:30–7:45 for Chamber. When others are rehearsing please be quiet! You are not to run around the church. Rehearsal assistants, please help to supervise.

5. Appearance at Rehearsals

   No bare midriffs, hats or bare feet please.

6. Parent Chorister Handbooks

   Please read the handbooks carefully. The chorister/parent agreement form should be handed in at the sign-in desk, if not today then next week at the latest.

7. Welcome to Visitors

   We would like to welcome the following observers to our rehearsal tonight . . .

   Ella K.; Mississauga Private          Marion R.; Russell D. Barber P.S.

   Jillian D.; Glenview Sr. P.S.          Lisa G.; Kent Sr. School

   Vanessa C.; Glenview Sr. P.S.

8. New Music Tonight

Here is the list of music you will receive tonight. Please check *very* carefully to see that you have everything. If you are missing a piece, you must call the librarian as soon as possible. This music *must* go in the coloured folders for next week's rehearsal. Please stay organized! Please refile all of your camp music into your coloured file folders before the next rehearsal.

RED FILE FOLDER

| | |
|---|---|
| Adams, Lydia (arr.) | *Micma'q Honour Song* |
| Bartle, Jean Ashworth (arr.) | *Hand Me Down My Silver Trumpet* |

BLUE FILE FOLDER

| | |
|---|---|
| Coghlan, Michael | *Nou is the Time of Christmas* |
| Daley, Eleanor | *And God Shall Wipe Away All Tears* |
| | *Each Child* |
| Davis, Katherine | *Little Drummer Boy* |
| Dedrick, Chris | *The Angel Choir and the Trumpeter* |
| | *Sweet Songs of Christmas* |
| Dubinsky, Leon/Adams, Lydia | *We Rise Again* |
| Duruflé, Maurice | *Tota Pulchra Es* |

GREEN FILE FOLDER

| | |
|---|---|
| Freedman, Harry | *Keewaydin* |
| Govedas, John (arr.) | *I'se the B'y* |
| Halley, Paul | *Freedom Trilogy* |
| Hayes, Mark (arr.) | *Go Down, Moses* |
| Henderson, Ruth | *Come, Ye Makers of Song* |

ORANGE FILE FOLDER

| | |
|---|---|
| Holcombe, Bill (arr.) | *George Gershwin Medley* |
| Holst, Gustav | *Ave Maria* |
| Honegger, Arthur | *Laudate Dominum* |
| Hurd, Michael | *A Song of St. Francis* |

YELLOW FILE FOLDER

| | |
|---|---|
| Naplan, Allan | *Al Shlosha D'Varim* |
| Peterson, Oscar | *Hymn to Freedom* |
| Poelinitz, Josephine (arr.) | *City Called Heaven (Chamber only)* |
| Prokofiev, S. | *Ivan at the Coffin of Anastasia* |
| Purcell, Henry | *Sound the Trumpet* |
| Raminsh, Imant | Songs of the Lights: |
| | *Song of the Stars* |
| | *The Sower* |
| | *The Sun is a Luminous Shield* |
| | *Daybreak Song* |

BEIGE FILE FOLDER

| | |
|---|---|
| Rutter, John | *Brother Heinrich's Christmas* |
| | *For the Beauty of the Earth* |

Sallinen, Aulis                           *Suita Grammaticale*
Smyth, Ethel                              *The March of the Women*

9.  Rehearsal Clean-up
    At 8:25 the following choristers please put away:

    Under Stage                                    On Stage
    a) The blackboards (Facing each                a) Large music stand
       other so that they do not scratch)
    b) Stool
    c) Lights in boxes (Please disconnect
       the electrical extension chords.)
    d) Chalk in box (Make sure that you
       do not switch boxes, they are labeled.)
    e) Carpet from podium
       1. Heather H.    2. Gabi E.    3. Julia B.    4. David S.

10. Tape Recorders
    Please make sure:
    a) *All* of you have them for *every* rehearsal.
    b) You have an extra tape in your bag.
    c) You have spare batteries in your bag.
    d) Your names are on them.

11. Uniforms
    Tonight you will receive the black pants you were fitted for at camp. This is part of
    your informal Toronto Children's Chorus uniform and will be worn with your red golf
    shirt and/or blue sweatshirt. Red golf shirts must be tucked into the waistband. These
    pants are to be worn at TCC functions only. *Please do not wear them at any other time.*
    *Girls' Dress Shoes*
    Girls must wear black FLAT patent shoes as part of their Performance Uniform. If
    you do not yet have a pair please find below information on where they can be ob-
    tained. We have located two different styles which can be obtained at many stores
    across Toronto. Cathy has a sample pair at the Rehearsal Desk tonight.
    Style name: "Veniceo" (#399-35) can be obtained at Softmoc at the following:
    Eaton Centre, Sherway Gardens, Bramalea City Centre, Square One, Pickering
    Town Centre
    Price: $59.95 sizes 6–10 ladies
    Style name: "Final Stretch": by Aerosole
    Price: $90.00 sizes 5 and a half–10
    Style name: "Final Stretch": by Aerosole can also be obtained at Naturalizer
    Shoe Stores at Sherway Gardens and other shopping centres. The Sherway store
    is willing to give a 20% discount for 6 or more orders.
    Price: $90.00 sizes 5 and a half–10
    Also available at Sears Stores.
    (Ladies size 5 1/2 equivalent to Girls size 3 1/2; Ladies size 6 equivalent to Girls
    size 4)

12. Calendar Update

Please make the following changes/additions to your calendars:

   i) Friday, Nov. 3       9:00–12:00 School Concert—*Cantare* only!

   ii) Friday, Nov. 3      5:00–6:30 Full rehearsal

   iii) Tuesday, Nov. 7    6:15–8:30 Chamber only

   iv) Friday, Feb. 16     8:00pm Concert/Macmillan Hall "Carla's Poems"

Reminder . . . Please call Mrs. Bartle at home if you are ill and must miss a rehearsal.

13. CHAMBER CHOIR—BILLET CHOICES FOR ROCHESTER/SYRACUSE

Choristers will be billeted with the Eastman Bach Children's Chorus in Rochester and the Syracuse Children's Chorus in Syracuse. Many of you have had the opportunity to host choristers from visiting choirs, including the Syracuse Chorus when they were here last Fall, and consequently will appreciate the unique and special privilege it is to live with a host family. Choristers will be accommodated in pairs. In order to assist us with billeting, please fill out the form below and return to the rehearsal desk next Tuesday, September 19th, 2000. Choristers must understand that we will try to place them with their first choice, but it is not always possible. Please hand this form in on time, or you will be assigned roommates.

✂ - - - - - - - - - - - - - - - - - - - - - - - - - - - - - - - - - - - - - - - - - - - - - - - - - - - - - - - - - - - - - - -

ROCHESTER/SYRACUSE BILLET CHOICES

Chorister Name: _____ #: _____

I would like to be billeted with the following:   1. _____

                                                  2. _____

                                                  3. _____

                                                  4. _____

Update on allergies/dietary restrictions

Medication:

_____

Allergies:

_____

Dietary:

_____

\* \* \* Return to the Rehearsal Desk on Tuesday, September 19th, 2000. \* \* \*

---

MEMO:    TCC #2

TO:        TORONTO CHILDREN'S CHORUS

FROM:    MRS. BARTLE

DATE:    September 19, 2000

We would like to wish Happy Birthday to Krista K. who turns 13 on September 21st!

1. THANK YOU

Our thanks to our volunteers who helped at New Auditions on Saturday, September 9th:

Ina, Camille, and Jennie.

2. Homework for Saturday, September 23rd

Practise with your tape recorders:

1. *Al Shlosha D'Varim* (YELLOW)
2. Memorize *Song for Canada* (GREEN)
3. Memorize *Haida* (ORANGE)
4. Memorize *Streets of London* (ORANGE)

3. Homework for Tuesday, September 26th

1. Chamber—Practise *Ivan at the Coffin of Anastasia* (YELLOW) and *"Suite" de Lorca* (BEIGE).
2. Cantare—Practise *Missa Brevis*—Britten (RED). (I suggest strongly that you purchase the TCC tape or CD "Mostly Britten" at this Friday's rehearsal. We will sell them to you at cost Tape—$7 CD—$14 so you can study the *Missa Brevis).*
3. Everyone—Practise *Suita Grammaticale*—Sallinen (BEIGE).

4. Sight Reading Exercise

All choristers who were in level one at camp come and sing this to me individually, before the rehearsal begins tonight, in tonic solfa.

(write the syllables in yourself)

There are 22 notes. I'll give you a mark out of 25. (The first three marks are *free!*)

5. Tapes—Tonight use your *second* tape. Don't tape over last week's tape. Listen to *both* tapes this week.

6. Happy Birthday in B Flat

Please leave them on my music stand. Make sure your *full* name and chorus number are on top. Would one of the rehearsal assistants please put them in alphabetical order for me after the break?

7. Seating Plan Changes

1. *C26*—Anna B. move to D24
2. *C25*—Leah F. move to C26
3. *C24*—Laura H. move to C25
4. *D24*—Shannon C. move to C24

Laura H. will now have two apprentices: Leah F. and Shannon C.

8. Other Apprentice Trainer Changes (because of the long distance telephone costs)

Janet S. (AT) with Sarah L. (Sr.App)

Brynne M. (AT) with Jessica R. (Sr.App)—no long distance fees applicable from Brampton to Don Mills.

*E18*—Sarah L. change seats with Jessica R. *C19*

9. Solo Try-outs

1. *Ballad*, #4 of *Songs of the Sea*—This Saturday at 12:30 in the Sanctuary.
2. *Benedictus*—This Friday at 4:30. Higher part only available. (The alto part was Gabi's two years ago.)

10. Staggered Break

Until we are able to find a second rehearsal space for Cantare, the breaks will be staggered.

Tonight: Cantare break—7:15–7:50

Chamber break—7:35–7:50

While Chamber rehearses for 20 minutes on own, Cantare must be quiet. *Cantare*— you must be accompanied by an ADULT SUPERVISOR if you go outside for the break. Please do not touch trees, bushes, shrubs, etc.

11. Error in Last Week's Memo

   1. The new music list only went to 'S' in BEIGE.

   2. Please put Tallis    *Glory to Thee*

           Thompson    *Pueri Hebraeorum*

and any other pieces whose composers come alphabetically after "Smyth" in BEIGE.

10. Rehearsal this Friday—5:00–6:30 everyone!

11. Concert/Demonstration *this* Saturday at LPCC!

Call Time: 12:45pm

1:00–2:00 rehearsal    2:00–3:00 concert    3:00–3:30 reception

Dress: Informal uniform: New black pants, good running shoes, red golf shirt tucked into waist, all three buttons fastened, no jewelry or make-up—no exceptions. Please ensure you are properly dressed before you leave home.

     This is a special concert/demonstration to celebrate ARTSWEEK in Toronto. We are inviting as many people with families as we can possibly squeeze into the church sanctuary, to come and learn the joys of singing. I will be teaching some new songs to you and them. You will be helping teach them some songs. It will be fun, educational, and informal. It's *FREE!* Doors open to the public at 1:45. First come, first served. (You will come to the gym please at 1:00 for a brief rehearsal.) Refreshments will be served to everyone in the gym afterwards (*guests first,* please!) You will meet many new people. Tonight we'll demonstrate how you meet a stranger and talk to him or her. Put in your black performance folder:

| | |
|---|---|
| *Song for Canada* | (GREEN) |
| *Haida* | (ORANGE) |
| *Go Where I Send Thee* | (RED) |
| *How Can I Keep from Singing?* | (YELLOW) |
| *Let the Bright Seraphim* | (GREEN) |
| *Streets of London* | (ORANGE) |
| *The Swallow* | (BEIGE) |
| *Ave Verum Corpus* | (Independent BLUE) |

12. Welcome to Visitors

We would like to welcome the following observers to our rehearsal tonight. . .

| | |
|---|---|
| Vanessa C.; Glenview Sr. P.S. | Maureen H.; T.C.D.S.B. |
| Jillian D.; Glenview Sr. P.S. | Ella K.; Mississauga Private School |
| Denise F.; Green Glad Sr. P.S. | Rachel S.; Brookhaven P.S. |
| Lisa G.; Kent Sr. School | |

13. CHAMBER CHOIR TO SYRACUSE AND ROCHESTER

    Please hand in your billet forms tonight at the Sign-in Desk, *not* my music stand!

    Choristers are required to travel with a valid Canadian passport when we travel outside of Canada. If you do not have a Canadian passport, applications for a child under 16 years of age are available at the Rehearsal Desk. Passport Offices are located at:

    74 Victoria Street, #300 (between Adelaide and Richmond) 8:00–5:00

    4900 Yonge Street, Joseph Shepard Centre, 1 block north of Shepard 8:00–5:00

    Scarborough Town Centre, 200 Town Centre Court, #828 8:45–4:30

14. Help! Fun Choristers Needed!

    I need 6 choristers to help with games this Sunday, September 24th, in the afternoon when I meet with TCII at LPCC in the gym from 2:00–4:30. You would need to be available from 2:30–3:00 and from 3:30–4:00. You need to devise four games (two for inside, two for outside) that 9 children could play—games that will help them get to know each other well. One game should be a mild "let off steam" game. Choristers interested in eventually becoming camp counselors are invited to apply. Speak to Gabi or Heather, our Head Choristers, if you are interested. (Gabi and Heather/Section Leaders get priority.) Gabi and Heather—please phone me with the names or give me a list on Saturday.

15. Absences

    PLEASE remember that if you are going to be absent you must:

    1. Call Mrs. Bartle beforehand.
    2. Fill out an absence form at the Sign-In Desk prior to the absence and either hand in to Mrs. Bartle or fax to the office.
    3. Send your TAPE RECORDER and a TAPE with another chorister so that you will not miss what was learned in a rehearsal.
    4. Call your section leader afterwards to see what you missed.

16. Ticket Reminder

    Just a reminder to parents that the early subscription deadline of September 30th is quickly approaching. In order to receive the discount on early subscription tickets all orders must be received by midnight on September 30th. Any orders received after that date will be charged full price.

    Tickets will not be ready until the end of September/beginning of October. The office has been busy with preparations for the beginning of rehearsals. If you have any concerns or questions about your orders please call Jennifer at 932-8666 ext.111.

17. Poinsettia Launch Campaign

    There will be a Parent Volunteer Meeting for all those who volunteered to assist with the Poinsettia Campaign on October 3rd at 6:15 downstairs in Rooms 1 & 2. Normally we do not hold this meeting for TCC volunteers but as there are a number of new policies this year, we would like to review them with everyone who volunteered. If you have volunteered, your attendance at this meeting will be greatly appreciated and expected.

MEMO:      TCC #3
TO:        TORONTO CHILDREN'S CHORUS
FROM:      MRS. BARTLE
DATE:      September 22, 2000

We would like to wish a Happy Birthday to:

1. Stacey H. who turns 13 today and
2. Stewart C. who turns 11 tomorrow!

1. New Seating Plan

   Tonight you have a Performance Seating Plan. This plan is used just before a concert. (Rehearsal seating plans are used for *most* rehearsals, where the apprentices sit next to their apprentice trainers.) For concerts, we use a Performance Seating Plan. Sit in your Performance Seating Plan tonight.

2. Update for tomorrow's concert:

   Please put in your folders:

   1. *Al Shlosha*
   2. *Song for Canada*
   3. *Haida*
   4. *Go Where I Send Thee*
   5. *Streets of London*
   6. *Swallow*
   7. *Hymn to Freedom*
   8. *How Can I Keep* (if time)
   9. *Let the Bright Seraphim* (if time)

3. Performance Times Tomorrow (an update from Tuesday)

   12:30–1:00—solo tryouts (Sanctuary)—voluntary, "Ballad—#4 Songs of the Sea"
   1:00–2:00—rehearsal (Sanctuary)
   2:00–2:30—break (in gym). Please bring your own snack!
   2:30–3:30—Concert/Big Audience sing/get to meet the TCC—Open House/Fun
   3:30–4:00—reception in gym for audience and choristers
   Parents: Here's a chance for *you* to dust off those vocal cords and sing with us!

4. Sallinen Divisi (BEIGE—#66)

   In *Suita Grammaticale,* please mark the following divisi in your scores:
   Page 8 Measures 109, 110, 111, 112./*Three Part Divisi* (Performance Seating Plan)
   Sop I —rows ABC—sing upper notes (G)
           —rows D & E—lower notes (F)
   Sop II—rows ABC—upper notes (E)
           —rows D & E—lower notes (D)
   Alto  —rows ABC—lower notes (B)
           —rows D & E—upper notes (C)
           similarly of page 9 and 10 and 11
   Please mark this in your score before rehearsal begins today. (Apprentice trainers need to help apprentices, please!)

5. Happy Birthday Homework

   I have marked about half of them. Katie M.'s version—enclosed on next page—gets full marks plus several bonus marks for creativity, imagination, going the second mile—*AND,* by the time I got to "M"—she made me laugh! Thank you, Katie! The following 9 choristers need to hand in "Happy Birthday" today: Sasha C., Evan G., Sydney H., Sarah J., Sally L., Brynne M., Gillian R., Charlie S. and Camille S.

6. ATTENTION CANTARE PARENTS

We are in desperate need of ushers for the school choir concert on Friday, November 3, 2000, 9:00 AM to NOON. If you are able to assist with this event, please contact Cindy G. immediately. Thanks!

7. POINSETTIA CAMPAIGN LAUNCH — October 3, 2000

The Poinsettia Campaign meeting announced in Memo #2 is a MANDATORY meeting for ALL TCC parents to launch the 2000 Poinsettia Campaign. Normally we do not hold this meeting because of the TCC's extensive experience with the campaign; however, we are introducing new products and policies and wish to review them with everyone. As always, your attendance at this meeting is greatly appreciated. The meeting will be held on October 3 at 6:15, downstairs in Rooms 1 & 2. If this meeting is absolutely impossible for you to attend (i.e., both parents are out of town), please let the office know by fax (932-8669) or email (singtcc@interlog.com) immediately!

8. Calendar Update

Please update your calendar with the following changes. The Michigan workshop on October 13th, 14th, and 15th has been cancelled. There will be a TCC rehearsal on October 13th from 5:00–6:30 at LPCC.

MEMO:    TCC #4
TO:       TORONTO CHILDREN'S CHORUS
FROM:    MRS. BARTLE
DATE:     September 26, 2000

We would like to wish a Happy Birthday to:

Thomas K. who turns 11 tomorrow and Polina K. who turns 14 on October 2nd!

1. No rehearsal Friday, September 29th!

There will be no rehearsal this Friday night due to Rosh Hashanah.

2. Homework for October 2nd

1. Fast on the heels of *"Happy Birthday",* please write out (*using* 8 1/2 x 11 paper—so it doesn't get lost,) printing *BOTH* names in the top right hand corner—and chorister #. Write out notes and syllables for *"The Farmer In The Dell!"* Please note 1) time signature (think!!), and the pick-up note (it does *not* start on doh). Write it in G+. (Independent, write it in G-.) Please leave them on my music stand on Tuesday, October 2nd.

2. Please work with your tape recorders on:

a. *Songs from the Sea*

b. *Suita Grammaticale* (apprentice trainers, help your apprentices with the German, French & Russian)

3. Please mark the following corrections in your scores: GERSHWIN

(Please do *NOT* erase these markings! I will explain to our librarian). Put the corrections in neatly, please!

| | | | |
|---|---|---|---|
| 1. | mm. 47 | 3rd beat | A flat (also in piano part) |
| 2. | mm. 54 | 4th beat | D and B flat—alto I & II |
| 3. | mm. 60 | 1st beat | D flat alto II |
| 4. | mm. 86 | change 'man' to 'one' | |
| 5. | mm. 99 | 4th beat | piano right hand G flat |
| 6. | mm. 126 | 4th beat | piano F sharp |
| 7. | mm. 133 | 3rd note | alto II B natural |
| | | 4th note | alto II B flat |
| 8. | mm. 158 | piano right hand | E natural, C natural |
| 9. | mm. 162 | 3rd beat | piano A natural |
| 10. | mm. 163 | 2nd beat | alto I A natural |
| 11. | mm. 212 | 4th beat | sop.II E flat |
| 12. | mm. 220 | 1st beat | sop.I A natural |
| | | 4th beat | alto A natural |
| | | piano | bass E natural |
| 13. | mm. 221 | 1st beat | sop.I A natural |
| | | piano | right hand A natural |
| | | 2nd chord | E natural |
| 14. | mm. 224 | 3rd beat | sop.II A natural |
| 15. | mm. 229 | sing "I am" not "I'm" | |
| 16. | mm. 254 | band | TA, TA, TA, TA (add words) |

    17. last bar shout "Hurrah" in the high part

3. Soloists

Thank you to *all* who tried out. There isn't one of you who couldn't handle it!

    1. Britten—Soprano    Aleha A.

    2. Ballad—I need to hear this in context so I have chosen 6 of you. I *likely* will choose 3, one for each verse; Gabi E., Andrea G., Sarah H., Jennie M., Laura R., Nellie S. Please work on word color, diction, and projection. I'll hear you in rehearsal tonight.

4. Independent

You will be singing the Daley—*Ave Verum* at our concert on October 20th, and also at the conference in Rochester and the concert in Syracuse. Please organize a rehearsal for yourselves at 5:30 some Tuesday. Use the stage, please.

5. Thank you!

For a great Open House/Presentation last Saturday! Congratulations to John C., Sally L., and Andrea G. for speaking so well, and to Conlin D. for playing his string bass!

6. Another Thank You!

A HUGE thank you to Jennie, Katie, Aleha, Laura, Emily and Silvi for doing a *great* job on Sunday, helping at Pizza and Games afternoon with TCII!

7. Staggered Break Tonight

7:15–7:50 Cantare        7:35–7:50 Chamber        (Cantare—you must *not* go out-
                                                   side unless there is an adult to
                                                   supervise you!)

8. GALA 2001

   Please review tonight's Chorister Package of information on the Toronto Children's
   Chorus Valentine Gala: *Sharing the Love of Music*. Next week, at the Mandatory Parent Meeting, you will have an opportunity to ask questions when this year's Gala
   committee representatives present the plans to date. Please bring the package with
   you, as the forms will be reviewed in detail.

9. Calendar Updates

   Please update your calendar with the following changes:

   1. No rehearsal this Friday—Rosh Hashanah
   2. Tuesday, October 10th         6:00–7:00 Everyone
                                    7:30–8:30 Chamber Only
   3. Tuesday, October 31st         4:45–6:15 Cantare Only
   4. Tuesday, November 7th         6:15–8:30 Chamber Only

10. TCIII Request

    Mr. B. would like four TCC members to assist on October 14th from 2:00–5:00 with
    their "Pizza—get to know you afternoon" (like the one we had last week for TCII). If
    you *can* help, please speak to Gabi or Heather. Heather and Gabi, please call Beth A.
    at 932-8666 x112 or fax the office at 932-8669. Beth looks after TCIII.

11. Parent Chorister Agreements

    Thank you to everyone who handed in his or her Parent/Chorister Agreement on
    time! There were a couple received that had illegible signatures. Please tell the re-
    hearsal assistants if your name is on the list at the sign-in desk, but you are SURE
    that you handed in your form.

12. POINSETTIA CAMPAIGN LAUNCH—October 3, 2000

    The Poinsettia Campaign meeting announced in Memo #2 is a MANDATORY meet-
    ing for ALL TCC parents to launch the 2000 Poinsettia Campaign. Normally we do
    not hold this meeting because of the TCC's extensive experience with the campaign;
    however, we are introducing new products and policies and wish to review them
    with everyone. As always, your attendance at this meeting is greatly appreciated.
    The meeting will be held on October 3 at 6:15, downstairs in Rooms 1 & 2. If this
    meeting is absolutely impossible for you to attend (i.e., both parents are out of
    town), please let the office know by fax (932-8669) or email (singtcc@interlog.com)
    immediately!

13. Toronto Children's Chorus Holiday CD Card

    A Message from David C., Board Member of the TCC . . .

    "The Board of Directors is currently offering to the business community an opportu-
    nity to send TCC Holiday CD greetings cards to their special clients. The Company's
    name and seasonal greetings will be customized and appear on the CD . Orders of
    up to 500 will cost $10.00 per card; or just $6.50 per card for a 1000 unit order.
    This year we are also offering a special package for smaller orders, for a minimum

order of 50 cards, your company's logo would appear on the card but not on the actual CD for the price of $11.50 per card. Last year many TCC families ordered non-logo cards to distribute as personal Christmas Cards."

      If you think your company might be interested in this special opportunity, further information can be obtained by calling our General Manager, Heather W. (932-8666, ext. 113).

14. ATTENTION CANTARE PARENTS

Thank you to those of you who volunteered to usher for the school choir concert on Friday, November 3, 2000. We are still looking for more volunteers. If you are able to assist on November 3rd from 9:00 AM to NOON, please contact Cindy G. immediately. Thanks!

15. REFRESHMENTS

Over the summer an attempt was made to have juice and cookies donated so that choristers would receive a free snack during long rehearsals (Tuesdays and weekends). At this time we have not succeeded. We will continue to pursue this and our fundraising committee is working hard to find a donor.

We have revised our price structure, which is as follows:

| | |
|---|---|
| cookies: | 2 for 25 cents |
| wafer cookies: | 4 for 25 cents |
| drinking boxes/bottled water: | 25 cents each |

Wendy H., our Rehearsal Refreshments Coordinator, will be calling parents who volunteered to donate juice boxes. Our thanks to Mrs. H. and all parents who donate juice and assist at rehearsals. Your assistance, as always, is deeply appreciated.

# Sight-Singing Curriculum Outline for the Toronto Children's Chorus

## Level 1

1. Use hand-signs while singing a descending E-flat major scale
2. Use hand-signs while singing "doh," "me," "soh," "me," "doh"; understand that this is the tonic triad
3. Know how to find and write all major key signatures; in sharp keys, call the sharp closest to the music "te" and count down to "doh"; in flat keys, call the flat closest to the music "fah," and count down to "doh"; write the tonic triad in whole notes
4. Know how to clap, count, and write four measures of rhythm in simple time—two-four, three-four, and four-four—from the chalkboard, using quarters, eighths, halves, whole notes, and rests; know how to write four measures of rhythmic dictation when it is clapped three times, the first and third times all four measures, the second time broken into two-measure phrases
5. Know how to sing in tonic-solfa syllables, using hand signs, the "Tallis Canon" in G major and "Baa, Baa, Black Sheep" in E-flat major
6. Know how to take melodic dictation on staff paper to write out the "Tallis Canon" in G major and "Baa, Baa, Black Sheep" in E-flat major by memory; know how to sing-count them

## Level 2

1. Use hand signs while singing natural, harmonic, and melodic scales
2. Use hand signs while singing "lah," "doh," "me," "doh," "lah"; understand that this is the tonic triad
3. Know how to find and write all minor key signatures by singing down from "doh" to "lah," a minor third, from the major key
4. Know how to clap, count (using "1 ee and uh" for four sixteenth notes; "1 and uh" for an eighth followed by two sixteenths; "1 ee and" for two sixteenths followed by an eighth), and write four measures in simple time using dotted quarters, eighths, sixteenths, halves, and whole notes and rests; rhythmic dictation as in Level 1, part 4
5. Know how to sing in tonic-solfa syllables, using hand signs, "Frère Jacques" in F major and D minor and the chorus of "Jingle Bells" in D major
6. Know how to take melodic dictation on staff paper to write out the preceding songs; know how to sing-count them

## Level 3

1. Know how to sing all exercises on the sequential and interval sheets
2. Review all concepts taught in Levels 1 and 2 until they are mastered
3. Know how to clap, count, and write four measures of rhythm in compound time; know how to write two measures of rhythmic dictation when it is clapped three times
4. Know how to sing in tonic-solfa syllables, using hand signs, "Silent Night" in six-eight time in D major, "Row, Row, Row Your Boat" in six-eight time in F major, "If You're Happy and You Know It" in G major, and "The Farmer in the Dell" in A major
5. Know how to take melodic dictation on staff paper to write out the preceding songs by memory; know how to sing-count them

## Level 4

1. Know how to sing the chromatic and whole-tone scales in canon; know how to sing "The Advanced Interval Song"
2. Know all concepts taught in Levels 2 and 3 until they are mastered
3. Know how to write and sing any interval
4. Understand mixed meter and know how to write in the twos with an L and the threes with a triangle
5. Know how to write more complex rhythmic dictation
6. Know how to take melodic dictation on staff paper to write out "Happy Birthday" in B-flat major, "The More We Are Together" in F major, and "Land of the Silver Birch" in D minor

## Level 5

1. Know all concepts from Levels 1 to 4 until they are mastered
2. Use hand signs while singing major triads, "doh," "me," "soh"; minor triads, "lah," "doh," "me"; diminished triads, "lah," "doh," "mah"; augmented triads, "doh," "me," "se";
3. Are able to hear, identify, and write any triad
4. Know how to take melodic dictation on staff paper to write out "The First Noel" and "O Canada" by memory
5. Know how to take melodic dictation of a two-bar phrase in two parts
6. Know how to add a simple alto part to an easy familiar song such as "Silent Night"

## Level 6

1. Know all concepts from Levels 1 to 5 until they are mastered
2. Use hand signs while singing dominant seventh chords ("soh," "te," "ray," "fah") and diminished seventh chords ("te," "ray," "fah," "se")

3. Are able to hear, identify, and write any triad, dominant or diminished seventh chord
4. Know how to take melodic dictation on staff paper to write out "Hark the Herald Angels Sing" and "Oh Come, All Ye Faithful" and "Three Blind Mice" in F major and F minor
5. Know how to write the alto or the second soprano line of a four-measure phrase of a dictated passage in three parts

## Independent

Should, given time, be able to sight-read ANYTHING—rhythmically and melodically

## Materials

1. *The Folk Song Sight Singing Series* (Oxford University Press)
   Level 1—Book 2
   Level 2—Book 2
   Level 3—Book 3
   Level 4—Book 4
   Level 5—Book 5
   Level 6—Book 6
   Independent—Choral Music
2. Scales, sequentials and interval sheets; Vocalises Sheet
3. Cheat Sheet that contains:
   a. all key signatures, major and minor (all choristers must have this memorized by the end of Camp)
   b. time signatures that illustrate simple time, compound time, and mixed meters
4. Blank manuscript paper, blank staff paper, 3 sharp pencils, and erasers
5. Tuning fork
6. Teachers need staplers; paper clips; five-line chalkboard liner; chalk and brushes

## Daily Work to Be Accomplished 3:10–4:10 P.M.

1. 5-minute individual and group warm-up drill to be taken from
   a. scales, sequentials, and interval sheets
   b. Key Signature Sheet
2. 8 minutes—*Folk Song Sight Singing* books
3. 8 minutes—aural and melodic dictation of individual intervals
4. 9 minutes—rhythmic dictation
5. 9 minutes—melodic dictation
6. 8 minutes—take everything up/ individuals go to boards to write answers (or assistant can mark overnight)

# KEY SIGNATURES SHEET - MAJOR/MINOR

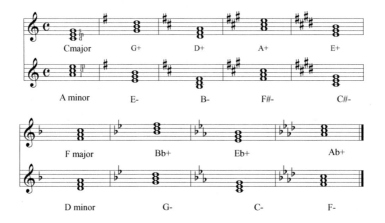

Cmajor   G+   D+   A+   E+

A minor   E-   B-   F#-   C#-

F major   Bb+   Eb+   Ab+

D minor   G-   C-   F-

# TIME SIGNATURES SHEET

**Simple Time:**

1   2 + 3   4   1 ee + uh 2 + 3 ee + 4   1   2 + uh 34   1234

**Compound Time:**

1   2   3   456   12   3   4   5   6   1   23   456   123456

# Rounds All Children Should Know

### 1. Make New Friends

Make new friends but keep the old,

One is sil - ver and the o - ther gold.

### 2. Health and Strength

For health and strength and dai-ly food, We praise Thy name, O Lord.

### 3. Frère Jacques

Frè-re Jac-ques, frè-re Jac-ques, dor-mez - vous, dor-mez - vous?
Are you sleep-ing, are you sleep-ing, Bro-ther John, Bro-ther John?

Son-nez les ma - ti - nes, son-nez les ma - ti - nes, Din, din, don! Din, din, don!
Morn-ing bells are ring-ing, Morn-ing bells are ring-ing, Ding, ding, dong, ding, ding, dong.

### 4. O Music

O—— mu-sic, sweet—— mu - sic, thy—— prai-ses we will sing: We——

will tell of the—— plea - sures and—— hap - pi - ness you—— bring.

Mu - sic, mu - sic, let the cho - rus sing.

## 5. Tallis Canon

Thomas Tallis (1505-1585)

Glo-ry to Thee, my God, this night, for all the bless-ings of the light. Keep

me, O keep me, King of Kings, Be - neath Thine own Al - might-y wings.

## 6. Oh How Lovely Is the Evening

Oh how love-ly is the eve - ning, is the eve - ning,

When the bells are sweet - ly ring - ing, sweet - ly ring - ing.

Ding, dong, ding, dong.

## 7. White Coral Bells

White co-ral bells up - on a slen - der stalk,

Lil - ies of the val - ley deck the gar - den walk.

Oh, don't you wish that you might hear them ring?

That can hap - pen on - ly when the elves all sing.

## 8. Die Music    [Music Alone Shall Live]

Him - mel und Er - de müs - sen ver - gehn;
*All things shall pe - rish from un - der the sky;*

a - ber die Mu - si - ci, a - ber die Mu - si - ci,
*Mu - sic a - lone shall live, Mu - sic a - lone shall live,*

a - ber die Mu - si - ci, blei - ben be - stehn.
*Mu - sic a - lone shall live, Ne - ver to die.*

**9. Jubilate Deo**                     Michael Praetorius (1571-1621)

**10. Three Blind Mice**

**11. Dona Nobis Pacem**

**12. Viva la musica**

### 13. Fire's Burning

Fire's bur-ning, fire's bur-ning, draw near-er, draw near-er, In the gloam-ing, in the gloam-ing, Come sing and be mer-ry.

### 14. Ars Longa

Ars Lon - ga vi - ta bre - va.

# Treble Choir Repertoire with Orchestral Accompaniment

The nucleus of the following comprehensive list of works for treble voices and orchestra was originally compiled for the *Choral Journal* and published in October 2000. My collaborator for this article was conductor Dr. Barbara Tagg, artistic director and founder of the Syracuse Children's Chorus and an affiliate artist at Syracuse University, where she conducts the Syracuse University Women's Choir. I have since updated and added to our list. We hope it will be a valuable resource for all conductors who wish to expand their knowledge of orchestral repertoire for treble voices. It is our hope that the high artistic standard achieved by the children's chorus over the past two decades will provide inspiration for composers to write new orchestral works for this instrument.

| Composer | Title | Publisher | Instruments | Rating Easy Medium Difficult |
|---|---|---|---|---|
| Adler, Samuel | A Whole Bunch of Fun (9 movements) | Oxford | full orchestra | M |
| Bach, J. S., arr. Stuart Calvert | Bist du bei mir | GVT/Warner/ Chappell | strings* | E |
| Bach, J. S. | Christe Eleison, from Mass in B Minor | Boosey & Hawkes | strings, continuo | M |
| Bach, J. S. | Domine Deus, from Mass in G | Boosey & Hawkes | strings | M |
| Bach, J. S. | Duet & Chorale, from Cantata 93 | Boosey & Hawkes | strings | M |
| Bach, J. S. | For Us a Child Is Born | Galaxy | string orchestra | M |
| Bach, J. S. | Jesu, Joy of Man's Desiring | E. C. Schirmer | full orchestra | E |
| Bach, J. S. | Now Let All the Heavens, from Cantata 140 | Thomas House | flute, continuo | E |
| Bach, J. S. | Schafe Können sicher weiden, from the *Birthday Cantata* | Kalmus | two flutes, continuo | E |
| Barab, Seymour | A Child's Garden of Verses | Boosey & Hawkes | full orchestra | E |

*(continued)*

| Composer | Title | Publisher | Instruments | Rating Easy Medium Difficult |
|---|---|---|---|---|
| Bartók, Bela | Six Children's Songs | Boosey & Hawkes | full orchestra | M |
| Bedford, David | The Rime of the Ancient Mariner | Universal Edition 16237 | children's orchestra, percussion | D |
| Bell, Leslie (arr.) | They All Call It Canada | GVT/Warner/ Chappell | full orchestra* | E |
| Berkey, Jackson | Cantata 2000 | SDG Press | piano, marimba, percussion | M |
| Bernstein, Leonard | Gloria Tibi, from Mass | Boosey & Hawkes | full orchestra | M |
| Bertaux, Betty | This is the Truth | Boosey & Hawkes | strings and percussion | E |
| Bertaux, Betty | To Music | Boosey & Hawkes | strings | E |
| Binkerd, Gordon | On the King's Highway | Boosey & Hawkes | chamber orchestra | M |
| Blake, Howard | All God's Creatures (Song Cycle) | Faber Music | full orchestra | M |
| Bolcom, William | Songs of Innocence and Experience (selected movements) | Theodore Presser | full orchestra | M |
| Borodin, Alexander | Choral Dance No. 17 from *Prince Igor* | Boosey & Hawkes | full orchestra | M |
| Brahms, Johannes | Ave Maria, Opus 12 | C. F. Peters | full orchestra | M |
| Britten, Benjamin | The Children's Crusade, Op. 82 | Faber Music | two pianos, organ, percussion | D |
| Brumby, Colin | Te Deum | Walton Music | brass | M |
| Brunner, David | Earthsongs (3 movements) | Boosey & Hawkes | full orchestra | M |
| Brunner, David | Jubilate Deo | Boosey & Hawkes | full orchestra | M |
| Burge, John | Simple Songs The Coat Silverly Secrets | Boosey & Hawkes | full orchestra | E |
| Cable, Howard (arr.) | Coventry Carol | Hinshaw | chamber orchestra | E |
| Cable, Howard | Sing—Sea to Sea | GVT/Warner/ Chappell | full orchestra* | M |
| Campbell, Norman, arr. Howard Cable | Anne of Green Gables | GVT/Warner/ Chappell | full orchestra* | M |

| | | | | |
|---|---|---|---|---|
| Carter, Andrew | Bless the Lord (3 songs) | Oxford | full orchestra | E |
| Chan Ka Nin | Carla's Poems | Canadian Music Centre | wind quartet | D |
| Chilcott, Bob | Hey! Now Mid-Winter Farewell! Advent | OUP | full orchestra | M E M |
| Chilcott, Bob | The Swallow | Oxford | full orchestra | M |
| Chilcott, Bob | The Time of Snow This Joy Gifts | Oxford | full orchestra | E M E |
| Copland, Aaron (arr.) | I Bought Me a Cat At the River Ching-a-Ring Chaw Little Horses Simple Gifts | Boosey & Hawkes | full orchestra | M |
| Corp, Ronald | Cornucopia | Oxford | full orchestra | D |
| Coulthard, Jean | Three Philosophical Songs | Hinshaw | strings | M |
| Debussy, Claude | Noël des enfants | Durand | full orchestra | M |
| Debussy, Claude | Salut Printemps | Editions Choudens: Theodore Presser | chamber orchestra | M |
| Delibes, Léo | Messe Brève | Roger Dean | string orchestra | E |
| Dengler, Lee | Christmas Sonnet | H. W. Gray/ Warner Bros. | piano or string quartet | E |
| Dexter, Harry | Old King Cole | Edwin Ashdown | violins, piano, celli, basses | E |
| Evans, Robert | Pie Jesu | GVT/Warner/ Chappell | solo French horn, strings* | E |
| Fauré, Gabriel, arr. Bartle | Cantique de Jean Racine | Hinshaw | low strings, harp (arr. John Rutter) | M |
| Fauré, Gabriel | Pie Jesu Requiem | Octavo: Boosey & Hawkes | organ, strings | E |
| Galuppi, Baldassare | Dixit Dominus | Roger Dean | strings | M |
| Gardner, John | Five Hymns in Popular Style | Oxford | strings, clarinets, percussion, piano/organ | M |
| Gibson, Paul | Suite: Alice Through a Looking-Glass | Ione Press, a division of ECS Publishing | chamber orchestra | E |
| Glick, Srul Irving | Psalm Trilogy: Psalms 92, 47, & 23 | earthsongs | strings | M |
| Hadley, Patrick | I Sing of a Maiden | Chappell (vocal: Oxford) | full orchestra | M |

*(continued)*

| Composer | Title | Publisher | Instruments | Rating Easy Medium Difficult |
|---|---|---|---|---|
| Handel, G. F., arr. Bartle | Art Thou Troubled? | Hinshaw | strings | E |
| Handel, G. F. | Let the Bright Seraphim | Novello | full orchestra | M |
| Handel, G. F. | Where'er You Walk, from *Semele* | E. C. Schirmer | full orchestra | E |
| Hanus, Jan | Three Hymns for Communion | Laurendale Associates | string orchestra | M |
| Hasse, Johann Adolf | Miserere mei, Deus, from Miserere in D Minor | Treble Clef Music | strings | M |
| Haydn, Michael, arr. Betsy Cook Weber | Dixit Dominus | Alliance Music | strings, continuo | M |
| Haydn, Michael, arr. Betsy Cook Weber | Kyrie | Alliance Music | strings, horns, continuo | M |
| Haydn, Michael, ed. Martin Banner | Laudate Pueri | Hinshaw | strings, continuo | M |
| Haydn, Michael | Missa St. Aloysii | Hug & Co./Kalmus | strings | M |
| Haydn, Michael | Missa Sancti Leopold | Peters | strings, continuo | M |
| Haydn, Michael, arr. Betsy Cook Weber | Regina Coeli, from *Litanie della Madonna* | Alliance Music | strings, horns, continuo | M |
| Haydn, Michael, | Stella Coeli | Harmonia-Uitgave | chamber orchestra | M |
| Haydn, Michael, arr. Banner | Vesperae Pro Festo Sancti Innocentium (8 movements) | Roger Dean | strings, two horns | M |
| Hayes, Mark | Sing Joy! | Alfred | full orchestra | E |
| Henderson, Ruth Watson | Adventures in Color | earthsongs | strings | M |
| Henderson, Ruth Watson | Barnyard Carols: | GVT/Warner/ Chappell | | E |
| | The Robin | | flute, cello* | |
| | The Lamb | | flute, viola* | |
| | The Duck | | viola, cello* | |
| | The Donkey | | viola, cello* | |
| | The Barn Owl | | flute* | |
| Henderson, Ruth Watson | Come, Ye Makers of Song | GVT/Warner/ Chappell | strings, winds* | M |

| | | | | |
|---|---|---|---|---|
| Henderson, Ruth Watson | Creation's Praise | GVT/Warner/ Chappell | piano, brass* | M |
| Henderson, Ruth Watson | Gloria | Boosey & Hawkes | brass, timpani, percussion* | D |
| Henderson, Ruth Watson | Lullaby for the Christ Child | GVT/Warner/ Chappell | strings, winds* | E |
| Henderson, Ruth Watson | The Travelling Musicians | GVT/Warner/ Chappell | piano, clarinet, cello* | M |
| Henderson, R. W. | Winter Store, from *Voices of Earth* | GVT/Warner/ Chappell | strings, flute, piano, percussion* | E |
| Henderson, Ruth Watson | Songs of the Nativity | GVT/Warner/ Chappell | strings, harp* | M |
| Hillert, Richard | Festival Te Deum | Augsburg | brass, bass, percussion, organ | E |
| Holst, Gustav | Choral Hymns from the Rig-Veda | Galaxy | full orchestra | M |
| Holst, Gustav | Seven Part-Songs | Novello | strings, continuo | M |
| Hurd, Michael | Charms and Ceremonies | Novello | strings | M |
| Hurd, Michael | Flower Songs | Novello | strings | M |
| Jacob, Gordon (arr.) | Brother James's Air | Oxford | strings, piano | E |
| Jacob, Gordon | A Goodly Heritage (12 movements) | Mills Music | strings, piano | E |
| Jager, Robert | I Dream of Peace | Hal Leonard | full orchestra | M |
| Kapilow, Robert | Elijah's Angel | G. Schirmer | full orchestra, baritone, bass-baritone, boy soprano | M |
| Kapilow, Robert | The Polar Express | G. Schirmer/ Hal Leonard | full orchestra, baritone | M |
| Leavitt, John | Festival Sanctus | Warner/CPP Belwin | brass quintet | M |
| Mamiya, Michio | Children's Field, Composition No. 4 | Zen-on Music | full orchestra | D |
| Mathias, William | Lear Songs | Oxford | clarinet, percussion, trumpet, string bass, piano (4 hands) | M |
| Mathias, William | O aulo nobilis | Oxford | 3 trumpets, timpani, 3 percussion, piano duet | M |
| Mathias, William | Salvator Mundi | Oxford | strings, percussion, piano duet | M |

*(continued)*

| Composer | Title | Publisher | Instruments | Rating<br>Easy<br>Medium<br>Difficult |
|---|---|---|---|---|
| Mechem, Kirke | Seven Joys of Christmas | E. C. Schirmer | chamber orchestra or piano/harp | M |
| Mozart, W. A. | Ave Verum Corpus | E. C. Schirmer | strings | M |
| Mozart, W. A. | Vesperae de Domenica K. 321, Vesperae Solennes de Confessore | Orch.: Kalmus Choral: Oxford | full orchestra | M |
| Neukomm, Sigismund | Mass in C | Boosey & Hawkes | string orchestra | M |
| Nuñez, Francisco | Three Dominican Folk Songs | Boosey & Hawkes | full orchestra | M |
| Page, Robert (arr.) | Behold, That Star | Hinshaw | full orchestra | E |
| Parry, C. Hubert H. | Jerusalem | Curwen | full orchestra | E |
| Perera, Ronald | earthsongs (Poems by e.e. cummings) | E. C. Schirmer | full orchestra | M |
| | O sweet spontaneous earth | | | |
| | in Just-spring | | | |
| | as in the sea marvelous | | | |
| | All in green went my love riding | | | |
| | when god lets my body be | | | |
| | i thank You God | | | |
| Pergolesi, G. B. | Stabat Mater | Hinshaw | strings, continuo | M |
| Pinkham, Daniel | Cantate Domino | Theodore Presser | brass quartet | M |
| Porpora, Nicola | Magnificat | Marks/Belwin-Mills | string orchestra, organ | M |
| Poulenc, Francis | Litanies à la Vierge Noire du Notre Dame de Roc Amadour | Theodore Presser | strings timpani | M |
| Powell, Anthony | Zlata's Diary (14 movements) | Oxford | full orchestra | E |
| Purcell, Henry | Sound the Trumpet | Roger Dean | full orchestra | M |
| Raminsh, Imant | Cantate Domino | Hinshaw | strings, solo trumpet, percussion | M |

| | | | | |
|---|---|---|---|---|
| Raminsh, Imant | Missa Brevis in C Minor | Plymouth Music | full orchestra | M |
| Raminsh, Imant | Songs of the Lights | Boosey & Hawkes | strings, flute, glockenspiel | M |
| Rautavaara, Einojuhani | Lapsimessu, Op. 71, A Children's Mass | Fazer | strings | M |
| Ridout, Godfrey (arr.) | From *Folksongs of Early Canada:* | GVT | full orchestra* | |
| | Ah! Si mon moine voulait danser! | | | E |
| | I'll Give My Love an Apple | | | E |
| | J'ai cueilli la belle rose | | | E |
| | She's like the Swallow | | | E |
| Runyan, Paul | Songs of Awakening | Boosey & Hawkes | full orchestra | M |
| Rutter, John | All Things Bright and Beautiful | Hinshaw | full orchestra | E |
| Rutter, John | Candlelight Carol | Oxford | full orchestra | M |
| Rutter, John | The Donkey Carol | Oxford | full orchestra | E |
| Rutter, John | For the Beauty of the Earth | Hinshaw | full orchestra | E |
| Rutter, John | Jesus Child | Oxford | full orchestra | E |
| Rutter, John | Shepherd's Pipe Carol | Oxford | full orchestra | E |
| Rutter, John | Star Carol | Oxford | full orchestra | E |
| Rutter, John | Three Opera Choruses for Upper Voices: | Oxford | full orchestra | M |
| | Tchaikovsky: Chorus of Peasant Girls (from *Eugene Onegin*) | | | |
| | Wagner: Spinning Chorus (from *The Flying Dutchman*) | | | |
| | Verdi: Witches' Chorus (from *Macbeth*) | | | |
| Sallinen, Aulis | Suita Grammaticale 1, 3, & 5 | Fazer | strings, percussion (2 & 4 strings only) | M |

*(continued)*

| Composer | Title | Publisher | Instruments | Rating<br>Easy<br>Medium<br>Difficult |
|---|---|---|---|---|
| Schuman,<br>William | Concert on Old | Theodore Presser | viola, orchestra | M |
| Smith, Gregg | Songs of Innocence,<br>from *Beware of the<br>Soldier* | G. Schirmer | woodwinds, or<br>piano 4 hands | M |
| | Infant Joy | | | |
| | The Grasshopper<br>and Cricket | | | |
| | The Blossom | | | |
| | Maying | | | |
| | Little Lamb | | | |
| Spitta, Heinrich | From Heaven<br>Above, Ye Angels All | Concordia | strings or winds<br>and continuo | E |
| Sutcliffe, James H. | Lo, How a Rose<br>E'er Blooming | Boosey & Hawkes | string quartet,<br>opt. Bass | E |
| Sutcliffe, James H. | Lullaby, My<br>Lovely Child | Boosey & Hawkes | string quartet,<br>clarinet, harp | E |
| Tallis, Thomas,<br>arr. Kenneth<br>Brown | Glory to Thee,<br><br>My God, This Night | OUP | strings, organ | E |
| Thompson,<br>Randall | From *Frostiana:* | E. C. Schirmer | full orchestra | M |
| | Come In | | | |
| | A Girl's Garden | | | |
| | Choose Something<br>like a Star | | | |
| Thompson,<br>Randall | A Hymn for Scholars<br>and Pupils | E. C. Schirmer | strings, flute,<br>2 tpts., trombone,<br>tuba, organ | M |
| Thompson,<br>Randall | The Place of the<br>Blest | E. C. Schirmer | strings, flute, oboe,<br>clarinet, bassoon | M |
| Tippett, Michael | Crown of the Year | Schott | strings, winds,<br>adult mezzo<br>soloist | M |
| Tomasi, Henri | Messe de la Nativité | Alphonse Leduc | full orchestra | M |
| Trew, Arthur (arr.) | Brother James's Air | Oxford | strings | E |
| Vaughan Williams,<br>Ralph | Folk Songs of the<br>Four Seasons | Oxford | full orchestra | M |
| Vaughan Williams,<br>Ralph | Magnificat | Oxford | full orchestra | M |

| | | | | |
|---|---|---|---|---|
| Vaughan Williams, Ralph | Six Choral Songs | Oxford | full orchestra | E |
| Walters, Edmund | As Joseph was A-walking | Boosey & Hawkes | full orchestra | E |
| Walters, Edmund, | Dance, Little Goatling | Boosey & Hawkes | full orchestra | E |
| Walters, Edmund | Little Camel Boy | Boosey & Hawkes | full orchestra | E |
| Walters, Edmund | Three Christmas Bird Songs | Boosey & Hawkes | full orchestra | E |
| Webber, Andrew Lloyd | Pie Jesu, from Requiem | Novello/ Hal Leonard | full orchestra | E |
| Wessman, Harri | Vesi Väsyy Lumen Alle (Water under Snow Is Weary) | Fazer | flute, strings | E |
| Willcocks, David | The Glories of Shakespeare: Who Is Silvia? Full Fathom Five Under the Greenwood Tree Fear No More the Heat of the Sun It Was a Lover and His Lass | Oxford | full orchestra | M |
| Willcocks, Jonathan | The Pied Piper of Hamelin (A Cantata) | Roger Dean | piano, brass, percussion | M |
| Williamson, Malcolm | Little Mass of St. Bernadette | Josef Weinberger | strings | M |
| Williamson, Malcolm | Ode to Music | Josef Weinberger | full orchestra | E |

*All GVT orchestral material is on hire from: Jean-Marie Barker, Counterpoint, 2650 John Street, Unit 24, Markham, Ontario, Canada L3R 2W6, phone: 905-415-0515, fax: 905-415-9232, E-mail: counterpointms@cs.com

# Repertoire Recommended List

## Unison

### First Grade

| | | | |
|---|---|---|---|
| To a Baby Brother | W. H. Anderson | Leslie Music* | 1018 |
| Children Singing | Violet Archer | GVT† | VG-259 |
| Four Sociable Songs for Infants | Elizabeth Barnard | Curwen/G. Schirmer | 72675 |
| Ride with Me | John Barron | Frederick Harris | ISBN 0-88797-402-3 |
| Mrs. Jenny Wren | Arthur Baynon | Boosey & Hawkes | 17301 |
| Spring Work at the Farm | Arthur Baynon | Elkin | 2381 |
| Just like Me and The Telephone Wires | Marilyn Broughton | GVT† | VG-1003 |
| Number Four | Winifred Bury | Paterson | 1712 |
| The Scarecrow | John Clements | Elkin | 16 0131 08 |
| Simple Songs | Compiled by John Feierabend | GIA | ISBN 1-57999-057-6 |
| Song for a Little House | Donald Ford | GVT/Warner† | G-147 |
| Dogs and Cats | Susan Jones | Oxford | U101 |
| Haircut | Burton Kurth | Leslie Music* | 1057 |
| New Shoes | Burton Kurth | Western/Vancouver | 1071 |
| Robin's Breakfast | Burton Kurth | Leslie Music* | 1060 |
| Adventure | Havelock Nelson | GVT/Warner† | VG-1016 |
| Three Songs for Very Young People | David Ouchterlony | Leslie Music* | 1124 |

1. Walk, Run, Jump; 2. Some Day; 3. Almost Asleep

| | | | |
|---|---|---|---|
| The Ferryman | Dorothy Parke | GVT† | 142 |
| If I Were . . . and the Moon | Elizabeth Pollmer | GVT/Warner† | G-151 |
| Candle-Light | Alec Rowley | Leslie Music* | 1026 |
| A Room of My Own | Eric Thiman | Curwen/Boosey & Hawkes | 72355 |
| Three Christmas Bird Songs | Edmund Walters | Boosey & Hawkes | 20494 |

1. Three Little Birdies; 2. Little Robin Redbreast; 3. Hop, Hop, Hop

| | | | |
|---|---|---|---|
| The First Christmas Night | Ashley Winning | GVT/Warner/ Chappell† | VA-1005 |

| The Grasshopper | Stuart Young | Curwen/Boosey & Hawkes | 72022 |
| My Boat | Stuart Young | Curwen/G. Schirmer | 71878 |

## Second Grade

| Four Seasonal Songs | W. H. Anderson | Leslie Music* | 1125 |
| My Caterpillar | Marilyn Broughton | GVT/Warner/Chappell† | G-185 |
| Nursery Rhyme Nonsense | Marilyn Broughton | GV.T/Warner/Chappell† | VG-184 |
| Skippets | Clifford Curwin | Curwen | 72589 |
| Rhythm of the Rain | Jerry Estes | Alfred | 17730 |
| Lullaby, Oh Lullaby | Gerald Finzi | Boosey & Hawkes | 6147 |
| Witch | Gordon M. Fleming | Leslie Music* | 1183 |
| Orion | Donald Ford | GVT† | G-140 |
| The Clucking Hen | Gordon Jacob | Oxford | U123 |
| Bessie the Black Cat | Peter Jenkyns | Elkin | 16 0110 |
| The Crocodile | Peter Jenkyns | Novello | 19091 |
| The Lizard | E. Markham Lee | Curwen | 72017 |
| Little Lambs, Where Do You Sleep? | Hilda Morgan | Waterloo | |
| Ghosts in the Belfry | Havelock Nelson | Elkin | EO2726 |
| Slumber Song | Roger Quilter | Elkin | 1513 |
| When the Wind Sweeps By | George Rathbone | Novello | 1706 |
| Lewis Bridal Song | Arr. Hugh Roberton | Roberton | 72507 |
| A Goblin Went A-hiking | Alec Rowley | Boosey & Hawkes (Winthrop) | |
| The Grandfather Clock | Alec Rowley | Leslie Music* | 1023 |

## Third Grade

| The Cowslip | W. H. Anderson, arr. Cohen | Leslie Music* | 1161 |
| The Owl and the Pussycat | Roy Boole | GVT† | VG-1020 |
| A La Claire Fontaine | Arr. Marilyn Broughton | GVT† | VG-1005 |
| Child of Bethlehem | William Bush | Leslie Music* | 1152 |
| The Wind | Henry Clark | Leslie Music* | 1098 |
| Trolls | Clifford Crawley | Leslie Music* | 1193 |
| Snakes | Peter Jenkyns | Elkin | 16 0115 06 |

| | | | |
|---|---|---|---|
| Haida | Gerber\Arr. Henry Leck | Plymouth | HL-516 |
| A Smuggler's Song | Christopher Le Fleming | OUP | OCS 1222 |
| Songs for Joanna | Havelock Nelson | Roberton | 75346 |
| Come, Enjoy God's Festive Springtime | Telemann, ed. Conion | Augsburg | 11-2443 |
| From Three Children's Songs, Spring | R. Vaughan Williams | OUP | OCS 1031 |

## Fourth Grade

| | | | |
|---|---|---|---|
| Lazy Summer | W. H. Belyea | Leslie Music* | 1127 |
| Winter-time | W. H. Belyea | Leslie Music* | 1179 |
| The Frost Is Here | Arthur Egerton | Leslie Music* | 1087 |
| Dream Pedlary | Armstrong Gibbs | Roberton | 75420 |
| Art Thou Troubled? | G. F. Handel, arr. Bartle | Hinshaw | HMC1431 |
| You'll Never Guess What I Saw | R. Watson Henderson | GVT† | G-177 |
| East Away O! | Derek Holman | Novello | 16 0177 06 |
| Blake's Lullaby | Antony Hopkins | Roberton | 75280 |
| The Owls | Peter Jenkyns | Novello | 16 0069 09 |
| Space Travellers | David Stone | Boosey & Hawkes | MFS 753 |
| Zumba, Zumba | Marie Stultz | Morningstar | MSM-50-9904 |
| The Path to the Moon | Eric Thiman | Boosey & Hawkes | 18160 |
| Vagabond Song | Alexander Tilley | Leslie Music* | HC-5024 |
| Orpheus with His Lute | R. Vaughan Williams | OUP | OCS 52 |

## Easy Two-Part Songs

## Fifth Grade

| | | | |
|---|---|---|---|
| Snow and Ice | D. Geoffrey Bell | Leslie Music* | 2101 |
| S'Vivon | Arr. Betty Bertaux | Boosey & Hawkes | OC4B6193 |
| Mary and Joseph | Keith Bissell | GVT/Warner/ Chappell† | VG-244 |
| Three Rhymes | Paul Bouman | earthsongs | |
| Three Rhymes Set II | Paul Bouman | earthsongs | |
| Lone Dog (Unison) | Benjamin Britten | Boosey & Hawkes | OCTB6738 |
| Winter Changes (Unison) | David Brunner | Boosey & Hawkes | OCTB6753 |

| | | | |
|---|---|---|---|
| City Songs | Bob Chilcott | Oxford | T123 |
| An Irish Blessing | Eleanor Daley | Alliance | AMP 0398 |
| Who Has Seen the Wind? | Victoria Ebel-Sabo | Boosey & Hawkes | OCTB6773 |
| Autumn Tints | Norman Gilbert | GVT† | G-210 |
| Storm | R. Watson Henderson | GVT† | VG-230 |
| Who Can Sail? | J. Julseth-Heinrich | Jensen | 43019015 |
| Misha, the Feline Queen | Valerie Shields | Mark Foster | YS401 |
| Fog | Audrey Snyder | Belwin | SV8931 |
| Moon at the Ruined Castle | Taki, arr. Snyder | Hal Leonard | 08551267 |
| When Cats Run Home | Eric Thiman | Boosey & Hawkes | OC2B5570 |

## Sixth Grade

| | | | |
|---|---|---|---|
| When I Set Out for Lyonesse | Keith Bissell | GVT† | G-235 |
| Hold Fast Your Dreams | David Brunner | Boosey & Hawkes | ISBN M-051-47123-2 |
| The Huron Carol | Arr. Howard Cable | GVT/Warner/ Chappell | VG-253 |
| The Jaybird Song (Unison) | Carlisle Floyd | Boosey & Hawkes | OCT5486 |
| Through Bush, through Brier | Armstrong Gibbs | Roberton | 75369 |
| Creatures Great and Small | Derek Holman | Boosey & Hawkes | OCTB6786 |

1. The Wonderful Derby Ram; 2. Unicorn; 3. The Ballad of Red Fox; 4. The Snail;
5. Rattlesnake Skipping Song

| | | | |
|---|---|---|---|
| Little Miss Muffet | Hal Hopson | Shawnee | E-128 |
| Linstead Market | Arr. Hazel Hudson | Boosey & Hawkes (Ashdown) | 332 |
| Evening Prayer | E. Humperdinck | Leslie Music* | 2003 |
| Shiru | Allan E. Naplan | Boosey & Hawkes | M-051-47201-7 |
| The Spiritual Railway | W. H. Parry | Oxford | 82.112 |
| Il yat un coq qui chante | Arr. Sid Robinovitch | earthsongs | |
| Three Hungarian Folk Songs | Matyas Seiber | Hal Leonard | HL 50308610 |
| Per Spelmann | Arr. Valerie Shields | Mark Foster | YS404 |
| Little Things | Bernard Tan | Neil A. Kjos | Ed.6230 |
| In Flanders Fields | Alexander Tilley | Leslie Music* | HC-5028 |
| Greensleeves | R. Vaughan Williams | Oxford | 82.004 |

## Easy Two-Part Songs for Ages Ten to Fifteen

| | | | |
|---|---|---|---|
| Jesu, Joy of Man's Desiring | J. S. Bach | Oxford | 1568 |
| Hand Me Down My Silver Trumpet | Arr. Bartle | Hinshaw | HMC1535 |
| The Swing | Paul Bouman | earthsongs | |
| The Ship of Rio | Benjamin Britten | Oxford | 54.123 |
| The Shepherd | Harry Brook | OUP | OCS-149 |
| Spirit of the Sun | Arr. John Butler | Leslie Music* | 2095 |
| Panis Angelicus | Arr. Franck, Howard Cable | Hinshaw | HMC1377 |
| Dodi Li | Chen, arr. Rao | Boosey & Hawkes | OCTB6679 |
| Can You Hear Me? | Bob Chilcott | Oxford | T129 |
| Sweet Songs of Christmas | Chris Dedrick | Hal Leonard | 08740256 |
| A Great Big Sea | Lori-Anne Doloff | Boosey & Hawkes | OCTB6914 |
| Sing Me a Song | Leonard Enns | GVT/Warner/ Chappell† | VG-1026 |
| Einini | Cyndee Giebler | Plymouth | HL-541 |
| Brother James's Air | Arr. Gordon Jacob | Oxford | 44.047 |
| Good Night | Kabalevsky, arr. Rao | Boosey & Hawkes | OCUB6441 |
| Winds | Larysa Kuzmenko | Boosey & Hawkes | M-051-46833-1 |
| Hine Ma Tov | Arr. Henry Leck | Colla Voce | 20-96890 |
| Soldier, Soldier | Tom Mitchell | Gene Thomas | GT-970012 |
| White Bird, Silver Bird | Robert Nelson | Alliance | AMP0031 |
| Silver the River | Stephen Paulus | European American Music Corp. | EA525 |
| Dona, Dona | Secunda, arr. Dwyer | Plymouth | HL-525 |
| Claude Is an Excellent Cat | Valerie Shields | Mark Foster | YS 400 |
| Irish Lullaby | Mark Sirett | Boosey & Hawkes | OCTB7134 |
| Sing Me a Song | Nancy Telfer | Leslie Music* | 2061 |
| Shining Moon | Thai Folk Song, arr. Snyder | Hal Leonard | 08551175 |
| Vem Kan Segla | Arr. Bob Walser | World Music | 018 |

## Songs Suitable for Boys' Choirs in Schools

| | | | |
|---|---|---|---|
| The Juggler | James Bennighof | Oxford | 95.420 |
| Lone Dog | Benjamin Britten | Boosey & Hawkes | Un OCTB6738 |

| | | | |
|---|---|---|---|
| The Ship of Rio | Benjamin Britten | Boosey & Hawkes | SA OCS170 |
| Hallowe'en | Marilyn Broughton | GVT/Warner/ Chappell† | Un VG-1013 |
| Hockey | Marilyn Broughton | GVT/Warner/ Chappell† | Un VG-1014 |
| Will You Walk a Little Faster? | John Carter | Bellwin-Mills | SA FEC10138 |
| City Songs | Bob Chilcott | Oxford | SA T123 |
| Old King Cole | Arr. Thomas Dunhill | Edward Arnold | Un/desc 16.0001 10 |
| Three Fine Ships | Thomas Dunhill | Cramer | Un 334 |
| Panis Angelicus | Franck, arr. Howard Cable | Hinshaw | SA HMC1377 |
| Pie Jesu | Gabriel Fauré | Boosey & Hawkes | Un OCTB6631 |
| Rolling Down to Rio | Edward German | Novello | 16 0096 06 |
| A Spider Danced a Cosy Jig | Srul Irving Glick | GVT/Warner/ Chappell† | SA VG-250 |
| I'se the B'y | Arr. John Govedas | GVT/Warner/ Chappell† | SA VG-267 |
| Where'er You Walk | G. F. Handel | GVT/Warner/ Chappell† | Un G197 |
| Cowboy Songs | Arr. Mark Hierholzer | Boosey & Hawkes | OCTB6754 |
| Creatures Great and Small | Derek Holman | Boosey & Hawkes | Two/Three OCTB6786 |
| Four Horses | Herbert Howells | Edward Arnold | Un EA855 |
| Jonah-Man Jazz | Michael Hurd | Novello | Un |
| The Gospel Train | Arr. Stuart Johnson | Oxford | SA 82.108 |
| Ave Maria | Simon Lindley | Basil Ramsey | Un 1057 |
| The King's New Clothes | Frank Loesser | Frank | SA F2011 |
| The East Indiaman | Arr. William McKie | OUP | Un OCS-1172 |
| I've Got a Song | Richard Osborne | Plymouth | SA HL204 |
| The Eddystone Light | Arr. Willard Palmer | Alfred | Un 6105X |
| Jerusalem | C. Hubert H. Parry | GVT/Warner/ Chappell† | Un VG-196 |
| Ave Maria | Franz Schubert, arr. Downing | G. Schirmer | SSA 41304 |
| Ave Maria | Franz Schubert, arr. Ehret | Bourne | Solo and SSA 2574-10-C |
| Benedictus | Franz Schubert | Neil A. Kjos | SA Ed.8730 |
| The Lord Is My Shepherd | Franz Schubert, arr. Higgs | Oxford | SA E147 |
| Three Hungarian Folk-Songs | Matyas Seiber | Hal Leonard | SA HL50308610 |
| Adventures | Cecil Sharman | Mills Music | Un 5021 |

| | | | |
|---|---|---|---|
| Sea Roads | Martin Shaw | Winthrop | Un 4554 |
| Two Native American Songs | Arr. Barbara Sletto | Plymouth | SA HLCC-200 |
| Beyond the Spanish Main | Meredith Tatton | Ascherberg | Un 387 |
| Johnny Todd | Arr. Edmund Walters | Roberton | SA 75330 |
| The Man from Okerboker | James Whicher | GVT/Warner/ Chappell[†] | Un G-180 |
| In Paradisum | Jonathan Willcocks | Oxford | SA E148 |

*GVT/Warner/Chappell, 15800 N.W. 48th Avenue, Miami, FL 33014, phone: 305-521-1697, fax: 305-621-1094, www.warnerchappell.com

†Leslie Music Publications, Box 471, Oakville, Ontario, Canada L6J5A8, phone: 1-905-844-3109, fax: 1-905-844-7637, E-mail: sales@lesliemusicsupply.com, www.lesliemusicsupply.com

# *Toronto Children's Chorus Compact Discs*

| CD Title | Title | Composer | Arranger | Publisher | Catalog # |
|---|---|---|---|---|---|
| *1. Adeste Fideles / CBC Records—SMCD 5119* | | | | | |
| 1 | Ave Maria | Bach-Gounod | Cable, Howard | Orig. manuscript | |
| 2 | Cantique de Noel | Adam, Adolphe | Cable, Howard | Orig. manuscript | |
| 3 | Carol of the Bells | Leontovich, M. Leon | Wilhousky, Pete | Carl Fischer | CM5276 |
| 4 | Cloche de Noel, La | French Canadian Folk Song | Cable, Howard | Orig. manuscript | |
| 5 | Coventry Carol | 16th-cen. Traditional English | Cable, Howard | Hinshaw | HMC1327 |
| 6 | Es Ist ein' Ros' entsprungen | Praetorius | Shand, David | G. Schirmer | Oct. No. 8954 |
| 7 | Flocks in Pastures Green Abiding | Bach, J. S. | James, Phyllis | Oxford | OCS1631 |
| 8 | Flambeau, un, Jeanette Isabella | Old French Carol | Cable, Howard | Orig. manuscript | |
| 9 | Fum, Fum, Fum | Old Spanish Carol | Cable, Howard | Hinshaw | HMC1379 |
| 10 | Huron Carol, The | Canadian Carol | Cable, Howard | GVT/Warner/Chappell | VG-253 |
| 11 | Medley (Christmas songs) | | Cable, Howard | Orig. manuscript | |
| 12 | Ninna Nanna a Gesu Bambino | Old Italian Carol | Cable, Howard | Orig. manuscript | |
| 13 | Panis Angelicus | Franck, Cesar | Cable, Howard | Hinshaw | HMC1377 |
| 14 | Pat-a-Pan | Old French Carol | Cable, Howard | Hinshaw | HMC1379 |
| 15 | Sleigh, The | Kountz, Richard | Cable, Howard | Orig. manuscript | |
| 16 | Virgin's Slumber Song, The, Op. 6, no. 52 | Reger, Max | Beckers, Anton | G. Schirmer | HL502284 10 |
| 17 | Gesu Bambino | Old Italian Carol | Cable, Howard | Orig. manuscript | |
| *2. Along the Road to Bethlehem / CBC Records SM5000—SMCD 5151* | | | | | |
| 1 | Star Carol | Rutter, John | | Oxford | U153 |
| 2 | The Kings | Cornelius | Henderson, R. W. | GVT/Warner/Chappell | VG-359 |
| 3 | Christmas Triptych | | Holman, Derek | Hinshaw | HMC1224 |
| 4 | Farewell! Advent | Chilcott, Bob | | Oxford | W117 |

| No. | Title | Composer | Arranger | Publisher | Catalog No. |
|---|---|---|---|---|---|
| 5 | Good King Wenceslas | | Jacques, Reginald | Oxford | W117 |
| 6 | Hey! Now | Chilcott, Bob | | Oxford | ECS141 |
| 7 | Jesus Christ, the Apple Tree | Poston, Elizabeth | | Banks Music Publ. | |
| 8 | Kings, The | Cornelius, Peter | Henderson, Ruth Watson | GVT/Warner/Chappell | VG-359 |
| 9 | Last Straw, The | Henderson, Ruth Watson | | GVT/Warner/Chappell | VG-347 |
| 10 | Mid-Winter | Chilcott, Bob | | Oxford | T121 |
| 11 | See amid the Winter's Snow | Goss, John | Willcocks, David | Oxford | |
| **3. A Boy Was Born / Toronto Children's Chorus—TCC 015** | | | | | |
| 1 | Folk Songs of the Four Seasons | Williams, R. V. | | Oxford | ISBN0-193-39086 |
| 2 | Brother Heinrich's Christmas | Rutter, John | | Hinshaw | ISBN0-19-3380463 |
| 3 | Salvator Mundi: Opus 89 | Mathias, William | | Oxford | OX26DP |
| 4 | Boy Was Born, A | Britten, B. | | Oxford | OUP 145 |
| **4. Come, Ye Makers of Song / Marquis Classics—Canada 81255, USA MAR 255** | | | | | |
| 1 | Agnus Dei | Mozart, W. A. | | Kjos, Neil A. | ED.9836 |
| 2 | Ave Maria | Holst, Gustav | | E. C. Schirmer (Galaxy) | 1-3121 |
| 3 | Come, Ye Makers of Song | Henderson, R. W. | | GVT/Warner/Chappell | VG-363 |
| 4 | Dixit Dominus | Galuppi, Baldassare | | Roger Dean | CMC108 |
| 5 | Freedom Trilogy | Halley, Paul | | Pelagos | |
| 6 | Glory to Thee, My God, This Night | Tallis, Thomas | Brown, Kenneth | Oxford | OUP 40.922 |
| 7 | Laudate Pueri Dominum: Op. 39, no. 32 | Mendelssohn, Felix | | E. C. Schirmer | ECS 1839 |
| 8 | Lift Thine Eyes | Mendelssohn, Felix | | E. C. Schirmer | 1017 |
| 9 | Petites Voix | Poulenc, Francis | | Salabert | ESA 16124 (1) |
| 10 | Psalm Trilogy—Psalm 23 | Glick, Srul Irving | | earthsongs | |

(continued)

| CD Title | Title | Composer | Arranger | Publisher | Catalog # |
|---|---|---|---|---|---|
| 11 | Psalm Trilogy—Psalm 47 | Glick, Srul Irving | | earthsongs | |
| 12 | Psalm Trilogy—Psalm 92 | Glick, Srul Irving | | earthsongs | |
| 13 | Song of St. Francis, A | Hurd, Michael | | Novello | 29 0560 04 |
| 14 | Stabat Mater | Pergolesi | | Hinshaw | HMB209 |

**5. *Dancing Day* / Marquis Classics—ERAD 135**

| CD Title | Title | Composer | Arranger | Publisher | Catalog # |
|---|---|---|---|---|---|
| 1 | Angels' Carol | Rutter, John | | Hinshaw | HMC986 |
| 2 | Carol | Telfer, Nancy | | Waterloo Music Co. | |
| 3 | Christmas | Archer, Violet | | GVT/Warner/Chappell | E.I. 1014 |
| 4 | Dancing Day | Rutter, John | | Oxford | ISBN 0-19-338065X |
| 5 | D'où viens-tu, bergère? | | Cable, Howard | Hinshaw | HMC1188 |
| 6 | Great Big Sea, A | | Fleming, Robert | GVT/Warner/Chappell | VG-228 |
| 7 | Mary and Joseph | Bissell, Keith | | GVT/Warner/Chappell | VG-244 |
| 8 | Nöel des enfants | Debussy, Claude | | Durand | 9418 |
| 9 | Nöel nouvelet | | Cable, Howard | Hinshaw | HMC1289 |
| 10 | Promptement levez-vous | Henderson, Ruth Watson | Henderson, R. W. | GVT/Warner/Chappell | VG-342 |
| 11 | Robin, The | | Henderson, R. W. | GVT/Warner/Chappell | VG-187 |
| 12 | Stille Nacht | Gruber, F. | Rutter, John | Oxford | VG-339 |
| 13 | Twelve Days of Christmas, The | | Henderson, R. W. | GVT/Warner/Chappell | |
| 14 | Two Christmas Carols | Willan, Healey | Middleton, J. E. | Frederick Harris Music Co. | FH1641 |
| 15 | Two Christmas Carols | Bissell, Keith | | GVT/Warner/Chappell | VG-127 |

**6. *Mostly Britten* / Marquis Classics—ERAD 133**

| CD Title | Title | Composer | Arranger | Publisher | Catalog # |
|---|---|---|---|---|---|
| 1 | Birds, The | Britten, Benjamin | | Boosey & Hawkes | OCTB6524 |
| 2 | Ceremony of Carols, A, Op. 28 | Britten, Benjamin | | Boosey & Hawkes | 16832 |

| | Title | Composer | Arr./Ed. | Publisher | Catalog |
|---|---|---|---|---|---|
| 3 | Friday Afternoons, Op. 7 | Britten, Benjamin | | Boosey & Hawkes | 19388 |
| 4 | Lord Bless You and Keep You, The | Rutter, John | | Hinshaw | HMC1169 |
| 5 | Missa Brevis in D, Opus 63 | Britten, Benjamin | | Boosey & Hawkes | B.H. M-060-01470-3 |
| 6 | Non Nobis, Domine | Byrd, William | | Hinshaw | HMC1161 |
| 7 | Psalm 150 | Britten, Benjamin | | Boosey & Hawkes | 19022 |
| 8 | Ride-by-Nights, The | Britten, Benjamin | | Oxford | OCS168/ Cat. no. 54.124 |
| 9 | Rainbow, The | Britten, Benjamin | | Oxford | 54.125 |
| 10 | Sound the Trumpet | Purcell, Henry | Lang, C. S. | Novello | 16 0017 06 |
| 11 | Ship of Rio, The | Britten, Benjamin | | Oxford | OCS170/ Cat. no. 54.123 |

*7. My Heart Soars / Marquis Classics—ERAD 199*

| | Title | Composer | Arr./Ed. | Publisher | Catalog |
|---|---|---|---|---|---|
| 1 | Away from the Roll of the Sea | MacGillivray, A. | Calvert, S. | GVT/Warner/Chappell | VG-340 |
| 2 | Ah! Si mon moine voulait danser | Patriquin | Patriquin, Donald | earthsongs | |
| 3 | Blue Eye of God, The | Telfer, Nancy | Powris, Barbara | earthsongs | |
| 4 | Blooming Bright Star of Belle Isle, The | Daley, Eleanor | | GVT/Warner/Chappell | VG-257 |
| 5 | Cape Breton Lullaby | Leslie, Kenneth | Calvert, Stuart | GVT/Warner/Chappell | VG-327 |
| 6 | Cantate Domino | Raminsh, Imant | | Orig. manuscript | |
| 7 | Clouds (from *Moments in Time*) | Glick, Srul Irving | | GVT/Warner/Chappell | VG-248 |
| 8 | I'se the B'y | Glick, Srul Irving | Govedas, John | GVT/Warner/Chappell | VG-267 |
| 9 | Keewaydin | Freedman, Harry | | GVT/Warner/Chappell | VG-334 |
| 10 | Laughter (from *Moments in Time*) | Glick, Srul Irving | | GVT/Warner/Chappell | VG-247 |
| 11 | Time (from *Moments in Time*) | Glick, Srul Irving | | GVT/Warner/Chappell | VG-251 |
| 12 | Orders (from *Moments in Time*) | Glick, Srul Irving | | GVT/Warner/Chappell | VG-249 |

(continued)

| CD Title | Title | Composer | Arranger | Publisher | Catalog # |
|---|---|---|---|---|---|
| 13 | Pie Jesu | Evans, Robert | | GVT/Warner/Chappell | VG-1010 |
| 14 | Song for the Mira | MacGillivray, A. | Calvert, S. | GVT/Warner/Chappell | VG-326 |
| 15 | Spider Danced a Cosy Jig, A (from *Moments in Time*) | Glick, Srul Irving | | GVT/Warner/Chappell | VG-250 |

*8. Songs of the Lights / Marquis Classics—Canada 81253, USA MAR 253*

| CD Title | Title | Composer | Arranger | Publisher | Catalog # |
|---|---|---|---|---|---|
| 1 | African Celebration | | Hatfield, Stephen | Boosey & Hawkes | OCTB6706 |
| 2 | Boar & the Dromedar, The; Don't Ever Squeeze a Weasel | Henderson, R. W. | | GVT/Warner/Chappell | VG-168 |
| 3 | City Called Heaven | | Poelinitz, Josephine | Plymouth | HL-105 |
| 4 | Daybreak Song | Raminsh, Imant | | Boosey & Hawkes | OC3B6273 |
| 5 | George Gershwin Medley | Gershwin, George | Holcombe, Bill | Orig. manuscript | |
| 6 | Go Down, Moses | | Hayes, Mark | Hinshaw | HMC1302 |
| 7 | Micma'q Honour Song | | Adams, Lydia | McGroarty Music Pub. | MMP08 |
| 8 | On Suuri Sun Rantas Autius | | Hyokki, Matti | Fazer | FM 06571-4 |
| 9 | Songs of the Stars | Raminsh, Imant | | Boosey & Hawkes | M-051-46270-4 |
| 10 | Sower, The | Raminsh, Imant | | Boosey & Hawkes | M-051-46271-1 |
| 11 | Sun Is a Luminous Shield, The | Raminsh, Imant | | Boosey & Hawkes | M-051-46272-8 |
| 12 | Somewhere | Bernstein, Leonard | | G. Schirmer | 44308 |
| 13 | Sing Me a Song | Enns, Leonard | | GVT/Warner/Chappell | VG-1026 |
| 14 | We Rise Again | Dubinsky, Leon | Adams, Lydia | GVT/Warner/Chappell | VA-2005 |
| 15 | World Music Suite | | Patriquin, Donald | earthsongs | |

# The Seating Plan

A seating plan is an invaluable tool. It is crucial that all children understand which part they are singing in works with multiple divisi. In this plan, three-part divisi are indicated by parallel lines and four-part divisi are indicated by curvy lines. In two-part divisi, the Soprano

**TCC Seating Plan**  Date:

| A | B | C | D | E |
|---|---|---|---|---|
| A1 Matthew D. MacDonald | B1 George Shipilov | C1 Alexandra Airhart A.T. | D1 Alana Hodge A.T. | E1 Claire Stollery |
| A2 Scott Reynolds | B2 Eric Rottman | C2 Julien Pileggi App. | D2 Calla Heilbron App. | E2 Nellie Stockhammer A.T. |
| A3 Duncan Cameron A.T. | B3 Nathaniel So App. | C3 Matthew A. MacDonald App. | D3 Julia Raffaghello | E3 Mabel Fulford App. |
| A4 Jeffrey Smith Sr. App. | B4 Karen Ng A.T. | C4 Heather Wilkie A.T. | D4 Katie Switzer | E4 Shaindel Egit |
| A5 Thomas Kais-Prial App. | B5 Andrew Chisholm App. | C5 Elizabeth Wong App. | D5 Andrea Grant A.T. | E5 Meg Moran Sr. App. |
| A6 Lauren Saunders Sr. App. | B6 Jonathan Mamalyga Sr. App. | C6 Nyree Grimes Sr.App. | D6 Alexandra Borkowski Sr. App. | E6 Elizabeth Convery A.T. |
| A7 Rena Ashton A.T. | B7 Elizabeth Lee A.T. | C7 Sarah Campbell A.T. | D7 Alison Price | E7 Emma Ratcliffe |
| A8 Elspeth Malcolm Sr. App. | B8 Alison Morin | C8 Cassandra Potichnji Sr. App. | D8 Cassandra Luftspring A.T. | E8 Hannah Woolaver |
| A9 Stewart Chisholm | B9 Isabelle Eckler | C9 Elliot Meyer | D9 Rebecca Boucher Johnson Sr. App. | E9 Alexandra Mealia |
| A10 Kyrie Vala-Webb | B10 Clara Tsui | C10 Matthew Quitasol | D10 Sydney Hodge | E10 Brynne McLeod A.T. |
| A11 Alexandra Rolland | B11 Curtis Ng | C11 Michael Saunders | D11 Sachi Marshall | E11 Claire Caldwell Sr. App. |
| A12 Fiona McLean | B12 Ben Walker | C12 Elizabeth Dalglish | D12 Aleha Aziz A.T. | E12 Emma Van Buskirk |
| A13 Anastasia Pasche-Arabczuk | B13 Grace Wong | C13 Clare King | D13 Sarah Copeland Sr. App. | E13 Sarah Lettieri |
| A14 Devin Campbell | B14 Faryn Stern | C14 Sarah Jacobs | D14 Krista Kais-Prial | E14 Polina Kukar |
| A15 David Walter Sr. App. | B15 Paige Halam-Andres Sr. App. | C15 Julianne Morin Sr. App. | D15 Sabina Saharatnam Sr. App. | E15 Heather Hurst A.T. |
| A16 Hannah Renglich A.T. | B16 Katie Mann A.T. | C16 Laura Cameron A.T. | D16 Gillian Robinson A.T. | E16 Claire Renouf App. |
| A17 Lauren Soo | B17 Lauren Mifflin | C17 Emily Shepard | D17 Sandra Sabaratnam | E17 Kathleen Hickey |
| A18 Alexandra Yellowlees | B18 Laura Goldsmith | C18 Anne Ma | D18 Valerie Conforzi | E18 Kate Van Buskirk A.T. |
| A19 Melissa Walter | B19 Malaya Sagada | C19 Poornima Narayanan Sr. App. | D19 Silvi Kuld A.T. | E19 Charlotte McGee Sr. App. |
| A20 Andrew Liu | B20 Jesse Williams A.T. | C20 Janet Sung A.T. | D20 Georgia Nowers Sr. App. | E20 Jennifer Harris-Lowe Sr. App. |
| A21 Bryan Allen | B21 Jenny Lemberg Sr. App. | C21 Jacqueline Tsekouras App. | D21 Amy Hammett | E21 Johanna Groenberg A.T. |
| A22 Elise Dostal | B22 Karen Mann | C22 Candy Chow | D22 Maxine Byam Sr. App. | E22 Frances Dorenbaum Sr. App. |
| A23 Carla Hartenberger A.T. | B23 Emily Houghton | C23 Beth Polese | D23 Michelle Laughton A.T. | E23 Angela Petz |
| A24 Oles Chepesiuk Sr. App. | B24 Samantha Jo Newman | C24 Shannon Chun | D24 Leah Frazer | E24 Sara Ho Sr.App. |
| A25 Peter Malcolm | B25 Carol Tse | C25 David Smith | D25 Desiree Abbey | E25 Jenny Sung A.T. |
| A26 Natasha Luckhardt | B26 Camille Shepherd | C26 Scott MacDonald | D26 Anastasia John-Sandy | E26 Stacey Hsu |

255

Is and IIs of four-part divisi sing Soprano I and the Alto Is and IIs of four-part divisi sing Alto. The seating plan also indicates where apprentices and apprentice trainers sit. The seating plan is also used to take attendance; children cross their names off the master seating plan as soon as they arrive.

SSA Divisi—3 parts ( ▬▬▬ double lines)          SSAA Divisi—4 parts (〜〜〜curvy lines)

| | Sop.I | Sop.II | Alto | | | Sop.I | Sop.II | Alto I | Alto II |
|---|---|---|---|---|---|---|---|---|---|
| Row A | A1–A10 | A11–A17 | A18–A26 | | Row A | A1–A8 | A9–A16 | A17–A26 | -------- |
| Row B | B1–B10 | B11–B18 | B19–B26 | | Row B | B1–B9 | B10–B17 | B18–B26 | -------- |
| Row C | C1–C11 | C12–C18 | C19–C26 | | Row C | C1–C10 | C11–C16 | C17–C22 | C23–C26 |
| Row D | D1–D10 | D11–D18 | D19–D26 | | Row D | D1–D7 | D8–D16 | D17–D18 | D19–D26 |
| Row E | E1–E9 | E10–E17 | E18–E26 | | Row E | E1–E7 | E8–E14 | E15–E17 | E18–E26 |

## Apprentice-Trainers and Apprentices

Soprano I
1. Apprentice-Trainer: Andrea Grant
   Sr. Apprentice: Alexandra Borkowski
2. Apprentice-Trainer: Cassandra Luftspring
   Sr. Apprentice: Rebecca Boucher Johnson
3. Apprentice-Trainer: Karen Ng
   Apprentice: Andrew Chisholm
   Apprentice: Nathaniel So
4. Apprentice-Trainer: Nellie Stockhammer
   Apprentice: Mabel Fulford
5. Apprentice-Trainer: Sarah Campbell
   Sr. Apprentice: Nyree Grimes
6. Apprentice-Trainer: Alana Hodge
   Apprentice: Calla Heilbron
7. Apprentice-Trainer: Heather Wilkie
   Apprentice: Matthew A. MacDonald
   Apprentice: Elizabeth Wong
8. Apprentice-Trainer: Rena Ashton
   Sr. Apprentice: Elspeth Malcolm
9. Apprentice-Trainer: Elizabeth Lee
   Sr. Apprentice: Jonathan Mamalyga
10. Apprentice-Trainer: Elizabeth Convery
    Sr. Apprentice: Meg Moran
11. Apprentice-Trainer: Alexandra Airhart
    Apprentice: Julian Pileggi
12. Apprentice-Trainer: Rena Ashton
    Apprentice: Lauren Saunders
13. Apprentice-Trainer: Duncan Cameron
    Sr. Apprentice: Jeffrey Smith
14. Apprentice-Trainer: Sarah Campbell
    Sr. Apprentice: Cassandra Potichnyj

Soprano II
1. Apprentice-Trainer: Brynne McLeod
   Sr. Apprentice: Claire Caldwell
2. Apprentice-Trainer: Aleha Aziz
   Sr. Apprentice: Sarah Copeland
3. Apprentice-Trainer: Katie Mann
   Sr. Apprentice: Paige Halam-Andres
4. Apprentice-Trainer: Laura Cameron
   Sr. Apprentice: Julianne Morin
5. Apprentice-Trainer: Heather Hurst
   Apprentice: Claire Renouf
6. Apprentice-Trainer: Gillian Robinson
   Sr. Apprentice: Sabina Sabaratnam
7. Apprentice-Trainer: Hannah Renglich
   Sr. Apprentice: David Walter

Alto
8. Apprentice-Trainer: Michelle Laughton
   Sr. Apprentice: Maxine Byam
9. Apprentice-Trainer: Carla Hartenberger
   Sr. Apprentice: Oles Chepesiuk
10. Apprentice-Trainer: Johanna Groenberg
    Sr. Apprentice: Frances Dorenbaum
    Sr. Apprentice: Jennifer Harris-Lowe
11. Apprentice-Trainer: Jenny Sung
    Sr. Apprentice: Sara Ho
12. Apprentice-Trainer: Jesse Williams
    Sr. Apprentice: Jenny Lemberg
13. Apprentice-Trainer: Kate Van Buskirk
    Sr. Apprentice: Charlotte McGee
14. Apprentice-Trainer: Silvi Kuld
    Sr. Apprentice: Georgia Nowers
15. Apprentice-Trainer: Janet Sung
    Sr. Apprentice: Poornima Narayanan
    Apprentice: Jacqueline Tsekouras

# Examples of Four-Measure
# Sight-Reading Passages

Level 6

# Transposing and Nontransposing Instruments

## Transposing Instruments

When these players play these notes, they sound as a C.

### B-flat Instruments

| | |
|---|---|
| Clarinet | Fr., clarinette; It., clarinetto; Ger., Klarinette |
| Trumpet | Fr., trompette; It., tromba; Ger., Trompette |
| Tenor Saxophone | Fr., saxophone; It., sazofono, sassofono; Ger., Saxophon |
| Bass Clarinet | Fr., clarinette basse; It., clarinetto basso, clarone; Ger., Bassklarinette |
| Tenor Trombone | Fr., trombone; It., trombone; Ger., Posaune |

### G Instrument

Alto Flute

### A Instrument

Clarinet

### E-flat Instruments

Alto Saxophone
Alto Clarinet
Baritone Saxophone
E-flat horn
E-flat clarinet

### F Instruments

| | |
|---|---|
| French horn | Fr., cor; It., corno; Ger., Horn |
| English horn | Fr., cor anglais; It., corno inglese; Ger., englisch Horn |

### D-flat Instruments

| | |
|---|---|
| Piccolo | |
| Flute | Fr., flûte, grande flûte; It., flauto, flauto grande; Ger., Flöte, grosse Flöte |

## D Instruments

Trumpet

## Nontransposing Instruments

| | |
|---|---|
| All strings | |
| Piccolo | |
| Flute | |
| Oboe | Fr., hautbois; It., oboe; Ger., Oboe, Hoboe |
| Trombone | |
| Bassoon | Fr., basson; It., fagotto; Ger. Fagott |
| Tuba | Fr., tuba; It., tuba: Ger., Tuba |